Build a House for My Name

"Awesome is His Name"

(Psalm 111:9)

Book II of the Barnabas Series

Cho Larson

Albertville, AL

Published by Warner House Press of Albertville, Alabama USA

Copyright © 2022 Cho Larson
Cover Design and Illustration © 2022 Ian Loudon, OKAY Media
Interior Design © 2022 Warner House Press

All rights reserved. No part of this book may be used or reproduced in any manner whatsoever without written permission, except in the case of brief quotations in critical articles and reviews. For more information, contact

Warner House Press
1325 Lane Switch Road
Albertville, Alabama 35951
USA

Published 2022
Printed in the United States of America

Cover image used under license from Shutterstock.com.

Unless otherwise noted, all scripture quotations are taken from HOLY BIBLE, NEW INTERNATIONAL VERSION®. Copyright © 1973, 1978, 1984 by International Bible Society. Used by permission of Zondervan Publishing House.

Scripture quotations marked ESV are from The Holy Bible, English Standard Version®, Copyright © 2001 by Crossway Bibles, a publishing ministry of Good News Publishers. Used by permission. All rights reserved.

Scripture quoted by permission. Quotations designated (NET) are from the NET Bible® copyright ©1996, 2019 by Biblical Studies Press, L.L.C. http://netbible.com All rights reserved.

Scripture quotations marked NKJV are from the New King James Version®. Copyright © 1982 by Thomas Nelson. Used by permission. All rights reserved.

Scripture quotations marked NLT are from the Holy Bible, New Living Translation, Copyright © 1996, 2004, 2007, 2013, 2015 by Tyndale House Foundation. Used by permission of Tyndale House Publishers Inc., Carol Stream, Illinois 60188. All rights reserved.

Scripture quotations marked NRSV are from New Revised Standard Version Bible, copyright © 1989 National Council of the Churches of Christ in the United States of America. Used by permission. All rights reserved worldwide.

26 25 24 23 22 1 2 3 4 5

ISBN: 978-1-951890-43-8

Dedicated to:
All those who are homeless, far from home and without a safe shelter.

"I will not enter my house or go to my bed, I will allow no sleep to my eyes or slumber to my eyelids, till I find a place for the Lord, a dwelling for the Mighty One of Jacob."
(Psalm 132:3–5)

"So that all the peoples of the earth may know your name and fear you, as do your own people Israel, and may know that this house I have built bears your Name."
(2 Chronicles 6:33)

"Heaven is my throne, and the earth is my footstool. Where is the house you will build for me? Where will my resting place be?"
(Isaiah 66:1)

Table of Contents

Part 1: The Ground Work
   1: Preparing the Building Site   3
   2: Majesty of the Name   13
   3: The Work of Generations   21

Part 2: A Crumbling House
   4: Lost Significance   33
   5: A Rejected Name   43
   6: Missing the Mark   53
   7: A Show of Contempt   63

Part 3: The Greatest House
   8: A New Name   75
   9: Baptized Into His Name   83
   10: Count the Cost   93
   11: A Covenantal Name   99

Part 4: A Beautiful House
   12: A Name that Reveals   111
   13: A House for Gathering   119
   14: Authority to Build   127
   15: A Cup of Cold Water   137
   16: Praise and Glorify   145
   17: Make Way for His Exalted Name   151
   18: Blessings of the Name   159
   19: Forgiveness and Mercy   169
   20: A Wise Builder   177
   21: A Worker's Songs   185
   22: No Other Name   193

Part 5: A Glorious House
   23: Blessed Be the Name   203
   24: Restoring the Temple   213
   25: A Redemptive Name   223
   26: A House Built True to Plan   231
   27: Blow the Trumpet in Zion   239

The Capstone   249

Definitions   257

Strap on Your Tool Belt and Plug In Your Power Cord

Building a house for your family is a challenging task that comes with great rewards. The planning, design work, and financing are monumental tasks, and when all that is finished the real work begins. This is the part of building that makes blisters and callouses on your hands and strains your back. Then the moment comes when the work is finished, the builder gives you the keys, and the truck arrives to deliver that favorite easy chair you've been missing. Now you can rest through the night in your own bed in fresh new surroundings. There's great satisfaction as you see your family safe in their new home.

This study leads the learner through the Scriptures with a clear purpose: to learn how to build a house for The Name that is above all names. The goal is not to impart theological concepts, but to show the practical, daily focus that is necessary to build this house alongside others in a community of faith. Every study chapter is interwoven with Scriptures to teach us how to use the tools we need for this construction project. With wisdom as our Master Builder, we'll build a dwelling place where the peaceful presence of God's name may dwell. We construct this abode with care because the Almighty's name is so much more than a way to know God who Created us. This house must be built true to spec so it is a place where we can worship in spirit and truth.

> *Above all, you must understand that no prophecy of Scripture came about by the prophet's own interpretation of things. For prophecy never had its origin in the human will, but prophets, though human, spoke from God as they were carried along by the Holy Spirit.*
> (2 Peter 1:20–21)

This study doesn't teach people to throw down what faithful generations of Christians have built before any of us came along. We can't deconstruct what others built during the first five hundred years of Church history. The house we build would only be weakened by backpedaling. Thinking that we should tear down and start all over again is not only arrogant, but impossible.

Israel's feasts, history, and prophetic record are useful to teach us about the fullness of Christ, but attempting to go back to subject ourselves to Old Covenant regulations is unwise.

Instead, this book builds on the work of faithful witnesses who laid a foundation that has proven true and right over time. The forerunners of our faith built with stone upon precious stone on the foundation of the Apostles and Prophets to prepare a house for us to expand. Martin Luther, Jonathan Edwards, George Whitfield, John Wesley, and Charles Finney made this house strong. Charles Spurgeon, D. L. Moody, R. A. Torrey, and Billy Sunday served as builders in their generations. Dietrich Bonhoeffer, Watchman Nee, and Corrie ten Boom offered faithful testimonies of overcoming in challenging times. Mother Teresa, Chuck Smith, and Billy Graham provided spiritual leadership to build on this strong house so that we may continue the good work.

Build up, build up, prepare the way, remove every obstruction from my people's way.
(Isaiah 57:14 ESV)

All Christians who are called by Jesus' name serve as builders in our day. But we have lost the significance of His name and this good work suffers for lack of authority. In postmodern cultures the vital nature of names and their purpose in society is often overlooked. Today, a name is little more than letters written on a name tag to wear on the first day of school. We are in danger of becoming nameless broods with no roots in any land anywhere.[1] Think about what happens when a person's name is thrown out and replaced with a number tattooed on their arm. Their personhood and identity are stolen away. Being a real person requires a real name.

In this tech-dependent world we invent new personas when we create various usernames to log on to our web accounts. Because of this it's easy to forget who we really are. We're in danger of becoming like parasitic plants that grow with no roots in the good earth that God created.

We've forgotten that a good name can make a real difference. It's a bit disconcerting if we introduce ourselves by our family name and the person says: "Huh?" But we are delighted when someone remembers our name, not just our face. Unless, of course, it's our super strict Aunt Bertha who calls us out by our first, middle, and last name and we know we're in big trouble.

A good name is more desirable than great riches; to be esteemed is better than silver or gold.
(Proverbs 22:1)

---
1. Job 30:8.

This prologue with its guiding Scriptures prepares us for the challenge of building a strong house with eternal value. We'll learn the significance and meaning of names, and especially the revelatory names and titles for our heavenly Father, His only Son, and the Holy Spirit. The inspiration for this book began with a question asked several years ago: "Why does the Bible say to 'exalt His name' instead of simply saying 'exalt the Lord God?'" No, they don't mean the same thing. Wouldn't exalting God be a more personal way to worship than praising His name? Those who ask this question reveal the disconnect we have in our day between the person and their name.

Scripture upon Scripture we examine this truth, like studying the blueprints before ordering building materials for our new house. Our blueprint is the Bible where the Great I AM reveals Himself to us by His name. We can know Him and His nature by His name and descriptive titles. Knowing His name teaches us who we are as sons and daughters of the Most High God. We find our identity in Christ by the name He bestows upon His brothers and sisters.[2]

The name we use to call upon our heavenly Father and the titles we use to address Him are more than revelatory. We exalt His name in worship, praise, and with our hands lifted up. But even more than this, He has given His name to His people so we may glorify Him. We are called by His name, known by His name, and find our identity by the name He gave us.

First, the Great I AM redeemed Israel out of Egypt so they would bear His name. Now, the Church is called by His name. Each member of the body of Christ is like a family living together in a great home. Each person is a precious living stone, like pillars called by our Savior's name.[3] Then every living stone is built into the kingdom where the Lord God's name is inscribed. All of us together are called by the name of our Lord Jesus Christ. We are many stones who God knows by name. He calls us by name and gives us His name to bring us together under one household name. By His name we can do this good work under authority. It's our family business.

So it is with Christ's body. We are many parts of one body, and we all belong to each other.
(Romans 12:5 NLT)

We must be clear about what we're building before we start. Jesus promised all of His disciples that He would go to prepare a house for us where we may dwell with Him forever.[4] The New Jerusalem is built upon a foundation of precious stones—the twelve Apostles of the Lamb.[5] We are the building

---
2. Matthew 12:50.
3. Revelation 3:12.
4. John 14:1–3.
5. Revelation 21:14.

stones of a spiritual house and we are built upon this foundation. As we tread upon created earth, we're like the tribes of Israel who wandered in the wilderness. The Bible likens us to tents; temporary dwellings where the Almighty comes to abide with us and carry us through to the eternal Land of Promise. Our Redeemer inhabits this temporary tent even when it sags and wrinkles with age. This is His habitation as we build and prepare an eternal house with many rooms—a home the Bridegroom is preparing for us.

This study gets personal. The Scriptures will hit as close to our hearts as our name. It's unlikely our neighbors will start calling us "Joe Christian" to our faces, but when we abide in Christ we become known by His name. Calling us "Jesus people" is out of fashion, but His name is forever written on our hearts. The name inscribed on our heart's door proclaims that we are one part of an eternal spiritual house whose Builder and Maker is God. During our time on earth, we are like temporary tents with pegs driven in the soil. But the dwelling we construct in the kingdom of heaven is built upon the sure and tested Cornerstone with precious stones. Such an abode will stand strong for eternity.[6]

The Scriptures in this book stand in contrast to a post-modern day culture. Today's people have forgotten the truth of these verses that have shaped relationships and the culture of marital unions for centuries. Every family is formed and defined by the foundations of truth the Creator established in the beginning by the power of the Word who was with God, and who spoke, "Let there be light."

As you come to him, the living Stone–rejected by humans but chosen by God and precious to him–you also, like living stones, are being built into a spiritual house to be a holy priesthood, offering spiritual sacrifices acceptable to God through Jesus Christ.
(1 Peter 2:4–5)

In many churches today expository teaching is in favor, and for good reason. It keeps us centered on the entire message of the Scriptures. Other Churches have a lectionary calendar for teaching through significant portions of the Bible, including the Old Testament, the Epistles, and the Gospels. Some Bible teachers conduct inductive studies that focus on key words. Studies through a book of the Bible are most common in adult groups today.

An in-depth topical study incorporates all of the above in the sense that the whole of Scripture is used to interpret the topic at hand. Studying key words in original languages serves to enlighten each topic. Every solid topical study must test what is taught by Scriptures from Genesis to Revelation.

---
6. Isaiah 28:16.

Teaching verse upon verse, the Gospels, writings of the Prophets, Apostles, the Pentateuch, Bible history, the Epistles, and the Apostle John's Revelation must all come together to complete a solid topical study. It's like taking good soil and blending it with nutrients and mulch to make raised planters where a garden will grow and produce plump tomatoes, sweet corn, climbing bean stalks, and giant orange pumpkins. Because Scripture interprets Scripture a topical study must be tested by every word of Scripture. The reader is encouraged to use the same standard to measure every word written here.

> *Above all, you must understand that no prophecy of Scripture came about by the prophet's own interpretation of things.*
> (2 Peter 1:20)

God's name is above all names, a most worthy name. His name is worthy of a house where He may dwell forever. This dwelling place is built with precious gemstones who are Abba Father's sons and daughters. This is a house worthy of the Great I AM, and the Prince of Peace. It's a dwelling place that is constantly refreshed by the four winds of the Spirit.

His holy name is all sufficient, more than enough to fill every house with many good things. His name satisfies every good desire from the heart. With the building materials at hand, tools in our belt, and power cords plugged in, let's get started with building a house for the Name that is above all names. We need a Zacchaeus-like enthusiasm for building. He invited Jesus to dinner as soon as he heard His precious words: "Zacchaeus, come down immediately. I must stay at your house today."[7]

With such a beautiful and glorious name given to us as our own we ought to sing out from our hearts with praise at every moment of every day. It is a great privilege to exalt our heavenly Father while serving side by side with wisdom as our Master Builder. We are incredibly blessed to serve as builders of the house for such an awesome name. Our hearts overflow with songs of joy as we join together in this great work.

Why do we only sing the Hallelujah Chorus during one season of the year? This choral exalts the Most High with glorious and harmonious words. It's no wonder the carpenters and masons of this house are thrilled to sing out in a mighty chorus while their hands are building.

---

7. Luke 19:5.

King of kings (Forever and ever Hallelujah! Hallelujah!)
And Lord of lords (Forever and ever Hallelujah! Hallelujah!)
King of kings (Forever and ever Hallelujah! Hallelujah!)
And Lord of lords (Forever and ever Hallelujah! Hallelujah!)
King of kings (Forever and ever Hallelujah! Hallelujah!)
And Lord of lords (King of kings and Lord of lords)[8]

---

8. "Hallelujah Chorus," from *Messiah, HWV 56*, G.F. Handel, public domain.

Part 1:
The Ground Work

Sow righteousness for yourselves, reap the fruit of unfailing love, and break up your unplowed ground; for it is time to seek the Lord, until he comes and showers his righteousness on you.

(Hosea 10:12)

Preparing the Building Site

Key Scriptures:

- "Thus says the Lord God, 'Behold, I am the one who has laid as a foundation in Zion, a stone, a tested stone, a precious cornerstone, of a sure foundation: "Whoever believes will not be in haste."'" (Isaiah 28:16 ESV)
- "You are no longer foreigners and strangers, but fellow citizens with God's people and also members of his household, built on the foundation of the apostles and prophets, with Christ Jesus himself as the chief cornerstone." (Ephesians 2:19–20)

This is your first training session to prepare you as a qualified builder. Roll out the blueprint, get out your tape measure and prepare to build. The holy Scriptures diagram this house in great detail so that you can build with care. The Word of creation is better than a laser measuring tape when it comes to making sure this dwelling is built true to plan. You'll learn why it's so important for everyone on the team to serve as tried and tested building stones for this eternal house. Every learner starts at the beginning where the Creator reveals Himself in the first words of the Bible. Genesis 1:1 sets the foundation for this good work with this powerful declaration: "In the beginning God created."[1]

This study emphasizes the day the Lord God revealed His name to Moses. As we read this account in Exodus 3:15, we learn that the Lord sent Moses to free the enslaved tribes from Egypt and told him, "Say to the Israelites, 'The Lord, the God of your fathers—the God of Abraham, the God of Isaac and the God of Jacob—has sent me to you.'" This study shows us that the foundation for Israel's deliverance began much earlier in time.

As we prepare the building site for this house we build for His name, we'll learn why Moses asked to know his heavenly Father's name when God called him to deliver Israel from slavery. The people would need to know by whose authority he spoke and what name gave him that authority. We'll learn the significance of changing Abram and Jacob's names to Abraham and Israel.

---

1. אֱלֹהִים 'ĕlôhîym.

This study shows us how the Creator's name advanced through time to establish the great renown of His name in all the earth.

We'll learn the importance of knowing our Father's name, the name of His Son, and the Holy Spirit. We'll come to see His awesome name imprinted on every element of our lives, enlightening every word of our intercessions and illuminating every prayerful plea.

Study Prayer

Father God; Out of your glorious riches strengthen us in our inner beings with power through your Holy Spirit so we may build a house for your holy name.

A prayer according to Ephesians 3:16

On the sixth day the Creator formed man out of the earth's soil. The Holy Spirit breathed into him the breath of life and he stood up on the earth, a living and breathing handiwork made in God's image. Then Creator God made a companion for the man. He gave both of them names, Adam and Eve. Their names have meaning: Adam means "Son of the Red Earth." Then the Creator formed a mate for the first man and called her Eve, meaning "Living one" or "Source of Life."

When Adam and Eve gave birth to children, they gave each one a name that had meaning. They named their firstborn son Cain because Eve declared, "I have brought forth a man." They gave their second child the name, Abel, meaning "Breath." Surely, earth's first mother named him "breath" as she held this child in her arms and watched as the Spirit breathe life into his lungs for the first time.

The wind of the Spirit hovered over the Creator's awesome new creation. The Almighty separated light from darkness and the water above from the water below. The Word brought heaven and earth into order. He planted a garden to sustain the man and woman, meeting their every need.[2] Before entering His rest on the seventh day the Lord God declared all He had made to be "very good." Moses, the author of Genesis, begins his account by writing: "In the beginning God," using the Creator's title. Then he writes a narrative of creation in chapter two, revealing the Creator's name: "Yehovah Elohim."[3]

---

2. An in-depth study on the Creator's work is available in the author's book, *Great Separations*.
3. The Name is written with the Hebrew letters Yod-Heh-Vav-Heh (YHVH). It is frequently spoken of as the "Unutterable Name."

This is the account of the heavens and the earth when they were created, when the LORD[4] God[5] made the earth and the heavens.
(Genesis 2:4)

Consider how the Creator's name advanced through time. People first called on the name of the Lord in the days of Seth and his son Enosh. Many years later God called Abram to a land he didn't know. By faith he traveled to Canaan with his family and flocks. In the land of promise God changed his name from Abram (exalted father) to Abraham (father of nations). Later the God of Abraham changed the grandson's name. Jacob shepherded his flocks and herds on his way back to the land promised to Abraham and his progeny. Then the angel of the Most High wrestled with him in his tent all through the night. Before heaven's messenger departed, he told him his name was changed from Jacob (grabber) to Israel. There, the Lord Almighty, El Shaddai established a nation called by Jacob's new name, Israel, meaning "Contender with God" or "God Prevails."

Now press the fast forward button and go to the Year of Our Lord. Jesus, who is the Christ, came to walk among His people. He taught the people, fed them, delivered them from demons, healed the sick, and raised the dead. Then, Jesus offered Himself as the Lamb of God. He suffered, died, was buried, rose again, and then resurrected. Then our Messiah ascended to the right hand of the Father and sent His Holy Spirit to establish the Church. Now He gives His gathered people His own name. Ultimately, in the Revelation of Jesus Christ His name will be fully revealed to all those who have called on His holy name. Look at how the Creator's name has advanced throughout time as His people build a house for His holy name.

In the days of Seth and Enosh people began to call on the name of the Lord.

At the age of ninety-nine God appeared to Abraham and said, "I am God Almighty;[6] walk before me faithfully and be blameless."[7]

God revealed His name as He commissioned Moses to deliver His people, saying: "I AM who I AM."[8] Then God gathered the children of Abraham's fourth generation as a holy nation to be called by a holy name, Israel.

Christ Jesus came humbly as a new-born child who was placed in a cow's trough to serve as His cradle. Thirty-three later, by means of a cruel Roman cross, He gained a mighty victory and then ascended to sit at the right hand of the Father. As promised, He sent the Holy Spirit with a fiery baptism to

4. יְהֹוָה Yᵉhôvâh
5. אֱלֹהִים 'ĕlôhîym
6. אֵל 'êl.
7. Genesis 17:1.
8. הָיָה hâyâh.

establish His Church. Now the Church is gathered from every tribe, nation, people, and culture. They are brought together as a remnant called by the name of God's only Son, our victorious Christ.

Christ, our Redeemer, has declared His victory over sin, Satan, and death. His victorious name and the power and authority of His name will be finally revealed in the Revelation of Jesus Christ. Our Father in heaven will exalt Him to the highest place and give Him the name that is above every name.[9] Upon hearing His name, every knee will bow and every tongue confess that Jesus the Christ is Lord of all. By His name everything is made subject to the Son by the One who put everything under His feet, "so that God may be all in all."[10]

We serve an awesome God who revealed Himself to Moses, saying: "I AM Yehovah Elohim." The God of Abraham, Isaac, and Jacob established His name for all generations to come. His reputation and renown became exalted among the nations who witnessed the deliverance of the tribes of Israel from bondage in Egypt. Ten plagues devastated the land of Israel's oppressors and forever established the power of God's mighty name. He commanded Moses to part the Red Sea, and then drowned the Egyptian army. From that time on, His name struck fear and awe in all His adversaries. Feeding the people in the desert, providing water in a dry and thirsty wilderness, and giving them His Law exalted His holy name. He performed all these miraculous works "to gain for Himself everlasting renown."[11] He guided His holy nation safely through the wilderness to make for Himself a glorious name.[12] The Lord who is mighty in battle gained great honor, and glory for His holy name by His mighty outstretched arm.

The Lord descended to the top of Mount Sanai and He called Moses to ascend to the peak of the mountain.[13] But after he was gone so long on the mountain, not returning to their encampment, the people gave up on Moses and decided to make their own god—a golden calf. In doing so they brought dishonor upon God whose name is Deliverer. They caused great shame to come upon the name of their God and they suffered the dire consequences of Yehovah's just and righteous wrath. We ought to learn from their egregious defamation of The Name. We are encouraged to wait on the Lord and keep ourselves free from acts that would dishonor His holy name. Then we can teach the next generation and the next to glorify and honor the Father's name in all <u>our words and deeds</u> so they may join us as builders of this awesome house.

9. Philippians 2:9.
10. 1 Corinthians 15:28.
11. Isaiah 63:12.
12. Isaiah 63:14.
13. Exodus 19:20.

God also said to Moses, "Say to the Israelites, 'The LORD, the God of your fathers—the God of Abraham, the God of Isaac and the God of Jacob—has sent me to you. This is my name forever, the name you shall call me from generation to generation.'"
(Exodus 3:15)

Since the days of Seth and Enosh a few people from every generation on earth have called on the name of the Lord. We often address the Father, His Son and the Holy Spirit by names that reveal the nature and attributes of the triune God. It's important to know His revelatory name and attributes because together we are building a house that will bear His holy name in all His majesty.

The desire of our hearts is for Yehova-Rapha, God who heals,[14] to have a place with us in this house? We yearn for Yehovah-Yireh, our Provider,[15] to join us at our table. Wouldn't we like to have Yehovah-Nissi as our Refuge and Banner[16] to safeguard our house? If it's our heart's desire to have peace reside with us, wouldn't we invite Yehovah-Shalom, God of Peace,[17] to inhabit our house? What an incredible blessing to have the ever-present Elohim[18] with us through the night hours. Consider the comfort of knowing Yahweh-Raah, our Shepherd who leads us beside still waters.[19] And what an awesome blessing to know Yahweh-Tsidkenu, our Righteousness,[20] who engulfs this tent where we dwell with His presence. If God in all His magnificence is what we desire, then we must build a house where He may reside with us in the fullness of His presence.

Yeshua, our Lord Jesus, is Savior, Redeemer, the Bread of Life, and the Word of Creation. Jesus is the Son of God, and Son of Man. Jesus Christ is Messiah, Lord, Master, and Immanuel. He is our Prince of Peace, High Priest, Advocate, and Head of the Church. The Good Shepherd is our High and Exalted One, Lily of the Valley, and the Bright Morning Star. His name is worthy of all praise because His name is Wonderful, Counselor, and Mighty God. We must ask ourselves: "Are there any human hands that can build a house for such an awesome name?"

The Holy Spirit is "Ruach" in Hebrew. He is the Spirit of Counsel, Comfort, and Knowledge. The Spirit of Christ is our Intercessor,[21] the Four

---

14. Exodus 15:26.
15. Genesis 22:14.
16. Exodus 17:15.
17. Judges 6:24.
18. Exodus 33:14.
19. Psalm 23:1.
20. Jeremiah 23:6.
21. Romans 8:26–27.

Winds on the Earth,[22] and the Breath of Life. The Spirit of Jesus is the Spirit of Wisdom, the Source of all knowledge and understanding, and the fear of the Lord. By wisdom this house is strengthened with Spirit's seven pillars of wisdom to support it.

> *Wisdom has built her house; she has set up its seven pillars. She has prepared her meat and mixed her wine; she has also set her table.*
> (Proverbs 9:1–2)

With great expectation we lay our petitions before Abba, our Father, the Lord Almighty, who is Creator of all Heaven and Earth. We know nothing is impossible for Him. The Holy Spirit helps us as we come to intercede before the throne of grace. We prayerfully ask for what we need in Jesus' name; a name honored above all names.[23] Jesus' name is more than a signature or seal to sign off on our prayers. When we pray, we ask for what is *in His name*. Our petitions are offered in agreement with every attribute revealed in the name of the Father, Son, and Holy Spirit. We ask for provision, healing, safety, peace, salvation, help, and comfort. In our prayers, praise, and worship we call out to Him in accord with the name and titles ascribed to Him. He is worthy of all praise because there is no name in heaven or on earth by which we may be saved.[24] This is the high and exalted name He gives to all His sons and daughters. Indeed, there is no house made by human hands, no stained-glass windows or buttressed rafters that can be built to contain such a holy name.

> *It was Solomon who built a house for him. However, the Most High does not live in houses made by human hands. As the prophet says: "Heaven is my throne, and the earth is my footstool. What kind of house will you build for me? says the Lord. Or where will my resting place be? Has not my hand made all these things?"*
> (Acts 7:47–50)

When a construction crew arrives at a vacant lot to start building a house, they begin by bulldozing out all the junk and leveling the ground. Christians who pray for renewal and revival find that the greatest challenge is getting the religious junk out of the way. We're stuck in our religious rut. We can't build a solid house until we fill in the deep ruts and level the land.[25] It's a challenge that begins on repentant knees. Restoration gains its wings by putting on our Gospel shoes and stepping out of our comfort zone to do the hard work of rebuilding. The reality is that repentance lays the groundwork for building an abode for the name that is above all names.

---

22. Daniel 7:2.
23. Philippians 2:9.
24. Acts 4:12.
25. Isaiah 40:3–5.

We've learned the importance of knowing our Father's name. How can we build a house for His name if we don't know the One who will dwell there? Our God has a glorious and awesome name, a name above all other names, and we must build an eternal house where He will dwell among all His sons and daughters who bear His name.

To qualify as builders, we learned how the Creator's name has progressed through history. By His name all things came into being and by His name He sustains all things. During Adam's lifetime, Seth and Enosh began calling on the name of the Lord. Then the Great I AM gathered a holy nation that is called by His name. Finally, by the power of the name our Lord and Savior gained the victory over sin, Satan, and death. All things are placed under the feet of our victorious and conquering Messiah. As our Redeemer looks to the day of His final victory, He is gathering a royal priesthood that is called by His name. It's a family name for all His adopted sons and daughters.

Every son and daughter of our Father in heaven is called to work in the power of Jesus' name to build a house where God may dwell with us in peace. This is a house that cannot be built by human hands, or by means of mortal strength. The dwelling we construct is holy, set apart for His name, a place where He alone will tabernacle with His people. He will not share this glorious abiding place with any other.[26] We learned from Israel's sin. With their own hands they made a golden calf to worship. We must not fall into the same trap, because any duplicity on our part brings shame upon our Father's holy name.

Those who are in Christ are the precious gems—the building stones of God's kingdom. Each one of us is a necessary part in the house built upon the seven pillars of the Spirit's wisdom for His holy name. The Lord Almighty inhabits us as His beloved building stones, and in the same way He inhabits the whole temple that is His Church.

> *For we know that if the earthly tent we live in is destroyed, we have a building from God, an eternal house in heaven, not built by human hands.*
> (2 Corinthians 5:1)

---

26. Isaiah 42:8.

Chapter 1

Preparing the Building Site

Q & A

1. Why are names and their meaning so important to know as we begin this building project?

   _____
   _____
   _____

2. How has our Creator's name advanced through time?

   _____
   _____
   _____

3. What do we learn from ancient Israel's duplicity? What effect did their idolatry have on their God's holy name?

   _____
   _____
   _____

4. Why is it important for us to know the majesty, glory, and attributes of the Father's holy name?

   _____
   _____
   _____

My Journal Notes:

Majesty of the Name

Key Scriptures:

- "Therefore God exalted him to the highest place and gave him the name that is above every name, that at the name of Jesus every knee should bow, in heaven and on earth and under the earth, and every tongue acknowledge that Jesus Christ is Lord, to the glory of God the Father." (Philippians 2:9–11)

- "His eyes are like blazing fire, and on his head are many crowns. He has a name written on him that no one knows but he himself." (Revelation 19:12)

Open your Bible and together we'll see the great and awesome beauty of the name of our God who is worthy of this house we build. His name is so awesome and glorious that only His Son can fathom the vast splendor it reveals. Could any dwelling we build encompass all the heavens and earth? Would it be sufficient for the majesty of His holy name? In this study we'll learn who is worthy to put their hand to the work of building this great house.

We'll come to know that every element of creation is imprinted with the Creator's holy name. With this truth imprinted on our spirit, our world view changes. The beauty of our great national parks and forests become a display of the wonders of God's holy name. In the comfort of His presence, you can settle down for the night and look up at the stars that glow with the wonders of Orion's Belt and the Pleiades cluster. As our eyes come to rest in the beauty and comfort of God's creation, it's too easy to forget the fearsome splendor of His majesty.

We'll learn that the grandeur of His name is also revealed in how He readily forgives us for the sake of His holy name. When our eyes are opened to see the splendor and vast treasures of the kingdom of heaven we must ask ourselves, "Is it even possible for mortal beings to build an eternal house?"

> **Study Prayer**
>
> *Father, we pray that the name of our Lord Jesus Christ may be glorified in us as we are in Him. Strengthen us to proclaim your holy name in every nation and tribe.*
>
> A prayer according to 2 Thessalonians 1:12

There are no words we can speak from any of earth's languages that can fully express the majesty and awesome glory of our Father's name. And yet, every word, letter, smallest punctuation mark, and smallest jot of the pen in the inspired Scriptures are interwoven with threads of our Father's holy name. Consider that every strike of a gavel where justice is done echoes on the courtroom walls with the sound of God's holy name. Indeed, our Creator's name is manifested universally. God's signature is inscribed on the subatomic particles of creation. The farthest stars in the outermost solar systems shine out with the glory of His name. The tiny veins in the leaves of the mighty oak tree contain the Almighty's beautiful imprint, and its branches joyfully clap their hands in earth's winds to glorify His name.[1] The mighty Redwood trees aspire to the heavens, reaching their branches to the sky, and every one of their thousand growth rings are imbedded with the majesty of our God's holy name.

The lion in the jungle roars and the fearsome sound resonates with his Creator's grandeur. Dolphins play in the ocean's currents, leaping, diving, and chattering in unison as if singing to the Lord of creation whose name is written deep in their genetic code.

Every ridge and rocky strata on the snow capped mountains have the Almighty's name inscribed in them and they quake at the sound of His name.[2] The waters of the great oceans are saturated with The Name, and they crash with a roar, creating a majestic display of our Lord's holy name on the shorelines of every jetty, island, and continent.

> Lord, *our Lord, how majestic is your name in all the earth! You have set your glory in the heavens.*
> (Psalm 8:1)

The Almighty called Job to account for speaking of things he knew nothing about. He confronted him with a pointed question: "Where were you when I laid the earth's foundation? Tell me, if you understand."[3]

Fallible humans are challenged when it comes to grasping the glory, majesty, and splendor of our Father's name. We know and cherish our Savior who comes to us as the Good Shepherd to rescue us, anoint us with healing

---
1. Isaiah 55:12.
2. Nahum 1:5.
3. Job 38:4.

oil, and then carry us home while holding us close to His heart. We cherish His intimate presence that is nearer than a touch, and closer than a breath. We speak His name, "Jesus," with familiarity, even casually because He calls us "brother," "sister," and "friend."

We are content in this closeness and enjoy the solace we find in His loving arms. But in His comfort, we tend to ignore the glorious and fearsome splendor of His presence as revealed in the Apostle John's Revelation of Jesus Christ. When we see our Lord and Savior face to face our knees buckle. As we look upon Him who is the Alpha and Omega our mortal strength evaporates. When the Apostle John came into His presence, he fully realized that there is no other name so worthy. What John saw was beyond understanding. He wrote His revelatory book to give us a glimpse of the glory of Jesus Christ that he saw in the spirit: "His feet were like bronze glowing in a furnace, and his voice was like the sound of rushing waters."[4] As John came face to face with the Alpha and Omega he fell down before Him as if dead until Christ Jesus reached out to touch him, saying, "Do not be afraid. I am the First and the Last."[5]

Our Shepherd carries us home on His shoulders and brings us into the fold of fellowship in His family; giving us His glorious name as our own. And yet, when we see Him face to face in the fullness of His majesty and come to know the full glory of His name, our knees buckle. We're blessed and comforted with the intimacy of His holy presence and we bow down as we come into the full majesty of His presence.

> *The L*ORD *reigns, let the nations tremble; he sits enthroned between the cherubim, let the earth shake. Great is the L*ORD *in Zion; he is exalted over all the nations. Let them praise your great and awesome name–he is holy.*
> (Psalm 99:1–3)

Because our heavenly Father's majestic name permeates every letter and punctuation mark in the inspired writings of Scripture, not one word ever fails to return abundantly fruitful.[6] His righteousness and faithful promises accompany all those who go out with tears, carrying seed to sow. They will return with joyful singing carrying baskets full of the bounty of the kingdom.[7]

Our Lord Jesus sends us out in His name. We serve as His hands extended to reach out to all those who come for His healing touch. By His command we have authority to extend a cup of water in His name to all those who thirst for the Spring of Living Water. We go out as ambassadors of all that is eter-

---
4. Revelation 1:15.
5. Revelation 1:17.
6. Isaiah 55:11.
7. Psalm 126:6.

nally trustworthy and true. Our mission compels us to carry with us the eternal Gospel that proclaims His love, mercy, forgiveness, faithfulness, justice, righteousness, and saving grace. We are sent as a covenant people, with our garden basket in hand, to pass on the Good News to every nation on earth so they may "taste and see that the Lord is good."[8]

O Lord, our Lord, how majestic is your name in all the earth![9]

The works of his hands are faithful and just; all his precepts are trustworthy. They are established for ever and ever, enacted in faithfulness and uprightness. He provided redemption for his people; he ordained his covenant forever–holy and awesome is his name.
(Psalm 111:7–9)

God's people are shown an abundance of grace for the sake of the name our Father gives us as adopted sons and daughters. When we bring shame on His name and then turn from our sin and repent, He is quick to forgive for the sake of His name. Our God is faithful and in justice He forgives us and cleanses us from even the stain of our sin. He also blesses us with consequences for our sin to restrain our wandering ways in the days ahead.

Because of His mercy and forgiveness, we love Him even more than ever. Be assured that our friends, family, neighbors, and our even own children notice our failings. The greatest witness to each of them is to admit that we fell down, but then realized our wrong, confessed our transgressions, and found forgiveness in Jesus Christ. In all this, His holy name is glorified among all those we rub elbows with, and especially to our little ones we feed around our table every day. By our faithful witness, His name is proven holy even in the eyes of the world.

I will show the holiness of my great name, which has been profaned among the nations, the name you have profaned among them. Then the nations will know that I am the Lord, declares the Sovereign Lord, when I am proved holy through you before their eyes.
(Ezekiel 36:23)

Our limited human intellect makes it challenging for us to understand the wonders our heavenly Father performs among all the inhabitants on earth. He establishes nations and throws down nations. He raises up rulers and deposes heads of state as He wills. He orchestrates Earth's climate, directing it according to His purpose and plan. The tides of the great oceans are stirred by His hands, bringing currents to warm the frozen northern shores. In God our Creator, the depths and richness of all wisdom and knowledge are pres-

---

8. Psalm 34:8.
9. Psalm 8:9.

ent. He gives His wisdom to all who ask. His just and righteous judgments are beyond our ability to comprehend. The paths of His footsteps are impossible for us to plot out.[10] By His Spirit he opens the minds of His people to understand things they could never have otherwise grasped.[11] The great mysteries of creation are His to reveal to those who seek to know the wonders of all He spoke into being.

How is it possible for us to build a house worthy of the name of our Sovereign Lord who is awesome in the splendor of His majesty?

Praise be to the name of God for ever and ever; wisdom and power are his. He changes times and seasons; he deposes kings and raises up others. He gives wisdom to the wise and knowledge to the discerning. He reveals deep and hidden things; he knows what lies in darkness, and light dwells with him.
(Daniel 2:20–22)

Every prayer begins with exaltation and is carried by the wind of the Spirit through heaven's gates accompanied with our thanksgiving. Jesus taught us to begin our prayers by glorifying our Father, because we serve an awesome and majestic God who is Lord of all creation. He is worthy of all praise because in Him we "live and move and have our being."[12] Indeed, we are His sons and daughters who are called by the greatest name known among humankind. He is worthy of all praise, honor, and glory and we come on prayer-bent knees because He is "holy, holy, holy." We come with our heads bowed because He is "the Lord God Almighty, who was, and is, and is to come."[13]

This, then, is how you should pray: "Our Father in heaven, hallowed be your name."
(Matthew 6:9)

If it was possible to bring together in one place all the riches, splendor, and trappings of every ruler over earth's great empires and kingdoms up to this present time; their gold, silver, jewels, beautiful tapestries, finest robes, and royal carriages would be a splendid sight to see. The shields of gold, helmets of shining silver, bejeweled crowns of every one of earth's kings and queens, princes and nobility throughout all time would be a display beyond anything we could ever imagine.

Now consider the awesome God we serve. The collective wealth and riches of all these grand rulers on the earth are a mere drop of water in the great oceans compared to the vast riches of the kingdom of heaven where our Lord

---

10. Romans 11:33–34.
11. Jeremiah 33:3.
12. Acts 17:28.
13. Revelation 4:8.

and God rules with majesty. David and Solomon in all their rich arraignments and royal splendor were less than a drop of water in earth's great seas compared to the glory of Israel's God whom they served.[14]

Our Father, who calls us by His name, is King over all of earth's kings. He is Master Builder over all master builders. He is Lord over all who call themselves lord, laird, landlord, or magistrate. Our Lord and Redeemer rises up victorious over every stronghold on earth with His that is worthy of all praise, honor, and glory.

This is the God whom we serve as builders of a house that is worthy of His holy name.

On his robe and on his thigh he has this name written: king of kings and lord of lords. (Revelation 19:16)

The sun, moon, and stars speak out as faithful witnesses to make known the glory of Creator God. They give glory to the Almighty One by whom all things were made and have their being. They have no need of earthbound words as they testify to the wonders of creation. The language they speak is neither Hebrew, Greek, Latin, nor English. That's a good thing because the tongues and dialects the nations use are wholly inadequate to proclaim the full revelation of the Father's holy name and the works of His hands.

An important takeaway from this study is that no human language on Earth is capable of expressing the glory and majesty of our Father's holy name. The only perfect expressions of the Creator's glorious name are spoken out by the sun, moon, and stars. Their voice speaks out perfectly and clearly to proclaim the Almighty's name to every nation and people on Earth.

Though our words are inadequate, we humbly raise up holy hands and lift our voices to shout out exaltations with words of praise from our spirit to the God of our Salvation. We shout out in our clearest voice with words to exalt our God who is above all gods. Our praises echo out into all the heavens.

As we build this house for our Father's holy name, stone upon precious stone, we must be cognizant, as best we are able, of the name for whom we build. The knowledge of His glorious name kindles a fire in us that cannot be extinguished. We must put aside our complacency, never forgetting that we serve God whose presence is fearsome and splendid. The fire of His holy presence is the catalyst for this great work. We undertake it with fear and trembling because of the sound of His name.

---

14. Matthew 6:29.

The heavens declare the glory of God; the skies proclaim the work of his hands. Day after day they pour forth speech; night after night they reveal knowledge. They have no speech, they use no words; no sound is heard from them. Yet their voice goes out into all the earth, their words to the ends of the world.
(Psalm 19:1–4)

Chapter 2

Majesty of the Name

Q & A

1. What is the best language for expressing our Father's holy name?

___

___

2. What language do the sun, moon, and stars use to speak out their faithful witness of God their Creator?

___

___

3. Describe the dichotomy of the comfort you enjoy as you abide in Christ and the fearsome splendor of His presence.

___

___

4. Do you know any person on Earth who is capable of building a house on their own where the glory, majesty, and holiness of our Father's name could dwell?

___

___

My Journal Notes:

The Work of Generations

Key Scriptures:

- "See, I have written your name on the palms of my hands. Always in my mind is a picture of Jerusalem's walls in ruins." (Isaiah 49:16 NLT)

- "Tell him this is what the Lord Almighty says: 'Here is the man whose name is the Branch, and he will branch out from his place and build the temple of the Lord.'" (Zechariah 6:12)

- "Lord, you have been our dwelling place throughout all generations." (Psalm 90:1)

One of the most important moments in an adult's life is when dad hands over the keys to the shop and says, "It's all yours. I'm heading out on a long fishing trip." The photos on his office walls offer a history of the family's hard work. It's a picture history of dad's expansion of the construction business his own dad began. Faded old black and white pictures show grandad Johansen and his four-man crew standing in front of post war houses they built for veterans coming home after World War II. The framed photographs progress to color and lead up to aerial views of grand housing developments with modern houses, banks, strip malls, and schools built by dad and scores of his subcontractors. With the keys in your shaking hand, you wonder: "What pictures will I add to the wall?"

When reading through our Bibles from Genesis to Revelation we tend to skip over the genealogies. It's hard to go through an exhaustive list of: the son of an unpronounceable name, who is the son of another name that twists our tongue. Parents and grandparents who attend Christmas pageants never hear the genealogy of Joseph read to them. It would take about three verses of begats to put everyone to sleep. But the long catalog of names serves several significant purposes and communicates many layers of revelation. First, we'll look at key points of vital truths and let the Scriptures open our eyes to see the greatest significance of these historic records. This study teaches us the significance of the Father's holy name in every generation throughout history. This Scripture by Scripture instruction turns the genealogies into a historic drama.

We begin with the first Adam as our teacher, and then we'll learn from the greatest teacher, Jesus Christ, the last Adam.[1]

As we delve into this study, consider the key Scriptures. The city our Father chose to inscribe His name is not just a place we pinpoint on a map where walls, houses, and a temple are built with earthen stones. Wooden beams and quarried rock cannot build a city in God's kingdom. We'll learn that those whom God has called and chosen are the building blocks, the living stones of the city of God.[2] We'll see that Generations of inhabitants threw down long-established barriers and allowed the idolatry of the nations around them to break down walls and bring them to ruin. We'll examine ourselves to see if the same spiritual problem exists today. Are we, the Church, more conformed to the world around us than we are to Christ?[3] Do false prophets in our day whitewash the crumbling Church walls that once separated us as a holy people? Have we breached our hedge of protection?[4] If so, who will stand in the gap?

This study brings us face to face with our sin so we may repent. It's a lesson that equips us to pick up the building stones from the rubble and begin to rebuild. We come into a great hope even as we see the piles of rocks and debris marred by flames and covered with soot. We take comfort in knowing they can be cleaned, refined and made into precious building stones.

Where do we start this great work? We begin by rebuilding close to home![5]

> Study Prayer
>
> *Father God; May our family roots grow deep in Springs of Living Water. May heaven's dew rest on our branches through all hours of night.*
>
> A prayer according to Job 29:19

We serve a risen Savior, the resurrected Christ who is the Alpha and Omega. With the first inspired words written by Moses in the holy Scriptures, the beginning and end is revealed. The Word of Creation spoke and formed Adam out of the earth's soil. From that day forward, every family name added to the genealogies and written in heaven's Book of Life becomes part of the house we build stone upon precious stone until that great day of the Lord when the Alpha and Omega is fulfilled and fully revealed. His promise is sure: "Yes I AM coming soon." We look forward to see that blessed day when

---

1. 1 Corinthians 15:45.
2. Isaiah 1:26; 1 Peter 2:4–5.
3. Ezekiel 11:12.
4. Ezekiel 13:14. (Chapter 9 in author's book, *Great Separations*, provides in-depth study of walls of separation.)
5. Nehemiah 3:23, 29–30.

the people from every tribe, nation, and language speak out, saying, "Amen, come, Lord Jesus."

Christians are a chosen people, a royal priesthood, and a holy nation. We are precious, living building stones—the Father's holy possession.[6] We are a house that is built with blood-bought gemstones. Sons and daughters of the Most High God are the rocks that cry out, singing the praises of our Father's holy name. With words of exaltation, we sing and lift up holy hands in praise. God's people are living sacrifices who bow in worship, shout out with praise, and lift up holy hands in exaltation. Walls built stone upon stone must measure up to be sure that what is holy is kept separate from what is common.[7] Every generation of faith born in Christ, from Adam and Abel to Zechariah and Zerubbabel are uplifted up into the light of our victorious risen Savior's holy name.

> *God also said to Moses, "Say to the Israelites, 'The LORD, the God of your fathers–the God of Abraham, the God of Isaac and the God of Jacob–has sent me to you.'" "This is my name forever, the name you shall call me from generation to generation."* (Exodus 3:15)

We are not only precious building stones but we are the builders—construction workers in Christ's kingdom. We build upon the Cornerstone who is Jesus, the Word of Creation who set the foundations in place. Our work is to build upon the work accomplished before us, building upon the Apostles and the Prophets. It's a family business; a family of faith. Only the Master builder knows when the work of each generation is ready for the next to build upon. Only the Father knows when every stone is in place and the house is ready to receive the bride of Christ.[8]

Stone upon stone, our family of faith builds a house worthy of the Name that is above all names. Our faithful grandmothers and grandfathers built according to the "blueprint" drawn out to chart their lives. Our spiritual mentors served to lift us up, to nurture us so that we too could build according to the Father's plan. It's as if we can stand back and look at the house and see layer upon layer built upon each other's good work. The work accomplished by each generation of true builders appears in layers, from Adam until our day. Every precious stone and every layer built has its distinct radiance and hue.

> *Such is the generation of those who seek him, who seek your face, God of Jacob.* (Psalm 24:6)

---

6. 1 Peter 2:9.
7. For an in-depth study on separating holy and common, see author's book, *Great Separations*.
8. John 14:3.

Consider the work accomplished before you came on the building site and strapped on your tool belt. Take God's word as your plumb line and check to be sure the building is true to plumb before you begin your work. When a wall that is not straight and true, the Master Builder will have it torn down. Then we can make a fresh start and rebuild according to the Creator's plan.

Walk about the construction site with the Scriptures as your plumb line and the Bible as your laser tape to make sure every detail is true to plan before you begin. Take an apprentice with you and teach them how to measure and examine the building so that they can learn the trade and continue the good work.

If the structure built before you came along is crooked and tilted, it must be torn down so you can build what is right and good. May your generation be known as those who repair broken walls, and those who restore streets with dwellings for the sake of His holy name.[9] May this age-old pile of rubble be rebuilt, constructing a house worthy of The Name for generations to come. May our work be strong for those who come after us to build upon.

Walk about Zion, go around her, count her towers, consider well her ramparts, view her citadels, that you may tell of them to the next generation.
(Psalm 48:12–13)

What legacy will we leave for our sons, daughters, and grandchildren to build on? Will we leave crooked and crumbling walls that disgrace the Lord's holy name?[10] Will we jeopardize their future by dumping a pile of rubble on them? Will we go into retirement and give up on training them how to build? The job of those with gray hair is to teach our children and grandchildren how to accomplish the work of the Great Commission. We teach and baptize, lifting new creations in Christ up from the water—precious, cleansed stones to construct a house worthy of the Lord's holy name.

We pack our work belts with tools of fervent prayer, intercession, words of wisdom, and words of knowledge. The working implements we pass on are love, peace, comfort, and strength in the Lord. Our tool pouch has everything we need. We plug into the Holy Spirit's power. Our tools are lubricated with the oil of the Spirit. Check every pocket in your tool belt to be sure you're fully equipped with patience, goodwill, humility, honor, generosity, tranquility, forgiveness, truth, trust, hope, and perseverance.[11] With all these good instruments we extend our hands to those who will come after us. We build a house that is true and right for the next generation to build on. May the work

---
9. Isaiah 58:12.
10. Nehemiah 2:17, Amos 7:7–8.
11. 1 Corinthians 13:4–7.

of our hands be found worthy of all who are called by The Name.

> *Even when I am old and gray, do not forsake me, my God, till I declare your power to the next generation, your mighty acts to all who are to come.*
> (Psalm 71:18)

Construction is a family trade. It may seem rude or dismissive to reject help from outside of God's family, but that is exactly what we are called to do. We cannot use any outside help or temporal means to build for eternity.[12] The empowering oil of the Spirit doesn't work in or through unworthy vessels. Building a house for God's holy name is not the work of those who reject The Name. That's because materials like wood, hay, and chaff will never do—they are not part of the building plan.

Before Moses built the tabernacle in the wilderness, God gave him explicit, meticulous plans for every detail of the tent structure where the Great I AM would dwell among His people. Even now, building this eternal kingdom requires refined gold, silver—tried and tested stones set in place according to plan.

The work requires redeemed men, women, and children who are shielded with God's armor. It's as if we take our tools in one hand and a sword in the other so we may build a strong house for all who are called by His name.[13] The Lord Almighty, Maker of all heaven and Earth is not like the gods whose houses are made by hands of mortal beings. Only the people of His inheritance may put their hands to this eternal work. We build a fire-proof house so that when we walk through the fire we will not be burned, the flames will not set us ablaze.[14] With reverent awe we build an awesome house for our Father's name, for He is our great and mighty King. Those who refuse to believe in His name are turned away from this holy work. They would only serve to discourage another generation of workers.

> *Then I replied to them, "The God of heaven will make us prosper, and we his servants will arise and build, but you have no portion or right or claim in Jerusalem."*
> (Nehemiah 2:20 ESV)

Heaven's record begins with the first man, Adam. Then the names of every generation of God's sons and daughters born on earth are also written down in glory. All those who are recorded with our Savior's holy name lift up holy hands in praise to God. He has written His name on our hearts. His name is indelibly written on our soul and spirit so that we may overflow

---

12. Zechariah 4:6.
13. Nehemiah 4:18.
14. Isaiah 43:2.

with praise. The Lord of the armies of heaven raises up an awesome troop of people from every generation who will offer themselves as precious, living building stones in the house we build for His holy name.[15]

Those who build in God's kingdom get tested and tried with fiery trials to strengthen their faith and produce a great hope in them. This refining process is necessary because we must build with gold, silver, and precious stones. If we build with temporal things like wood, hay, and straw, the house will not stand. Generations who build with sticks may still be saved, but like burning branches snatched from the fire.[16]

Tried and tested spiritual fathers and evangelistic mothers begat sons and daughters of faith in every decade of time. Their cherished names are recorded in heaven's record book. What a blessed day it will be when the manifest is opened and we hear our name read; "Listen up Steffen. You built this house by bringing Simone, Jimmy, and Theresa to Christ. Well done, good and faithful servant. Enter into the joy of the Lord."[17]

Let this be written for a future generation, that a people not yet created may praise the LORD.
(Psalm 102:18)

What is the portion allotted to you in this life? Turn your focus away from temporal material things and personal assets and abilities and you will see yourself in a whole new light. You have been given favor and a new name in the sight of God.[18] By this name you are called to live in the fullness of Christ as a builder in the kingdom of heaven. You've been adopted into a family as a son or daughter of the Most High God. This new family name written on your heart, soul, and spirit establishes you in the family's construction business. You are a rightful heir to an awesome portion allotted to you in the work of the kingdom of heaven.

Now, as a son or daughter of the Lord Almighty you are a precious stone, refined like pure gold and silver made useful in building a house for The Name that is above all names. Building this house will not be done *for* you, but it's impossible on your own. You must strap on your tool belt, put on your hard hat, learn to read your tape measure, and put your hands to work building a house for all who are called by God's holy name. We take great care in what we build because it must be a rock-solid structure for future generations to build on; all for the glory and honor of His holy name.[19]

---
15. Psalm 46:7.
16. 1 Corinthians 3:10–15.
17. Matthew 25:23.
18. Proverbs 3:4.
19. 1 Corinthians 3:10.

He allots their portions; his hand distributes them by measure. They will possess it forever and dwell there from generation to generation.
(Isaiah 34:17)

The genealogies recorded in the Bible are small fragments compared to the records kept in heaven's cloud drive.[20] Like the Bible's generational records, the Book of Life chronicles the bloodline of our Lord, Savior, and soon coming King. Heaven's manifest keeps a record of our family tree—the Tree of Life. This is a record of redemption, forgiveness, and mercy. It's written proof of our inheritance; our portion in the kingdom of God. God's sons and daughters are recorded name upon name on our High Priest's breastplate. The family roots go deep to draw from springs of Living Water.[21]

Heaven's family tree is a record of branches grafted in to become builders.[22] It shows us where shoots have gone wild, been broken off and tossed aside.[23] The records are evidence of the work of saving grace, giving testimony of smoldering branches snatched from the fire.[24] Above all else, the record of generations provides a witness of the Savior's name given to mortal, fallible human beings. These are families redeemed from a fallen creation—men, women, and children who are set apart as holy unto the Lord God, Almighty. Every name recorded in heaven's accounts is made into a unique and precious building stone in the house we build for all who will answer the call to come and tabernacle in Jesus' holy name.

You, LORD, reign forever; your throne endures from generation to generation.
(Lamentations 5:19)

When we read through thousands of years of Biblical begats our minds tend to drift to something more interesting. Maybe we wonder, "What do these obscure names have to do with the Gospel message?" In this study we learned that the record of each family name is more than a historical record for Bible Scholars to contemplate—it's a chronicle for the Tree of Life. Now we see it as a historic drama. We understand that begetting a son or daughter whose names are recorded in the Book of Life is more than contributing a man's seed for their issue or adding a father's name to a certificate of birth. It is a living and eternal legacy.

To serve as a covenantal father or mother is to raise up godly offspring. When seeds of faith are planted in good soil, they grow and flourish in the

---
20. Revelation 20:12.
21. Jeremiah 17:8, Psalm 1:3.
22. Matthew 1:5.
23. Jeremiah 22:28–30, Matthew 1:11. Jeconiah (also spelled as Jehoiachin) was a branch broken off. None of his offspring would ever sit on the throne of David.
24. Zechariah 3:2.

kingdom of heaven.[25] Indeed, parents are the greatest evangelists, the best builders in every generation. Home is the frontline of the Good News message that brings a son or daughter to believe in Christ as Savior. Parents and grandparents are frontline kingdom workers who help to mold little pebbles who are brought to saving faith. This is the groundwork of building the kingdom of heaven.

> *We will not neglect the house of our God.*
> (Nehemiah 10:39)

We learned that Bible history is like a logbook that records the names of builders from every generation. We build on the work of the champions of our faith that came before us. With our hands set to this good work, we're inspired by great expectations, and we sing out: "Amen, Come Lord Jesus."

All those who are called by Jesus' holy name are part of the crew for this house we establish on Christ the Cornerstone. We build on the work of the generations who came before us. We prepare ourselves for this work with proper tools for the project so we can be diligent workers. When someone shows up without the proper tools, we quickly realize they are only there to discourage and distract us from our work. Indeed, this house can only be built with tried, proven, and tested precious stones.

We've learned that every name recorded in heaven's "cloud" is one unique and treasured building stone in the house we build for His holy name, where all who are called by His name may come to tabernacle in Jesus' holy name.

> *Who will not fear you, Lord, and bring glory to your name? For you alone are holy. All nations will come and worship before you, for your righteous acts have been revealed.*
> (Revelation 15:4)

---

25. Luke 8:15.

Chapter 3

The Work of Generations

Q & A

1. Why is the work of previous godly generations so important to us today?

   _____
   _____

2. Describe the precious building stones of the Father's holy dwelling place.

   _____
   _____

3. What tools do we need to do the work of building a house for God's holy name?

   _____
   _____

4. Who is qualified to join in the work of building?

   _____
   _____

5. Why are the right building materials so important?

   _____
   _____

My Journal Notes:

Part 2:
A Crumbling House

Look, your house is left to you desolate. For I tell you, you will not see me again until you say, "Blessed is he who comes in the name of the Lord."

(Matthew 23:38–39)

Lost Significance

Key Scriptures:

- "A good name is more desirable than great riches; to be esteemed is better than silver or gold." (Proverbs 22:1)
- "For this reason I kneel before the Father, from whom every family in heaven and on earth derives its name." (Ephesians 3:14–15)

What is a "good" name? How does someone earn a good or bad name? Good name or bad name, does it even matter in a world where we can just move away and leave our troubles behind? In this study we'll learn about the great treasure we have in an honorable name. We'll gain a whole new perspective on the importance of names. As an example: when people come to know and trust a name like Sam Walton, he can build an international business empire based on his name. People trust the name Ben Franklin so much that banks and financial institutions use this name. But in a post-modern society, names have become little more than what you scribble on a name tag at a Chamber of Commerce meeting. We have thrown away the foundational meaning and impact of names, but is there really anything we can do about it?

When the foundations are being destroyed, what can the righteous do?
(Psalm 11:3)

This study topic prepares us to do the groundwork for restoring the significance and meaning of names, especially the family name given us by our heavenly Father. With this truth burning in our hearts, we come to know the awesome glory and majesty of our heavenly Father's holy name. The learner will come to see the importance of the new name we are given as sons and daughters of the Most High God. This name is so much more than a reinvented persona, or a fresh outlook on life. We receive a new name and the Father writes it on His hand. Jesus, our High Priest, wears our name close to His heart on His priestly breastplate of righteousness.

See, I have engraved you on the palms of my hands; your walls are ever before me.
(Isaiah 49:16)

> **Study Prayer**
>
> *Father, we kneel before you with thanksgiving and praise, because your family in heaven and on earth derives its name from your name.*
>
> A prayer according to Ephesians 3:14–15

Narratives in the Bible give us a full picture of real people living all their days on Earth with the same challenges, temptations, and weaknesses we have. The genealogies enlightened us to the full meaning of lineages written in the Bible. Why are these long lists of names recorded, and what do these Bible characters' names teach us? The extensive records are important to real-life Christians and not just to Bible scholars and theologians. They serve many good purposes:

- The names prove the historical reliability of the Biblical account.
- Name by name we are led to the fulfillment of prophecies about Jesus, our Lord and Savior.
- Ancestral names verify a lineage of priests who were in line to serve before the Yehovah God in the temple.
- A record of a father's name established the inheritance of fields, forests, and springs in the Promised Land, Israel.
- Before Jacob passed away he prophesied blessings on his sons and the generations to follow. They kept a family record because they treasured these precious blessings.
- The genealogies are an account of the Great I AM's history of redemption for His many sons and daughters.
- Real people with real names had a place in the Creator's story, from the very beginning.
- The lists of sons and daughters prove that ordinary people make a difference in the fulfillment of God's eternal purpose and plan. They are names the Almighty has written down in glory, and treasures stored up in the kingdom of heaven and kept safe.
- A family record proved who was qualified as a kinsman redeemer to purchase land when there was no immediate heir. This law provided for a family name to be carried on to the next generation.
- The begats prove the Righteous Branch is the One who spreads out to produce the branches that strengthen the house that every generation builds for the Almighty's holy name.

Therefore my people will know my name; therefore in that day they will know that it is I who foretold it. Yes, it is I.
(Isaiah 52:6)

The meaning of names is often lost in post-modern American culture. We name our children after celebrities, sports stars, or people we admire. A gun enthusiast might name his first-born son "Ruger." After the ultrasound image comes back and we know the child's gender we select a name from a Google search of popular names and then plan a gender reveal party. Then the boy grows up and changes his name from Charles to Chip because that's how he sees himself. Some people pick a new name because their given name associates them with infamous people. Other monikers get changed because the name is too foreign and associates don't want to do the work of learning how to pronounce the name Xiomara. Authors may use pen names to create a writer's image. A name change may help a person recover from the trauma of growing up with the parents who gave them their name. In reality, when we hear a good name spoken it ought to bring up the sense of a family tree with the sweet and fragrant aromas of fruitfulness. There's a sense of hopelessness if a name given to a new-born child ends up as nothing more than a moniker chiseled in stone on a grave marker where it's obscured by moss that grows thick and green.

A good name is better than fine perfume.
(Ecclesiastes 7:1)

The entertainment culture understands a name's importance more than Jesus' followers do. They take on a name that conveys an image to their audience. Self-descriptive stage names like Stevie Wonder, Bad Bunny, or Lady Gaga create their persona. The name Johnny Cash brings up images of a Ring of Fire and Folsom Prison. Our favorite performers have a grasp of the importance of a name.

Consider the names of heroes of our faith in the Bible. When we hear of David in the Bible we think of a shepherd Psalmist with his harp who slayed a giant with a stone. Solomon's name is associated with wisdom and splendor. The disciple Peter's name brings up images of denial that's soon forgiven. Remembering the Apostle John's name will bring up images of God's love. We can see him leaning his head upon Jesus' shoulder as the disciples gathered around the table.

As people mature, they start to think about their legacy—what will they leave behind? We might be able to leave a generous inheritance to our children, but money is often like sand that slips away between their fingers.

Leave your favorite car that you've washed and polished a thousand times to a grandson and who knows if it will turn to rust in the backyard.

The best heritage is a good name passed on to our sons and daughters. But today we think of names as little more than a moniker on a keychain with a made up verse about what the name means. Our names are transient as a breath. They have lost their significance and meaning. For families today it's less common to name our children after an honored grandparent or an ancestor. But the name we give a child can shape their lives. Try naming your newborn boy "Sue." He'll have to grow up tough to defend himself. A girl with an odd name will struggle to find her place with girls who are called Amy and Olivia. Isn't it better to give a child a name like Stephen, that means "crowned"? Indeed, a man with this name rose up in the church where he lived up to his name and became known as a man crowned with faith and filled with the Holy Spirit. The elders selected him to serve in the first Church as a deacon. Then he was privileged to serve as the first martyr of the Church. With this good name He served honorably and then died in keeping with his name.

They chose Stephen, a man full of faith and of the Holy Spirit.
(Acts 6:5)

After the tribes of Israel entered the Promised Land, Zelophehad's five daughters showed exceptional concern for their father's name.[1] They determined that their father's heritage must continue on through every generation. All five of them stood up boldly to plead their case before Moses, Eleazar the priest, and their leaders, where the whole assembly gathered at the entrance of the Tent of Meeting. Their father had no son to inherit his allotted land and his name would be lost among the nation. But Zelophehad's five unmarried daughters acted with wisdom like the five wise the virgins in Jesus' parable.[2] In godly wisdom they stood up to defend their family name.

It was considered brash for women to present such a petition in the culture of their time because women had no right of inheritance. But their plea was worthy because a good name is better than great riches.[3] Why should their father's name be written in the dust?[4] To keep his name alive they asked for property among their tribe's lands. The Lord Himself answered their plea. He instructed Moses, in keeping with the spirit of kinsman redeemers, to give them land with springs so their father's name would not disappear in the dust of the earth. Zelophehad's daughters acted in godly wisdom, knowing that their good father's name should be honored in every generation.

---

1. Numbers 27.
2. Matthew 25:1–13.
3. Proverbs 22:1.
4. Jeremiah 17:13.

We tend to skip over the numerous genealogies in the Old and New Testaments. What purpose do they serve beyond proving a man's right to serve in the Levitical priesthood? The long lists of names show us the importance of preserving a good family name. The record of fathers and sons also displays God's abundant grace with the inclusion of harlots and aliens.

The Great I AM's everlasting name must be lifted up with honor. We ought to live every day of our lives in a way that will not bring dishonor upon our heavenly Father's name. We are called to live our lives with God's word as our light. The Scriptures illuminate our pathway and the oil of the Spirit fuels the fire in our lamps. Indeed, the Lord God's name, Yehovah Elohim, is likened to oil—a fragrant anointing oil poured out upon all who are called by His name and who live to honor His name.

Your anointing oils are fragrant; your name is oil poured out.
(Song of Songs 1:3 ESV)

Today, when we greet a new acquaintance and they learn our name there is rarely a light bulb moment when they say: "Oh yeah. I know your family. You've got some good genes." Instead, they note our fashion savvy by the holes in our jeans. In today's culture, when we introduce ourselves, we're a blank slate instead of a living lineage. We're strangers in a world filled with pointless and meaningless names.

Now step into heaven's kingdom realm where the Lord God's name is above all other names. In Christ we are made a new creation, adopted, and given a new name. This new name is written on a white stone to prove that we are proclaimed "not guilty," no longer condemned with a bad name.[5] When our Lord and Savior gives us His name he absolves all our past, including bad names and all that tarnished us. Our old name is no longer a burden. We can throw off the yoke of a name that is like an old bag full of dusty, dirty lumps of coal strapped on our aching back.

Consider the power of a new name. The honored father, Abram, who had no children became Abraham, the father of many nations. Zacchaeus, the tax collector, became Zacchaeus, a true son of Abraham's faith.[6] Simon became known as the disciple Simon Peter the "rock" who "has heard."[7] Was Jesus also saying that His church is built upon rocks that hear?

---

5. Revelation 2:17.
6. Luke 19:8–9.
7. Peter means "rock" and Simon means, "he has heard."

> *Blessed are you, Simon son of Jonah, for this was not revealed to you by flesh and blood, but by my Father in heaven. And I tell you that you are Peter, and on this rock I will build my church, and the gates of Hades will not overcome it.*
> (Matthew 16:17–18)

Our Father's name and the name of His only Son serve a greater purpose than beginning and ending our prayers. Consider that the Creator's name is emblazoned on every fiery star in the universe. Earth's core radiates with the supremacy of our Father's holy name. The Son of God is the Firstborn of creation and the power of His name holds all of creation together. Seed-bearing fruit from every flourishing garden reveals a living miracle with the Word of creation encoded inside "according to their various kinds."[8] The DNA of every newborn child is imprinted with the Good Shepherd's love and care. As we look at the stars in the sky above, we see His name is ablaze in the heavens. Now we can see that the Lord God's holy name is so much more than a signature for our petitions. Jesus' name is more than an endorsement after our prayers.

> *Therefore God exalted him to the highest place and gave him the name that is above every name, that at the name of Jesus every knee should bow, in heaven and on earth and under the earth, and every tongue acknowledge that Jesus Christ is Lord, to the glory of God the Father.*
> (Philippians 2:9–11)

All redeemed sons and daughters are called by Christ's name. He makes us family and gives us His name. Our neighbors ought to know us by the name of our Savior, Jesus Christ. Because of this holy name some will persecute us and reject us. The Father and the Son's glorious names are given to us because we are His adopted sons and daughters. Now the Almighty One desires that each of us serve as a precious building stone, one building block in a house where His holy name may dwell. Those who reject Christ the Cornerstone will also reject the building stones of His house.

Good name, bad name, is it all the same in a contemporary culture? Have we progressed to a higher level of civilization where names are of little consequence? Is the handle our parents gave us little more than an identifier on government tax forms? Are our contemporaries in American culture living at the pinnacle of human evolution where meaningful names are obsolete?

There's so much we can learn from thousands of years of human history. The Bible is filled with accounts of real people with real names that have real meaning. They are remembered as heroes of our faith who built a solid spiritual house that we can build on. We can place our names with other precious

---

8. Genesis 1:12.

stones etched with names like Priscilla and Aquila who worked in the early church with the Apostle Paul to complete the work of suffering for the sake of Christ Jesus and His Church.[9]

In post-modern American culture we have a lot of different reasons for the names we give our children. Some of us get stuck with nicknames for the silly things we say or do as kids. When we become adults there may be good reasons or wrong reasons for changing our names. Celebrity entertainers know the value of creating an image to establish a fan following, but it's all a façade.

Christians need to recapture the significance of names, for the sake of our children who build upon our faith. Even more important, we do well to cherish our new name in Christ. We treasure the awesome name that is given to us as adopted sons and daughters. We are the bearers of our Father's name. It is for us to be reflections of His name and to shine out with the renown of His holy name.

As we mature in years we become concerned with the legacy of our name and our family name. The reality is that a good family name is the best inheritance we can leave for a child who has to make his or her way in the world. We see an example of this in Zelophehad's daughters who still teach us the importance of a name. These five daughters, guided by wisdom, stood up against the system and presented their case for the preservation of their father's name. The Lord God Almighty gave a judgment in their favor. In their father's name they received an inheritance of property in the land of promise.

As adopted sons and daughters we are called to press on for the glory and honor of our heavenly Father's holy name. We are heirs of His promise who bear His holy name as our own. Because of His awesome name we are called to serve as witnesses, representatives, and ambassadors to proclaim the renown of His name throughout all the Earth.

---

9. 1 Corinthians 16:19.

Chapter 4
Lost Significance
Q & A

1. Is a good name or bad name of any significance today?
___
___
___

2. Are meaningful names important in a post-modern culture?
___
___
___

3. What legacy will you leave behind for your namesake?
___
___
___

4. What do Zelophehad's daughters teach us about the importance of a good family name?
___
___
___

My Journal Notes:

A Rejected Name

Key Scriptures:

- "They got up, drove him [Jesus] out of the town, and took him to the brow of the hill on which the town was built, in order to throw him off the cliff. But he walked right through the crowd and went on his way." (Luke 4:29–30)

- "Blessed are you when people hate you, when they exclude you and insult you and reject your name as evil, because of the Son of Man." (Luke 6:22)

The rejection Christians suffer cuts deep to the heart, soul, and spirit. It wounds us right where our Father's name is written. The world's dark side screams out with hateful words, "Be like us and you won't get hurt." Throughout the centuries since the Holy Spirit established the Church countless people have been beaten down and martyred because of the name they carried like a cross. They wanted to throw Jesus over the cliff, and now they think we should get heaved over.

Our adversaries assault us like an army on the offense. Our attackers' intent is to leave behind ruined lives like charred stumps in a desert wasteland. This study serves to remind us that all those who reject Christ will be shaken out, while we stand strong in the victory we have in Him. This teaching session brings people of faith together as a mighty troop, armored up in the power of the resurrected Christ.

Too often, a Christian's complacency also serves as a rejection of His name. To our own ruin we reject His authority to rule over every aspect of our lives. God's holy name gets trampled down by those who turn away from His name and become like, or worse than those the Lord has never Shepherded.[1]

Study Prayer

O Lord, who is mighty in battle, strengthen us in the power of your might so we may stand strong in the day of battle.

A prayer in agreement with Ephesians 6:10

---

1. Isaiah 63:18–19.

When we see Jesus' name rejected it hurts and it's personal, because we're family. The hatred spewed at Christ and His followers can divide a home. Jesus warned that because of His name a father would turn against his son, and mother against daughter.[2] This contempt started with the first family in Genesis when Cain murdered Abel just four chapters after "Let there be light." Now fast forward to the rapidly approaching Revelation of Jesus Christ. All around the world persecutions of the Church have hit an exponential curve. Synagogues, temples, and church buildings are burned to the ground. Witnessing for Christ is punishable by death in many countries. In this nation, originally founded on godly principles by devout men and women, God's word and the name of Christ Jesus is shunned in the public square, schools, and universities.

But beware! The same people who turn their backs on us because of Jesus' name speak such beautiful and pious words, quoting Scripture after Scripture as if they really believed what it says. They spew hateful curses out of one side of their mouths and then pour saccharin sweet words out of the other side. It's like they pelt us with words thrown like stones and then say, "What's your problem? You need to get in line. You know what wonderful, loving people we are. Be like us and you won't get hurt."

But those who bear the name of Christ must never compromise their faith or give up hope under pressure. We need to remind ourselves that in times of persecution we gain a great and lasting confidence—a hope that will never disappoint because Christ Jesus has given us His Holy Spirit to secure us. Indeed, our Lord God is a righteous Judge and He has the final word.[3] We grieve for those who bring reproach upon His name. We weep knowing that those who refuse to live according to the Promise will be shaken out, never allowed to enter this holy house.[4]

> *Hear the word of the L*ORD*, you who tremble at his word: "Your own people who hate you, and exclude you because of my name, have said, 'Let the L*ORD *be glorified, that we may see your joy!' Yet they will be put to shame."*
> (Isaiah 66:5)

As the day of the Lord draws near the enemies of the kingdom of heaven become desperate to keep people bound in the chains of sin and death. They're frantic as they feel their sway over the nations slipping through their fingers and their alliance of evil unraveling. The principalities and powers of the air ramp up their warfare with barrages of fiery arrows.[5] They fight

---

2. Luke 12:53.
3. John 12:48.
4. Nehemiah 5:13.
5. Ephesians 2:2, 6:16.

against the advancing armies of God's people. Satan with his fallen angels is prepared to scorch the earth. With their assaults they intend to leave behind a desert-like wasteland of rubble, chaos, and ruined lives.

In this dark hour the forces of darkness muster their armies. "Before them the land is like the garden of Eden, behind them, a desert waste."[6] They are like an army with flamethrowers, trying to turn to ashes what the Creator made beautiful. In their desperation they seize God's people and torture them with their terrors. They assault God's people because the name of the Most High God and the name of His Son are written on our hearts. They hate us because our names are inscribed on the palm of the Father's hand. The forces of darkness despise us because God's covenant is written on our hearts.[7] The principalities and powers of the air assault us when they see the Almighty's name written on our foreheads.[8]

But in every battle we gain the victory in Christ. Even when our lives look like a pile of ashes, we know our Redeemer makes streams in the wasteland.[9] We are overcomers who stand fast, armored up in the power of the resurrected Christ, and the gates of hades will not overwhelm us.[10]

But before all this, they will seize you and persecute you. They will hand you over to synagogues and put you in prison, and you will be brought before kings and governors, and all on account of my name.
(Luke 21:12)

Jesus headed for Jerusalem with a clear purpose: redemption of sin-captured souls. With every step he took, the awareness of Judas' betrayal loomed before Him. At every turn in the path, He looked ahead and saw His arrest and illegal trial before the Sanhedrin. It seemed like a dead end to the disciples when that decisive moment came when the temple guards arrested Jesus. The entrenched powers of the religious elite collided with the advancing kingdom of heaven. They clashed at the front line of battle. The fickle crowds stood on one side, incited by religious forces in collusion with Rome. Their leaders stirred up the mob to choose a murderer, Barabbas be released. Then they rejected Jesus, thrusting their fists at Him and screaming out: "Crucify Him! Crucify Him!"

They forgot that He came as Immanuel, God with us. He led them beside still waters of truth, wisdom, grace, and mercy. He brought God's kingdom into their lives and homes. He healed their sick and raised their dead. He fed them with the bread of heaven and released those held captive in their sinful condition.

---
6. Joel 2:3.
7. Hebrews 8:10.
8. Revelation 22:4.
9. Isaiah 43:19.
10. Matthew 16:18.

Then the moment came when choosing between light and darkness confronted those who heard Jesus teach. Would they continue in the traditions of men or walk in the light of life? They had to decide: Would they come to the Lord's table or to the table of demons? Would they drink from the cup of the Lord or the cup of the Deceiver?[11]

Why would they choose a rebel and murderer like Barabbas over their Messiah who came to give them life? Because people's natural inclination is to love darkness more than light.[12] Our choices are rarely as momentous as for those who stood before Pilate as he washed his hands of them. We must stand firm in the name whom we serve. These choices begin at the moment we slip our feet into our slippers in the morning and continue until we go into REM sleep in the night.

> *I have come in my Father's name, and you do not accept me; but if someone else comes in his own name, you will accept him.*
> (John 5:43)

Consider a town's mayor who is an honest and fair man and whose dealings in the community are honorable in every way. People admire him and continue to vote for him because he's a straight shooter and treats them right. But he has six children who haven't learned much, if anything, from their dad. They violate the city's quiet enjoyment laws with their all-night parties. Driving at high speed through a school zone is cool because the local cops never bother them. In local restaurants the mayor's kids are rude and demanding. Before long Mr. Mayor's good name falls into disrepute because of the attitudes and actions of his arrogant kids. His name turns from "Model Mayor" to "Mud."

The Almighty God and Creator of all heaven and Earth has given people His holy name in every generation. This awesome name is written on our hearts, and everything we do in our community reflects upon our Lord and Savior. When we head to the restaurant with the after-church crowd, will we tarnish God's name with rude and demanding behavior? When we throw our debris into the neighbor's yard, we dishonor God's name. A boss thinks much less of the God we serve when we shirk our duties and refuse their instructions.

It's important for Christians to be aware that our every action reflects on the new name given to us in Christ. We must not be the cause of someone rejecting Jesus, the Church, and anything that has to do with His name. This isn't a call to perfection that we gain apart from Christ, but a call to know what is good, what is required of us, and then to act accordingly.[13]

---

11. 1 Corinthians 10:21.
12. John 3:19.
13. Micah 6:8.

As it is written: "God's name is blasphemed among the Gentiles because of you."
(Romans 2:24)

Persecution of the Church has hit that proverbial exponential upward curve in our day and time. What is true and right is mocked as false and corrupt. In today's world what is dark and deceptive is exalted as enlightened and trustworthy. People are whiplashed between fear and greed as they seek to fulfill their deepest-felt needs in a dark void.

What about those who desire to live a life that is conformed to Christ and honor His name? Every day we are confronted with assaults of deceit and violence. Our hearts break as we see people in despair all around us, groping about for something solid to hang onto, but finding nothing. We reach out our hands to offer hope, but desperate people turn on us and rip into us in the fury of their violence. They imagine that godly people are the problem. They rage against us, convinced that if they could be rid of devout Christians the world would be just fine. Indeed, the closer we come to the Revelation of Jesus Christ the greater their rage against the name and the people who bear His name.

In fact, everyone who wants to live a godly life in Christ Jesus will be persecuted, while evildoers and impostors will go from bad to worse, deceiving and being deceived.
(2 Timothy 3:12–13)

This is one great mystery of the Gospel. When people hear the Word of God proclaimed, one of two things occurs. Either the seed of faith is planted in their hearts to take root and flourish, or their hearts are hardened like a rocky pathway and birds come to eat the seed.[14] When the Good News is proclaimed people will either build their lives on the Rock, who is Christ Jesus, or they will stumble over Him and fall down.

Those who trip up are like a drunk who hates to be around sober people. The inebriated man shouts his curses and lashes out at those who refuse to join his party. People whose trip along on a hardened pathway throw hateful rocks at those who flourish and bear good fruit in fertile ground. Not only do they reject the seed of truth, they despise and abuse those who lift up the name of Christ.

A stone that causes people to stumble and a rock that makes them fall. They stumble because they disobey the message–which is also what they were destined for.
(1 Peter 2:8)

---

14. Matthew 13:4.

Christians are ambassadors for an eternal kingdom where Christ Jesus reigns in all power, glory, and majesty. We are the hands, feet and mouths that lift up the name of Christ and the cross. The Father glorifies the Son, and our Lord and Savior lifts us up to share in His sufferings so that we may also share in His glory.[15] We persevere in suffering for the name of Christ, knowing that our character is strengthened with an eternal hope.[16] God's people stand together, united in Christ who has given us the glory the Father gave to Him.[17] We have heard and answered the Gospel's call so that we may share in the glory of our Redeemer who is Yeshua HaMashiach.[18]

Those who reject The Name are caught in the chains of sin and depravity. In desperation they lash out at those who walk the well-lit path of freedom and righteousness. All those who are blessed to bear the name of Christ are targets of hate because of His name written on our hearts. But take heart and rejoice in Jesus' promise to bless those who are persecuted because of His righteous name.[19]

If you are insulted because of the name of Christ, you are blessed, for the Spirit of glory and of God rests on you.
(1 Peter 4:14)

All who are in Christ get rejected and despised simply because of the Lord's name written on our hearts. Jesus, our Lord Jesus, was scorned, crucified and then raised up victorious as the Chief Cornerstone and the Gate.[20] Christians are spurned and hated but we are made victors in Christ to serve as building stones of the City of God. We follow in the footsteps of the fathers of our faith, and the Apostles who walked the road of suffering and came into a great hope to pave the way before us.

Generation after generation we build stone upon precious stone so that every nation and tribe will hear the call and come to the throne of grace. Those who answer the call in every native tongue are welcomed to enter through the Gate who is Jesus our Lord and Savior. Our Redeemer made the way clear and simple when He answered Thomas: "I am the way and the truth and the life. No one comes to the Father except through me."[21]

---

15. Romans 8:17.
16. Romans 5:3–5.
17. John 17:22–23.
18. 2 Thessalonians 2:14. Yeshua HaMashiach means Jesus the Messiah, or Jesus the Anointed One.
19. Matthew 5:10.
20. John 10:9, Ephesians 2:19–22.
21. John 14:6.

> *It had a great, high wall with twelve gates, and with twelve angels at the gates. On the gates were written the names of the twelve tribes of Israel. There were three gates on the east, three on the north, three on the south and three on the west. The wall of the city had twelve foundations, and on them were the names of the twelve apostles of the Lamb.*
> (Revelation 21:12–14)

As the years progress, it becomes painfully obvious that rejection of Creator God, His Son, the Holy Spirit, and all who bear His holy name increases dramatically. This rejection began in Genesis with Abel who was slain by his brother. The violent rejection of Abel has carried on throughout history to the Zachery's who are rejected because of Jesus' name in our day. Cain brought an offering to the Lord before he killed his brother. Even today people speak beautiful, religious, and pious words while holding a knife behind their backs. They demand that we conform to their way of doing things—or else.

When persecution comes our way, we are reminded that we have the greatest hope. Torments because of Jesus' name are proof that God's holy and righteous judgments will come against the ungodly and violent. We are called to persevere in our faith for the sake of Jesus' name so that we will be counted worthy in God's kingdom.[22]

Those who desire to walk faithfully must examine themselves to be sure that they continue to do what is right and good. We need to make wise choices every day so we will act with justice, loving mercy, and walk humbly with our God.[23] We need to check our heart's attitude to keep us from blazing our own trail and going our own way by creating our own Jesus in our own image. Rejection of the Way, the Truth, and the Life is often subtle, but deceptively evil and always leads to a downfall. By continuous rebellious actions we reject our Savior's holy name.

> *You will be ashamed because of the sacred oaks in which you have delighted; you will be disgraced because of the gardens that you have chosen.*
> (Isaiah 1:29)

We must remain true to our heavenly Father, Son, and Holy Spirit so that we may be strengthened in the power of His might as we build a house for His name.

---

22. 2 Thessalonians 1:4–10.
23. Micah 6:8.

Chapter 5
A Rejected Name
Q & A

1. When did the rejection of the Creator's name begin?
   _____
   _____
   _____

2. Persecution has hit an exponential curve. Why is that reassuring to Christians today?
   _____
   _____
   _____

3. How do Christians dishonor their Father's holy name and ruin their witness?
   _____
   _____
   _____

4. How do we know when people's sweet, religious, and pious words are just a coverup for their evil intentions?
   _____
   _____
   _____

My Journal Notes:

6

Missing the Mark

Key Scriptures:

- "For many will come in my name, claiming, 'I am the Messiah,' and will deceive many." (Matthew 24:5)
- "But avoid foolish controversies and genealogies and arguments and quarrels about the law, because these are unprofitable and useless." (Titus 3:9)

This study focuses on Jesus' teaching; leading us to come to His Father in heaven with a simple faith. We'll start to see ourselves as a part of the work crew that builds one eternal house, rather than many houses. We construct a house where all God's sons and daughters are brought together in His name. Our team comes from every part of the worldwide Church to build stone upon living stone. Even if the stones are called Pentecostal, Lutheran, Presbyterian, Calvary Chapel, Baptist, Mennonite, Amish, or Catholic stones—out of these denominations, people of true Christian faith are raised up to build one house. All who are grafted into the one Vine, who is Jesus Christ, share the work of building a house for the name of the Father, Son, and Holy Spirit. We come together to build a house, not according to one denomination's plan, but a house true to the Master Builder's blueprint.

Jesus teaching challenges our divided perspectives. He reveals the duplicity that distracts us from the narrow way of truth, justice, love, and righteousness. We'll learn that God's realm is an upside-down kingdom when viewed from a human perspective. In this study a learner is strengthened to keep free from deceitful distractions about controversies and words. Builders of the house for God's holy name will learn how to use a standard tape measure, which is God's Word. This vital topic leads us to treasure the name of our Lord and God, by sustaining us in the glory of His holy presence.

One, two, three strikes and you're out. But that's only at the old ballgame. In the realm where Christ reigns there is forgiveness and mercy for those who miss the mark.

> ### Study Prayer
> *Change our hearts, O Lord, so that we may come to you with like little children. Give us a simple and pure faith so we may enter into the fullness of Christ.*
>
> A prayer according to Matthew 18:3

The name of Jesus Christ is awesome and powerful. There are many good reasons for Jesus to command that we be baptized in water. The water and the Word make us new creations and give us right standing before the Father. We continue to live in agreement with our baptism and try to walk just as Jesus walked. We live like Jesus' followers when we're at church and even more so when we're at work and on our time off. As we abide in the power of Jesus we remain true, serving in agreement with His example as a servant. We refuse to hide under a false cover, with only a veneer of Christianity. We claim our Father's name because we are His adopted sons or daughters. Our love keeps us from misusing this glorious name. We don't use "Jesus talk" just to impress others. Our every word is surrendered to Christ. Anyone can say Jesus' name with their words but we are called to take it to heart and live in agreement with His name. When we hit their thumb with a hammer, our words still honor Him. We don't say "Jesus" as if it's a magic incantation. We will not live a lie knowing that those who do are easily duped. We dwell in the house built for His name and come to know its dynamic power. To do anything less is to miss the mark.

How do we stay on course knowing we are in Christ and that He is in us? We know because, by faith, we have been given a new family name. It's a sign of a vibrant new life in Christ when we hunger to partake of Christ at the Lord's Table. God's promises certify our adoption, and by faith we have an assurance of the Spirit of Christ's indwelling. The evidence of this is what we produce: an outcropping of the fruit of the Spirit. Our confidence comes from being grafted into the Vine, who is Christ, and bearing good fruit.[1] This bold, unifying faith is possible because we live in agreement with Christ who indwells us.[2] Those who are "IN" Christ are empowered to serve as His hand extended. When we abide in Christ and walk according to the Spirit of Christ, we are His ambassadors who are sent to speak what He is speaking—words of healing, deliverance, redemption, freedom, and saving grace.

---

1. John 15:5.
2. See the first book in the Barnabas Series; *The Mystery Which is Christ in You.*

> *Some Jews who went around driving out evil spirits tried to invoke the name of the Lord Jesus over those who were demon-possessed. They would say, "In the name of the Jesus whom Paul preaches, I command you to come out." Seven sons of Sceva, a Jewish chief priest, were doing this. One day the evil spirit answered them, "Jesus I know, and Paul I know about, but who are you?" Then the man who had the evil spirit jumped on them and overpowered them all. He gave them such a beating that they ran out of the house naked and bleeding.*
> (Acts 19:13–16)

We must press on toward the mark. It's important to understand that people are not attracted to Christ because Christians drive new BMWs with an "I ♡ Jesus" sticker on the bumper. Coworkers don't decide to come to our church because they see Christians living in nice houses in the best neighborhoods. Temporal attractions cannot change a person's eternal destiny. Instead, we look to the power of God's name in the light of the Scriptures. The prophet Zechariah's word from the Lord may well be rephrased: "Not by luxury cars, nor by McMansions, but by my Spirit, says the Lord." This declaration of truth could be amplified to read: "Not by the strength of human will, nor by the power of material things we gain, but by the power of the Holy Spirit and the Word."[3]

From the world's point of view, Christians live in an upside-down kingdom. We're generous with our material things so we may save up eternal treasure in the kingdom of heaven. The humble are exalted. The orphan is given a family. The homeless are brought home. But those who stand up proud trip over in their pride. People who arrogantly applaud themselves are applauded when they go to their grave.[4] Those who blow their own horn run out of hot air. A man who arrogantly exalts himself and shows off all his toys ends up with nothing.

In the work of the kingdom, choosing to serve others is the first step toward leadership.[5] Indeed, status and material benefits do not draw people to Christ. The latest fashions are not a good hook to get people through the church doors. Instead, people come to dwell in Christ by hearing the Word and believing what they hear—all by the power and work of the Holy Spirit. So, instead of tearing down our house to build a bigger one with a four-car garage, let's keep our eyes on the prize and build a house for the name that is above all names—a spiritual house filled with abundant and eternal blessings.

> *So he said to me, "This is the word of the Lord to Zerubbabel: 'Not by might nor by power, but by my Spirit,' says the Lord Almighty."*
> *(Zechariah 4:6)*

---

3. Zechariah 4:6.
4. Proverbs 11:10.
5. Luke 22:26–27.

When you buy tickets for front row seats at a concert to hear the Boss with his band singing all your favorite songs, you expect to get what you paid for. But what if you plunk yourselves in your seats and get settled with your date only to get some look-alike band you've never heard of? You might be yelling at them, "You ain't the Boss!"

When it comes to spiritual matters it seems the opposite is true. Human nature is quick to accept things that never confront our sin. Too often, we're willing to accept a lie because we have first deceived ourselves, saying, "I'm just fine the way I am." What is real and true offends our self-image. But when we see the true Christ as Redeemer and Savior, we will either be broken and repent, or we'll look for another name that comforts us in our deceit. Too often we custom design a savior to fit with our own needs and then tack on the name "Jesus" to make it sound right. But there is no other Name, and we must not accept any other who is not the true Redeemer.

I have come in my Father's name, and you do not accept me; but if someone else comes in his own name, you will accept him.
(John 5:43)

In order to build a house for our Father's name, we must get our tool box in order, sharpen our tools, throw out the old bent hardware, and stick to the plan. To accomplish this we have to ask ourselves some hard questions. Without the proper spiritual tools, we're only left with distractions and we can't build walls that are straight and true. Consider each of the following questions to prepare for this good work.

Let's stay on the right path so we don't miss the mark. If all Christians learned to speak the Father's name in Paleo Hebrew and prayed to Yehovah Elohim in Yeshua's holy name, would this restore the post-modern Church? Would learning the seventy-two letters of the Creator's name overcome our shortcomings and renew the Church? Is it possible that restoration of "The Name" in Christian circles would serve to revive us? If we pronounced and spoke God's name in the original Bible languages would this restore HaShem, "The Name"?[6] Would our prayers be more effective if we prayed to El Shaddai, instead of the Lord Almighty?[7] These are hard questions and we must answer them. Our answers must measure up to the standard of the holy Scriptures.

The truth is, because of our human nature, a controversy over our heavenly Father's name may further divide us. Why do we attempt to create man-made hoops to jump through? The reality is that the full richness of the Creator's name is greater than we can pronounce. His holy name is inexpress-

---
6. Deuteronomy 28:58.
7. Genesis 17:1.

ible, and too awesome for earthbound words to articulate. If we go no further than learning original Hebrew script, we'll become more divided than we are now. We will end up with a few who proudly proclaim they're right and every other Church has it wrong. They'll accuse the others of spiritual ignorance because they don't speak the true spiritual language. They'll point fingers and say, "They're calling the Creator by a name corrupted by other languages."

Fallible people who limit themselves to human reasoning could never agree whether our Father should be referred to as YHWH, YHVH, Yahweh, Yahveh, Yehovah, or Jehovah. Are prayers only heard when our petitions are raised before HaShem, "The Name?" Is the Creator's name too holy to speak out loud? Because we're so fallible, pressing people to use the Creator's historic Paleo Hebrew name would likely embroil us in more divisive controversies.

Would the end result of this controversy be a new division or a new denomination of the Church called Yehovites? Do we honor the Creator of all heaven and earth by being historically correct in the way we speak His name? It's a good thing to exalt God and take time to know His name and the meaning of His name and titles. It's important to know all we can learn about the God we serve. Knowing our heavenly Father is an honorable pursuit and helps us to live in agreement with His holy presence. But we must never promote our own agenda above Christ and the cross, and at the expense of the work of the Great Commission.

It's obvious that every nation, whether Greece, Israel, Spain, or Japan has their own language. Christians around the world pray in the name of Christ Jesus, our Lord and Savior in their own tongue. By faith, people of every island and continent come to believe in Jesus as their Lord and Messiah. We must avoid meaningless controversies that destroy faith and divide us. Instead, we are called to hold fast to the unifying truth of Christ and Christ crucified for the sins of the world.

When Jesus walked among us, He taught us how to address Creator God. His disciples heard him pray to "Father in heaven." Jesus taught His followers to pray to the same "Father in heaven." Jesus prayed to and referred to His Father over one-hundred-seventy times in the Gospels. It's clear and simple. We pray to Abba Father who watches over us with a fatherly love. We must not create a new redemptive hurdle for people to jump over. Instead, we are called to build an eternal spiritual house for The Name even while living in our temporary earthly tents. Our work is to come together to glorify His holy name in tents of worship as we build an eternal house.

The foundation, sinews, filaments, structure, and presence of our heavenly Father's name permeates all the living stones who are raised up from every language; whether Hebrew, Greek, Spanish, Mandarin, or any other. We are the building blocks of the house for God's holy Name. We must not get tangled up in disputes about such an awesome and holy name and get distracted from the work we are called to accomplish.

> *For there are many rebellious people, full of meaningless talk and deception, especially those of the circumcision group. They must be silenced, because they are disrupting whole households by teaching things they ought not to teach—and that for the sake of dishonest gain.*
(Titus 1:10–11)

Don't let your walk of faith be ruined by disputes over words.[8] The power of The Name is not manifested in correct pronunciation in original Hebrew. We don't enter into power and authority by using His name exactly as the angel Gabriel pronounced it to Mary. We are holy sanctuaries whom the Spirit indwells and we are called to lift up His name to its rightful place in our heart of hearts. This temple is not made by human hands, nor is it built by learning to speak to our heavenly Father just as Abraham did. All who hear the word, come to believe, and call on the name of the Lord will make a place in their hearts where the glory of His name may reside forever.

Some have a desire to restore honor to our Savior's name by calling Him Yeshua, Y'shua, Yahusha, or Ieshuah. But the only historically correct spelling is ישוע. To honor the Lord in this way is good if our heart is right. If it isn't, it's like putting a bandaid on a wound. If all we do is learn a correct name and how to pronounce it, we are worse off than before. English speaking people use the Greek form for the name of the Son of God, calling Him "Jesus," and this is a wonderful name. His name will soon be spoken uniquely in every language all around the world. It's awesome to hear Hispanic believers pray in the name of their Redeemer "Jesuchristos." Our Hindi speaking brothers and sisters exalt the name with praise to Yīsu Masīha. Filipino Christians intercede in the name of Hesukristo. Home churches in China gather in the name of 耶穌基督 "Yēsū Jīdū."

If we assembled all the nations to speak with one voice and proclaimed Yehova's name and the name of our Savior in original Hebrew and in unison, would this restore the power of His name? Do prayers spoken in Paleo Hebrew get preferred treatment in heaven? Are our prayers true and right if we pray in the Hebrew or Aramaic name as spoken by the prophets? Learning ancient names of our Creator and praying in an ageless language might be

---
8. 2 Timothy 2:14.

exhilarating and satisfying, but if it's nothing but words, we're still a spiritually impoverished people. If this knowledge divides us, or keeps us from Christian fellowship, it does more harm than good.

> *We know that "We all possess knowledge." But knowledge puffs up while love builds up.*
> (1 Corinthians 8:1)

In Christ there is a majestic union formed out of many nations. A remnant is brought together as a holy nation. Each one speaks of the Savior in their native language and exalts the Almighty Creator.[9] We are united in Christ so we may come into His power that is at work in our lives. The dynamo of the indwelling Holy Spirit empowers us to live, serve, and minister according to all that is in our Lord's name that He bestowed upon us. This is a powerful name given to all adopted sons and daughters of the Most High God. We are called to exalt Him by living our lives accordingly, in our temple that is likened to a tent. Our every word, no matter our language, dialect, or accent ought to strengthen and glorify The Name that covers each one of us who are followers of Christ. We were first called "Christian" at Antioch and this is what our family is called. Now our family name is heard in the farthest corners of the earth: Christianós, Cristiano, Քրիստոնեա, Christen, and Chrześcijanin.

> *May his name endure forever; may it continue as long as the sun. Then all nations will be blessed through him, and they will call him blessed.*
> (Psalm 72:17)

Our focus is on Christ, a Savior crucified in our place and for our sins on a cruel Roman cross. Because of the work of the cross the greatest promise of all became possible—we are made whole new creations as we are baptized into Christ. But the job of getting us totally cleaned up isn't quite finished. We are called to live in repentance and forgiveness every day of our lives. This kind of lifestyle keeps us in harmony with our baptism. To live any other way is to miss the mark.

We have a great confidence, knowing we are our Father's sons and daughters because we bear his name as our family name. His name is written on our heart's door. Because of His abundant forgiveness we love our Lord and God with all our hearts and we live lives that bring glory and honor to His name. We can't just fake it by wearing a gold cross necklace. Instead, we delight in living in an upside-down kingdom where choosing to serve is the first step toward leadership. We don't offer artificial incentives to draw people to our church because we know this would lead them to a counterfeit savior and a false hope.

---
9. Revelation 7:9.

People try out churches because the Spirit of Christ is tugging on their heart strings. We must be sure that they aren't fed cheese-puff snacks instead of the true milk and meat of the Word. Cheese snacks send them away feeling empty. Their spiritual void remains and they seldom return.

Join our crew in this good work. We must get our tool boxes in order, sharpen our tools, and plug in our power cords. Let's throw out the dead weight from old, bent nails and broken fasteners buried in sawdust in the bottom of our toolbox. We can't allow ourselves to be distracted by baseless controversies. We must free ourselves of this dead weight so we don't miss the mark as we build a strong and eternal house for our heavenly Father's holy name.

Chapter 6
Missing the Mark
Q & A

1. How does baptism in water serve to change our lives?

_____

2. Why is the kingdom of heaven considered an upside-down kingdom?

_____

3. What kind of spiritual food should be on the menu for those who gather to worship with us?

_____

4. What will you do to get your tool box in order?

_____

My Journal Notes:

A Show of Contempt

Key Scriptures:

- "You shall not misuse the name of the Lord your God, for the Lord will not hold anyone guiltless who misuses his name." (Exodus 20:7)

- "They speak of you with evil intent; your adversaries misuse your name." (Psalm 139:20)

This is a challenging study because it calls for us to take a personal inventory.[1] It's good to examine ourselves to see if we are showing hidden contempt for God's holy name. In this study we'll learn about hidden sins that we justify by compartmentalizing our lives. We'll come to understand the importance of remaining in the comfort of the Holy Spirit and the security of our Father's house. We must ask ourselves if we claim God's name as our own, but then use His name as to cover up for part of our lives. We'll check up on ourselves to see if the family name we post over the front door of our home shines out with the light of Christ.

God's Word serves as a yardstick to measure the words we speak. Do we speak with the authority of the Spirit of Christ or do we speak what we wish was true? There are so many warnings spoken out with many voices and through many messengers—but will we listen? Wisdom warns us not to use God's name as a stick-on name tag that gets tossed the minute we walk out of a gathering for Christian fellowship and worship. This training session leads us to take a hard look at our job review, and then redirect ourselves and come to be forgiven.

In repentance and rest is your salvation, in quietness and trust is your strength. (Isaiah 30:15)

---

1. 2 Corinthians 13:5.

> **Study Prayer**
>
> *Teach us to examine ourselves to see if we are truly in the faith. Give us honest hearts so we may test ourselves. For those of us who pass our self-examination, give us a sense of Christ's indwelling presence.*
>
> A prayer according to 2 Corinthians 13:5

Every child ever born has a deep felt need for a secure place to grow and mature. This place of safety should be a home with protective, loving, and encouraging parents. A nurturing household ought to post the family's honorable name on a placard over the front door to remind the children that their home is a shelter from the assaults of the world around them. The children can enter into the safety of the Martins', Rodriguez's, or the Yang's front door and breathe a sigh of relief. The familiar sweet aroma of mom's dinner in the oven is a comfort every child should know.

But what if Dad clicks on illicit graphic images on his break time at work so he can have a good laugh with the guys? What happens to a child's sense of safety when Mom is playing secret intimate games with a man not her own? It's as if these wayward parents compartmentalize their lives and come home pretending that all is well—but it's not. Children have a sixth sense of their own safety and well-being. They know, deep down, when their good family name is being violated. Parents must realize that there is nothing truly hidden from a child's wide-open eyes and ears. We think we've kept it secret until we see our children act out what we thought was well hidden. They act according to the family name the parents establish.

Too often, by our actions we take those in our care outside the safety and security of the home we build for the Father's holy name. We live like hell for six days and then pack up the kids for an hour of church so that our family will be known as good people. We come to the Lord's Table with a repentant look on our faces, pretending to be pious. But the pretense isn't even skin deep. The point is clear. We cannot remain true to Christ, abide in His promises, and be kept safe under His wings when the name over our front door is tainted with filth that we refuse to clean up. A safe home is one with our Savior's holy name written on our heart's door. It's a house where Mom and Dad provide security so the whole family may live in the safety of His holy name.

> *Will you steal and murder, commit adultery and perjury, burn incense to Baal and follow other gods you have not known, and then come and stand before me in this house, which bears my Name, and say, "We are safe"—safe to do all these detestable things? Has this house, which bears my Name, become a den of robbers to you? But I have been watching! declares the LORD.*
> (Jeremiah 7:9–11)

A seven-year-old who started his first year at a Christian school was quick to learn about the power of God and the authority of His name. He tried it out one day at his grandparents' house after school. When grandma saw him with his hand in the cookie jar, she asked him, "Who said you could have another cookie so close to dinner time?"

He gave her a confident reply: "God said I could."

It's all too common in today's Church to hear people speak out, inspired only by their own intuitions or personal needs, and they use God's name as their authority. The words they proclaim sound so sweet to our ears because they claim God's name as their source. They say to their friends, "Listen, I had a dream last night and it touched my heart."[2] They overlook the spiritual condition of those who gather as they speak out our favorite Scriptures, saying, "'For I know the plans I have for you,' declares the Lord, 'plans to prosper you and not to harm you, plans to give you hope and a future.'"[3] But is this what the Spirit is speaking in the moment, or is it what we wish was true? Will we speak like Wish-tians or witnesses of Christ? There are times when the Spirit of Christ needs to warn us from the Scriptures. Christians and their church leaders who wander from the truth (we all wander) need to be admonished so they can see the consequences if they refuse to turn around: "For I am watching over them for harm, not for good."[4]

When teaching God's people, will we speak what we hear the Holy Spirit speaking, or what our feelings tell us? Will our preachers warn when a warning is needed, or will they soothe our convicted souls with nice words from their own thoughts? It's a natural impulse to quote nice verses to our church friends because we love them so much and want them to love us. But a true friend in Christ speaks what the Father is speaking in the time of need. We are called to be like Jesus and speak only what we hear the Father speaking.[5]

---

2. Jeremiah 23:25.
3. Jeremiah 29:11.
4. Jeremiah 44:27.
5. John 12:49.

We cannot build an enduring house upon falsehoods and lies, falsely using God's name as our authority. Words spoken out from human reasoning and heartfelt emotions alone show contempt for our Father's holy name. The house we attempt to build will crumble.

> Then the LORD said to me, "The prophets are prophesying lies in my name. I have not sent them or appointed them or spoken to them. They are prophesying to you false visions, divinations, idolatries and the delusions of their own minds. Therefore this is what the LORD says about the prophets who are prophesying in my name: I did not send them, yet they are saying, 'No sword or famine will touch this land.' Those same prophets will perish by sword and famine."
(Jeremiah 14:14–15)

When the truth is spoken, who will listen? A messenger who comes with a seemingly obscure warning is scoffed at and thrown over the cliff. Words are thrown at him like rocks as he makes a hasty retreat. Instead of repenting we sing out, "Tell me lies." The age-old saying is true. We "shoot the messenger" who brings news bad news; i.e., news we don't want to hear.

If a man or woman comes to us with words of warning, all too often their message falls on deaf ears. When the holy Scriptures proclaim a warning, we refuse to hear it. Hardened hearts tend to stop up our ears.[6] Our self-centered attitudes deny the truth even when all of God's creation speaks out with alarm to warn us. The ground beneath our feet shakes. Stormy winds carry thundering messages. The seas rage with rogue waves that stir up the deep. Clouds become thick and dark and rumble in the night hours, disturbing our rest. But will we listen? The prophet Micah implores us to "Heed the rod."[7] Jesus made it clear. When disasters strike, the question is not, "Did this disaster happen to people because they are more guilty than others?" Instead, the question should be, "Will we turn from our sin and repent, or will we also perish?"[8]

The Lord God speaks in many ways and through countless voices. He sent Elijah with warnings. Elisha took up his mantle and spoke out God's warnings. Jeremiah and Ezekiel prophesied warnings but the people scorned and rejected them. God sent His only Son and the religious leaders crucified Him. Apostles came to teach and admonish us, but will anyone listen to their words that have echoed throughout the Earth for over two-thousand years? The Earth thunders and shakes to warn us, but will we heed the call?

---

6. Zechariah 7:11–12.
7. Micah 6:9.
8. Luke 13:1–5.

> *We have not listened to your servants the prophets, who spoke in your name to our kings, our princes and our ancestors, and to all the people of the land.*
> (Daniel 9:6)

The house we build must be strong, true, and secure. Every building stone must be tested in the Spirit's fire so the house will measure up according to God's purpose and plan. But there are imposters—building stones who are no stronger than chalk or talc.[9] They crumble easily under the Father's just and righteous judgments and a cutting wind erodes them and blows them away like sand and dust. What they build takes away from God's glory. The walls of the house they build will fall down into a heap of rubble and ruin as soon as they are tested.

Idolatrous stones still claim the name of our Lord and Redeemer, but they wear His name like a name tag that's tossed away after the show. They stand before the Lord's Table acting like true sons and daughters of the Most High God. But the label they stick on themselves falls to the floor.

The prophet Zechariah saw a flying scroll with words of woe written on both sides, indicating that it contained a true and inescapable message. Jesus spoke out the words of the scroll declaring seven woes over the hypocrisy of the religious elite who opposed the truth He taught.[10] Again, the scroll written on both sides with laments, mourning, and woes is doubly true with added emphasis. The Apostle John writes about the Lion of the tribe of Judah who is worthy to open these sealed scrolls in the book of Revelation.[11]

Let's get rid of stick-on labels and turn to Christ who writes His name on our hearts. With His name inscribed on our heart's door we can build a house on the Rock. We will build with tried and tested stones refined in the fires of affliction. We will not show contempt for God's holy name by building with untested stones. Instead, we build a secure and eternal house, and the gates of hell will not prevail against it. This house must be built as strong as a fortress, secured from all who come to steal, kill, and destroy.[12]

> *The LORD Almighty declares, 'I will send it out, and it will enter the house of the thief and the house of anyone who swears falsely by my name. It will remain in that house and destroy it completely, both its timbers and its stones.'"*
> (Zechariah 5:4)

Too many Christians are only hearers of God's word. When it comes to doing what it says, they conveniently forget what they heard. Even in their

---
9. Isaiah 27:9.
10. Matthew 23,
11. Revelation 5:5.
12. John 10:10.

wayward ways they still see themselves as right. Because of this, instead of seeing a forgiven and cleansed Church, our neighbors see God's people living contrary to faith. We go to Church, repent, take communion, and say "praise the Lord." We sound so sweet when we tell people we'll pray for them, but then we live like hell. In doing this we profane the name of our heavenly Father. We show our contempt for His holy name.

There's a much better way. Our God and Father desires that His name be renowned as holy, because in Him there is no darkness at all.[13] In Christ we are light to illuminate His name to the nations. Those who are called by His name are called to serve as living proof; witnesses before our neighbors, friends, and coworkers that our God's name is holy.

> *I will show the holiness of my great name, which has been profaned among the nations, the name you have profaned among them. Then the nations will know that I am the LORD, declares the Sovereign LORD, when I am proved holy through you before their eyes.*
> (Ezekiel 36:23)

Hear our prayer. "Call us to repentance, O Lord. May the Lord God, the Great I AM, wash over us like a pent-up flood.[14] We have left your house in ruins. We must repent of the dust and rubble we have left in our wake. Come, Anointed One, turn our hearts from our self-serving ways. Change our hearts. Change our minds and conform us to Christ. By the power of the Word and the Holy Spirit bring our hearts to repentance, for you are faithful and just to forgive us our sins and to cleanse us from all unrighteousness.[15] Renew a right spirit in us and restore to us the joy of your salvation so that we, your Church, may sing out in harmony; 'Blessed is He who comes in the name of the Lord.'"

> *Look, your house is left to you desolate. I tell you, you will not see me again until you say, "Blessed is he who comes in the name of the Lord."*
> (Luke 13:35)

There's an old saying that goes: "Get a check-up from the neck up." But in reality, checking our attitude is just a good start. We need to examine ourselves from our toenails all the way up to our hair bun to know the root cause of our conduct. As parents it's important for us to remember that we're the adults who are responsible for creating a safe home for our children. We're responsible for examining our words and actions that affect our children's sense of well-being, whether we do them in secret or in public.

---

13. 1 John 1:5.
14. Isaiah 59:19.
15. 1 John 1:9.

As Christians who dwell in God's holy presence, it's not possible to fake it or live a double life. Putting on a churchy mask or wearing a custom-made Jesus superhero suit to make us look good doesn't cut it in God's kingdom where everything is exposed to the light.[16] We need to put on God's armor from head to foot.[17]

> *Woe to him who builds his palace by unrighteousness, his upper rooms by injustice.* (Jeremiah 22:13)

We are called to be conformed to Christ. Christians are instructed to serve as the light of Christ to the world around them. We speak out as witnesses, saying what we hear the Holy Spirit speaking. We reach out to those whom our Savior reaches out to touch. The words we speak when everything turns against us must be our Lord Jesus' words, not the curses the world speaks.

If we refuse the Scripture's warnings that urge us to check up on ourselves, it's as if we toss the messenger over the cliffside. Mocking the messenger is like throwing words at them like rocks. Our stopped-up ears and stone-hard hearts block out more severe warnings to redirect our attention. If we turn our spiritual hearing aids off, then we need to consider warnings that come from every direction—the four winds of the Spirit.

Those of us who are active parts of the body of Christ—members of the post-modern day church—need to be brought to the throne of grace with contrite hearts so that the Church will be renewed in us, restored to us, and revived in our hearts.[18]

> *Unless the* LORD *builds the house, the builders labor in vain.* (Psalm 127:1)

---

16. Ephesians 5:13.
17. Ephesians 6:11.
18. Psalm 51:10.

Chapter 7
A Show of Contempt
Q & A

1. What does a child's need for a safe home teach us about the house we build?

2. Describe what it means to be "conformed to Christ." How does this affect what we say and do?

3. What kind of warnings ring out all around us?

4. Why are contrite hearts so crucial to revival for those who build the house for our Father's holy name?

My Journal Notes:

Part 3:
The Greatest House

By wisdom a house is built, and through understanding it is established.
(Proverbs 24:3)

A New Name

Key Scripture:

- "The nations will see your vindication, and all kings your glory; you will be called by a new name that the mouth of the Lord will bestow." (Isaiah 62:2)

There's a great old hymn of the church that says, "There's a new name written down in glory, and it's mine."[1] In this study we'll learn why we are given a new name in Christ and the significance of our new name. We'll see the futility of trying to change our own name in an effort to rescue ourselves from our past wrongdoing. This lesson opens our understanding to know that when we hear the Word, come to saving faith, and are baptized into Christ we are made part of our heavenly Father's household and receive a new family name. His miraculous name changes our lives now and forever.

We'll learn about the Bible characters whose names were changed. The good purpose for giving them new names will become clear. Every learner will come to treasure the white stone of absolution they hold in their hands. We'll see the imprint of our new name forever inscribed on it. With the promise of absolution held tight in our grip, we are brought from the pit of ashes where we wallowed in mourning, and into the beauty of Christ and the oil of joy. Our Bridegroom wraps His bride with a garment of praise as He goes to prepare a place for us.

Now you're ready to take these learning steps to know our new name and its miraculous effect on your life.

Study Prayer

Heavenly Father, may your name be glorified in your sons and daughters. Mold us and shape us so we may honorably represent your name–the new name you have given us as you brought us into your family.

A prayer inspired by Jeremiah 18:6

---

1. *A New Name in Glory*, hymn by C. Austin Miles. Public domain.

People tend to get stuck in the muck, and it keeps us bogged down for most of our lives. Even the brightest and strongest of us can't pull ourselves out of the dirt from our past. We might try moving to a new town and changing our name, but the reality of life is that we will likely pack up our old baggage and take it with us. Changing our eternal destiny requires a strong hand, a nail-pierced hand, to release us from the chains of our past. Getting rid of an impoverished mindset requires the miraculous work of a Deliverer. Being set free from our sins requires a Savior who holds the keys to our prison. Overcoming a life pattern of failure requires a Redeemer who has overcome death and the grave.

Abram offers us a good example. The Almighty gave him a new name that meant "exalted father." How many times did he chuckle a bit when he heard his name called for dinner where there would be no children around the table? It's as if his name added insult to the shame of his childless life. He had no heir, no son or daughter to pass on his legacy of faith. He had to face the stark reality that his body was as good as dead when it came to fathering children.[2] He had no power to change this. He pleaded with the Almighty for a son. Abram's Lord and God heard his plea and began this great miracle by changing his name to Abraham: "father of nations."

> *This is my covenant with you: I will make you the father of a multitude of nations! What's more, I am changing your name. It will no longer be Abram. Instead, you will be called Abraham, for you will be the father of many nations. I will make you extremely fruitful. Your descendants will become many nations, and kings will be among them!*
> (Genesis 17:4–6 NLT)

In ancient times a barren womb cast a dark shadow of shame over a woman. Sarai lived with this disgrace every day of her life. As an elderly childless woman she had to face reality and let go of an unrealistic dream. She could have changed her own name and stitched baby images to her tent door. She might have tried to knead her wishes into every batch of dough. She might have visited her neighbors who had lots of kids, hoping it would rub off. But on her own no plan would ever work; not even her scheme to give her handmaid to Abram. The best way is always to wait on the Lord alone.

The God of Abraham began this miraculous work in her by changing her name from Sarai (princess) to Sarah (noblewoman). In one miraculous moment the Lord spoke and changed her from being a princess of shame to a woman with a noble heritage who gave birth to a promised son. A son, Isaac, whose name meant "Laughter."

---

2. Romans 4:19.

God also said to Abraham, "As for Sarai your wife, you are no longer to call her Sarai; her name will be Sarah. I will bless her and will surely give you a son by her. I will bless her so that she will be the mother of nations; kings of peoples will come from her."
(Genesis 17:15–16)

When Jesus called His twelve disciples, He chose common fishermen, a tax collector, a zealot, and one radical Zionist.[3] They had one thing in common. When Jesus said: "follow me," they dropped what they were doing and devotedly pursued Him. Simon reeked of fish and Matthew smelled of tainted Roman tax money, but they obeyed Jesus' call. We can't be sure why James and John were called "sons of thunder." But in reality, each disciple was baptized into a new name; our Savior's name. The name above all names wrote His name on their heart's door.

We can identify with them because when Jesus found us we were spiritual paupers; dirty, smelly, broken, ruined, and wandering about, lost in our sin. We were self-serving scoundrels. But when we answered His call to follow Him, He forgave our sin, washed us clean, healed our wounded soul, and gave us His name as our own.

These are the twelve he appointed: Simon (to whom he gave the name Peter), James son of Zebedee and his brother John (to them he gave the name Boanerges, which means "sons of thunder").
(Mark 3:16-17)

Every redeemed soul is given a new name—the name of their Savior. A white stone of absolution with a new name engraved on it is presented to all who are brought to the Throne of Grace with contrite hearts and receive forgiveness. With this stone in hand, we can hold tight to the promise of our new name; the name of Christ Jesus our Lord and Savior whose name is also written on our heart's door and on our forehead.[4]

Only the person who holds this witness stone in his or her hand can know this new name is theirs as an adopted son or daughter of the Most High God. No one else can judge their standing before our Father in heaven. Only those who are victorious in Christ Jesus can know He has overcome sin, Satan, and death on their behalf. This new family name is our ticket to the table where we partake of the Bread of Life.

---

3. Many Bible scholars consider it likely that Judas belonged to the Sicarii, the most radical Jewish militants.
4. Revelation 22:4.

Whoever has ears, let them hear what the Spirit says to the churches. To the one who is victorious, I will give some of the hidden manna. I will also give that person a white stone with a new name written on it, known only to the one who receives it.
(Revelation 2:17)

All Christians together from every tribe, nationality, and culture dwell together in one house and feast at one table. We are the building stones of this dwelling place, built upon the Cornerstone, and in keeping with the inspired word written by Apostles and the Prophets. This house is home because we are one with Christ who gained the victory by giving His body to be broken and His blood to be shed so that He could pay the price to redeem us from sin's death sentence.[5]

You can look forward to the victorious wedding celebration you're invited to attend. You came ragged, soiled, and with your clothes torn. Your hands were stained with the world's corruption. But then He cleansed you in the blood of the Lamb of God. He washed you in the waters of baptism. He wrapped a sparkling white robe around you. He gave you new sandals for your feet and jewels to adorn your neck. And then your Savior ushered you before the throne to present you to the Father. You stand there overwhelmed with awe as you see your new name is written down in heaven's eternal record.

The one who is victorious will, like them, be dressed in white. I will never blot out the name of that person from the book of life, but will acknowledge that name before my Father and his angels.
(Revelation 3:5)

The stones used for building a sanctuary for God's name serve as pillars of this eternal abode. Each precious stone is tested, tried, and measured to fill its ordained place and purpose. Every pillar is brought through the fires of affliction to refine and strengthen it. Then each stone is set in place, one upon the other, to build a house as strong as a mighty fortress. Each one of us is a part of this awesome dwelling place. Jesus' followers are the radiant stones with their new names written on them; stones that shout out with praise. The Father's name is also inscribed on our forehead and on our heart's door. Our Father cherishes us because we are jewels on the breastplate worn by Christ Jesus, our High Priest, who serves in the temple in the city of the living God.

Israel's high priest wore a breastplate with twelve gemstones set in gold mountings. Each precious stone had one tribe's name inscribed on it.[6]

---

5. Romans 6:23.
6. Exodus 28:21.

Now, our High Priest, who is Jesus Christ, wears His breastplate close to His heart. We are the precious stones set on His breastplate and mounted in gold filigrees—each one with one saint's precious name.

> *The one who is victorious I will make a pillar in the temple of my God. Never again will they leave it. I will write on them the name of my God and the name of the city of my God, the new Jerusalem, which is coming down out of heaven from my God; and I will also write on them my new name.*
> (Revelation 3:12)

In modern times, 144,000 doesn't seem like a big number. Hundreds of cities in the USA have populations over 150 thousand. So, what does the 144,000 stand for in the Bible's final book? This number in the book of Revelation is obviously not literal. It represents a complete number. The number is fulfilled when every precious stone whose name is written in the Book of Life from the beginning of time has filled his or her place in the walls of the house we build for the Father's holy name. They serve as pillars in this eternal home—the eternal city whose Builder and Maker is God. Not one is missing.[7] Every wanderer and every soul who got lost along the way has been found, forgiven, cleansed, washed by the blood of the sacrificial Lamb of God, and restored to its place in this house.

Every stone the Father chooses to refine and make precious has a special place prepared for it. Each one fulfills a unique place and purpose. This means that every one of us has a job to do, custom made for our time and place in the building of the kingdom of heaven. When we have completed this good work, we can rest assured we will hear those awesome words: "Well done, good and faithful servant."[8]

> *Then I looked, and there before me was the Lamb, standing on Mount Zion, and with him 144,000 who had his name and his Father's name written on their foreheads.*
> (Revelation 14:1)

When Jesus healed the blind man in Bethsaida, He used water from His mouth to create new, seeing eyes for him, but He did this in two stages for good reason. After first touching him, Jesus asked the man, "Do you see anything?" The man saw people looking like trees walking around. Again, Jesus put his hands on the man's eyes and he saw everything clearly.[9]

The Apostle Paul taught how we are like the man who Jesus gave new eyes. Our spiritual eyes are opened in two stages. Today our eyes are like looking in an old mirror in an antique store—what we see is not perfectly

---

7. Isaiah 40:26.
8. Matthew 25:21.
9. Mark 8:22–25.

clear. We see dimly.[10] In other words, we don't understand everything God has done and is doing from beginning to end. We need to trust that God knows what He's doing. We must walk by faith, not by natural eyesight.[11] But there will come a great and glorious day when we will see him clearly, face to face. As we stand before our heavenly Father, He will know we are His sons and daughters by the name inscribed on our foreheads. It's a name that is more permanent than any inked tattoo you can get today.

They will see his face, and his name will be on their foreheads. (Revelation 22:4)

If Luke, the Gospel writer, told the story of your sin-wrecked life, you might want to get a new name and leave your reputation behind. Jesus gave an example of leaving the past behind. He was invited to dinner one evening and He told His pious host a simple truth about those who are forgiven much: "They love much!" His host pointed at a woman with an accusing finger, but Jesus said to her, "Your sins are forgiven." He went on to make it very clear that she was forgiven, cleansed, and made a new creation when He said, "Your faith has saved you, go in peace."[12]

Changing our eternal destiny requires more than a reinvented online persona with a made-up name. Getting on the right path requires us to become new creations in Christ. Christ's suffering, death, and resurrection make it possible for us to become part of the family of God and receive a new family name. Abram and Sarai's name changes, ordained by God Almighty, changed the direction of their lives and planted the seeds for a holy nation that would be set apart for the Great I AM. We learn the value of a name change as Jesus added Peter to Simon's name. With the new name, Simon Peter, became a "rock who has heard," a living and precious stone for building the Church. Perhaps Jesus called James and John "The sons of thunder" because He knew they would become mighty witnesses who boldly spoke out with the thunderous message of the Gospel.

Under the covering of one holy family name, we dwell together in one house. By this name our house is known as a place of redemption where blood-bought sons and daughters may dwell in the presence of the Most High God. The Bible gives us many various descriptions to help us understand who we are in Christ. We are whole new creations, and adopted children. We are pledged as a bride, forgiven and made clean. We are dressed in fine, white linen, adorned with heaven's precious jewels, and given a crown for our heads. How awesome it is to know that our name is written down in glory.

---

10. 1 Corinthians 13:12.
11. 2 Corinthians 5:7.
12. Luke 7:44-50.

As we meditate on these awesome truths, we must also consider that we are tried and tested stones, set in place to build up a house for our Father's holy name. It's a house as strong as a fortress. We are the precious stones mounted in gold settings on our High Priest's breastplate. There is great comfort knowing that Jesus keeps our names so close to His heart.

Chapter 8

A New Name

Q & A

1. How do we become new creations in Christ and made part of the family of God?

\
\
\

2. Why is it significant that God gave Abram a new name? Why did Jesus give Peter a new name?

\
\
\

3. What is the significance of the white stone referred to in Revelation 2:17?

\
\
\

4. What truth does the Old Testament high priest's breastplate picture for us today?

\
\
\

My Journal Notes:

9

Baptized Into His Name

Key Scriptures:

- "Go ye therefore, and make disciples of all the nations, baptizing them [into] the name of the Father and of the Son and of the Holy Spirit." (Matthew 28:19 ASV)[1]
- "So in Christ Jesus you are all children of God through faith, for all of you who were baptized into Christ have clothed yourselves with Christ." (Galatians 3:26–27)

Most of our studies in this book include teaching to help us see ourselves as the bride of Christ. Old Testament religious practices offer illustrations that serve as shadows of spiritual realities for the church today. One teaching moment from ancient Israel is when a bride is immersed in the mikveh, a ritual bath, before she is wed.[2] In shoulder deep water, the bride dips three times. Dipping the third time, she quotes the words of the prophet Hosea: "I will betroth you to me forever; I will betroth you in righteousness and justice, in love and compassion."[3]

Israel's wedding mikvah is a cleansing rite of passage to prepare the bride and groom for a life together as one. Is it possible that Jesus' baptism by John the Baptizer in the Jordan River also served as a mikveh, preparing Jesus to be joined as a Bridegroom to His bride?[4] This study opens the learner's understanding to the miraculous mystery of baptism and the command to "believe and be baptized."[5]

Baptism was given as a life changing rite for God's people on the day of Pentecost when the Holy Spirit came with fire to establish the Church. When we come into Christ through the water and the Word, we are transformed to become representations of our Redeemer for our friends, family, and co-workers. We'll learn that all who are called and chosen must enter into God's

---
1. According to original Greek, "into" is the best English translation.
2. Bridegrooms could also be immersed in a mikveh bath.
3. Hosea 2:19.
4. Jesus fulfilled all the Old Testament's external ordinances of the flesh, as seen in Hebrews 9:10.
5. Mark 16:16.

kingdom through water, just as the children of Israel passed through the water to be baptized into Moses who led them to the Promised Land. We'll come to understand the desperate cry from the crowds after they heard Peter's anointed message. They cried out, "What shall we do?" The reader will come to know why this penitent plea is a sure sign when people first thirst for the Spring of Living Water.

> Study Prayer
>
> *O Lord God Almighty, we call upon you to teach us the unsearchable mysteries of your glorious kingdom that we have never known.*
>
> A prayer according to Jeremiah 33:3

We are called and prepared as a bride so we may be joined together with Christ, our Bridegroom. But how is this great mystery possible? Our Redeemer makes a way. In the waters of baptism we are made one with the Father, Son, and Holy Spirit. By the power of the Word and in water, we are brought into the family of God and given His name as our own.

The second half of the following verse must break our hearts, especially when those who don't believe are beloved family or close friends. They can see the power and effect of God's forgiveness and mercy in our lives. They watch us as we reflect the light of Christ to them. They notice when our words and conversations honor Christ. What we do every day of our lives is in the likeness of Christ. At every opportunity we give witness of faith in our Lord and Savior. But it breaks our hearts if they simply won't hear it or see it.

Whoever believes and is baptized will be saved, but whoever does not believe will be condemned.
(Mark 16:16)

Sons and daughters of the Most High God are called and chosen to enter through the narrow gate, who is Christ. Then we step out onto a narrow pathway that is blazed before us by our Savior. We walk in His footsteps, firmly placing our feet on the stepping stones of this path. Each step opens our eyes to another attribute of our Redeemer. As we step forward, we see a pathway paved with love, faithfulness, joy, forgiveness, and saving grace. When we answer Jesus' call to saving faith, we embark on a path to strength, peace, comfort, and victory. How is it possible that these miraculous blessings are poured out on us?

In the name of the Father, Son, and Holy Spirit we are baptized *into* the name of the Father, Son, and Holy Spirit.

Our heavenly Father knows our sorrows, encompasses us with His loving-kindness, surrounds us with the riches of His grace, redeems us out of darkness, and He is faithful even when we are not. Our God pours out the riches of His mercies. He mounts up, mighty in battle on our behalf. The Lord Almighty is ever-present with us and quick to forgive. The Great I AM rises with healing in His wings to restore us to health. Yehovah, our God, is mighty to save, to redeem, and to deliver us. He provides our daily bread, shelters us, and gifts us with fulfilling work.

This is our Father whose name we are baptized into.

A father to the fatherless, a defender of widows, is God in his holy dwelling. (Psalm 68:5)

The Son of God is the way, the truth, and the life. Because of His great love for us He gave His body to be broken, and His blood shed to redeem us from the clutches of sin, Satan, and death. Our Savior is the holy One sent from God above. He is the Word of creation. He is the Alpha and Omega—the beginning and end of all things. All authority is given to Him and He serves as Prophet, Priest, and King. He reigns in justice and righteousness. Our Redeemer is the Spirit of counsel and wisdom who is constantly at the Creator's side, delighting in humankind. He is the Head of the Church and ministers in heaven's sanctuary as our High Priest.

This is Christ Jesus whose name we are baptized into by the water of baptism and the promise of the Word.

Greater love has no one than this: to lay down one's life for one's friends. (John 15:13)

The Holy Spirit is the Spirit of Christ who is sent as our Helper, Advocate, and Counselor. He is sent from the Father to guide us in all truth. He is our Teacher who opens God's word to us. He gives us understanding hearts and minds. The Spirit of Jesus produces good fruit in us—the fruit of love, joy, peace, patience, faithfulness, gentleness, and self-control. He gives us ears to hear so the seed of faith is planted in our hearts to grow and flourish. The Holy Spirit helps us in our weaknesses and leads us in paths of righteousness.

This is the Holy Spirit whose name we are baptized into.

When the Advocate comes, whom I will send to you from the Father–the Spirit of truth who goes out from the Father–he will testify about me. (John 15:26)

The Spirit of Creation breathed into Adam and he became a living soul. Then Adam and Eve fell, and through this one man, sin entered the world.[6] But our heavenly Father made a way for lost souls to be redeemed. This is only possible through water and the blood.[7] This cleansing flow came from Jesus' pierced side to become a mighty river that satisfies all who thirst and who will come by faith to be made new creations in Christ.[8] The blood that flowed is the sacrificial blood of the Paschal Lamb who takes away the sins of the world. Then, as victors in Christ, when we come to the end of our life's journey, we are welcomed into the Father's eternal kingdom where we will dwell with Him forever. In the water of baptism, we cross the threshold. We're like the tribes of Israel who crossed the Jordan River into their Promised Land. We too are ushered into the land of promise where there is a bountiful wedding banquet prepared for us in His garden of delights.

> *Jesus answered, "Very truly I tell you, no one can enter the kingdom of God unless they are born of water and the Spirit."*
> (John 3:5)

Try to imagine baptizing three thousand men and their families in one day. How did this happen? The rush of the Spirit's wind grabbed the attention of the pilgrims who came to celebrate the feast of Pentecost in Jerusalem. The mighty Wind of the Spirit captured their attention. Then Peter stood before the people filled with fresh fire of the Holy Spirit's anointing and spoke God's word to the crowd. Everyone heard words of life, liberty, and saving grace in their own tongue. God fearing Jews from other nations gathered in Jerusalem and they heard men speaking Gospel truths in the languages of their homelands.

The people responded with a plea. This plea gave a sure sign they heard and acted according to the call of the Spirit of Christ. They reached out their hands, hungry for the Bread of Life. The crowds called out because of their thirst for Living Water, saying: "What shall we do?"[9] The Holy Spirit gave Peter the right answer and as a result the Church grew by three thousand families on that first day of the week. Each baptized convert received the Holy Spirit who sealed them "for the day of redemption."[10]

> *Peter replied, "Repent and be baptized, every one of you, in the name of Jesus Christ for the forgiveness of your sins. And you will receive the gift of the Holy Spirit."*
> (Acts 2:38)

---

6. Romans 5:12–21.
7. 1 John 5:6.
8. "Come, all you who are thirsty, come to the waters." (Isaiah 55:1)
9. Acts 2:37.
10. Ephesians 4:30.

When the Holy Spirit led Peter to Cornelius' house in Joppa, the New Testament Church expanded its reach. Before this time Peter focused on leading his Jewish brothers to Christ, but now he saw that God welcomed all people of every nation to be His sons and daughters. Peter spoke just a few words, proclaiming the resurrected Christ who was crucified, when the Holy Spirit came upon the people with an undeniable, visible manifestation of power. The house then filled with praises to God, each one speaking in Spirit-inspired languages.[11] This offered a sure sign of the Spirit spreading the tent curtain wide to include the Gentiles.[12]

And that day, without delay, all who heard and believed the Gospel message stepped into the waters of baptism. Their hunger to hear more of Christ who saved them became clear evidence of their new faith in Christ Jesus. They asked Peter to stay a few more days to teach them and baptize those who believed.

So he ordered that they be baptized in the name of Jesus Christ. Then they asked Peter to stay with them for a few days.
(Acts 10:48)

The tribes of Israel held back, afraid. They stared at the deep waters of the Red Sea and saw them as an uncrossable barrier. The tribes of Israel grumbled against their leader because they were trapped between deep water and the Egyptian army. But God had an awesome plan. The Almighty made a way. The words in the following verse echo what God spoke to Moses just before the people stepped onto the dry bed of the Red Sea: "Why are you crying out to me? Tell the Israelites to Move on."[13] In obedience to God's command, Moses raised up his hand over the sea.

The Almighty One pushed back the water of the Red Sea and they made their escape. They reached the other side on dry ground. God still makes a way for us today. When we first hear precious words of saving grace and believe the Good News Gospel of Jesus Christ, we get caught in the battle between the forces of light and darkness. Darkness presses in to destroy the sprouting seed of faith to keep it from taking root in our heart and soul.[14] But there is no need to fear. The waters of baptism make a way for us. Through water and the Word we are sealed from destruction just as the Almighty sealed Noah's ark from earth's devastation.

The light of Christ draws us to the throne of grace to receive forgiveness and become new creations in Him. We are victorious in Christ because the

---
11. Acts 10:44.
12. Isaiah 54:2.
13. Exodus 14:15.
14. Matthew 13:4.

One who is in you is greater than he who is in the world.[15] We are raised up from the waters of baptism to live in the power of resurrection, and there is no need to fear the forces of darkness.

The tribes of Israel went through the Red Sea as their baptism into Moses, who foreshadowed Christ.[16] Now, we are called to cross the threshold into Christ through the waters of Christian baptism—waters set apart for a holy purpose. By means of the water and the word we are made new creations in Christ and so we may be refined as the precious building stones of the kingdom of heaven.

> *And now what are you waiting for? Get up, be baptized and wash your sins away, calling on his name.*
> (Acts 22:16)

The miraculous work that baptism accomplishes is a great mystery. In the water and by the authority of the Word, we are powerfully transformed. The realities of this miracle are awesome to consider. In this water we enter into Christ and His sacrificial death. We die to our old self and enter into new life in Christ Jesus who died to pay sin's penalty for us and for the forgiveness of our sins. Our old self is buried—dead and gone. In the water of baptism, we are made one with the Father, Son, and Holy Spirit, and we are blessed to enter into our Savior's suffering. By baptism we become one with Christ in the power of His resurrection. In Him we are new creations and our past is left behind us. We are made victors over sin, Satan, and death. We are brought into a family of faith under the protective covering of our heavenly Father. We are forever sealed from God's just and righteous wrath.

> *Or don't you know that all of us who were baptized into Christ Jesus were baptized into his death?*
> (Romans 6:3)

In the water of baptism we are made whole as a functioning part of His Church. This wholeness is made possible because Jesus' body was broken. By His brokenness the Church (His body) is restored. Each person who comes to saving faith and obeys Christ in holy baptism is a building stone for the sanctuary.[17] We are made whole; unbroken building stones, so we may fulfill our place of the whole body of Christ. Every new building stone set in place is celebrated as one vital part of the body of Christ—a good work completed.[18]

---

15. 1 John 4:4.
16. 1 Corinthians 10:2.
17. 1 Peter 2:5.
18. This miracle is prefigured in Joshua 4:1–10, when men from each tribe were commanded to take twelve stones from the river bed of the Jordan to create a memorial monument as their first campsite in the Promised Land.

We are made whole as a part of the whole when we are baptized into Christ and His body, the Church. Jesus gave His body to be broken so that His body, the Church, might be made whole and complete.

Baptismal water is not meant for washing the outside of the body. The flow of this cleansing fountain permeates our whole being. This is water that is separated for a holy purpose. Our soul and spirit drink in the Spirit of Christ. Jesus beckoned us saying, "Let anyone who is thirsty come to me and drink.."[19] So let us answer His call and come to Him in the waters of baptism and be satisfied in the Springs of Living Water.

> *For we were all baptized by one Spirit so as to form one body–whether Jews or Gentiles, slave or free–and we were all given the one Spirit to drink.*
> (1 Corinthians 12:13)

If we could just leave behind all the crazy, stupid stuff we did earlier in our lives—what a relief that would be. That's exactly what our Savior does for us in baptism. We ruined our lives by our own actions, and now we come to these holy waters where our past lives die off to be buried for good. Even those who have been violated, their innocence stolen away, are restored and made pure in Christ who died for us to cleanse us. Every stain and bruise of the evil done to us is cleansed away and we are made new.

The new creations we become in Jesus Christ are a good beginning. This new life keeps getting better because, by faith, we are also raised to a new life in Christ. We are raised up in the power of our resurrected Redeemer to live in the eighth day of His creation—the day of renewal. Now, by the power of the Word and the Holy Spirit, we can overrule the crazy, stupid temptations that try to drag us back down. By the power of Jesus' name we cast down and take captive every evil thought that crosses our minds.[20] In Christ we have the confidence to stand up against those who would steal away the good gifts we received in Jesus' name.

> *Your whole self ruled by the flesh was put off when you were circumcised by Christ, having been buried with him in baptism, in which you were also raised with him through your faith in the working of God, who raised him from the dead.*
> (Colossians 2:11–12)

Sunday school children always enjoy hearing the story of Noah and the ark. They can visualize old Noah with his white beard standing on the rampway into the great ship as the animals pass by, two by two. The lion came with the lioness. The stallion galloped up with the mare. The giraffe came with his mate. All of them together with Noah's family show us the essence of God's saving grace through water.

---

19. John 7:37.
20. 2 Corinthians 10:5.

Eight people and a lot of animals were all sealed safely inside the ark while waters surged around them to flood the earth. They were kept safe from the Almighty's holy and just wrath unleashed against a world that defied all that He established in creation. Then the waters receded, the ground dried, the trees sprouted, and the Earth began anew. This served as their baptism; a beautiful foreshadowing that gives witness to the power of baptismal water for us today that forever shields us from God's just and righteous wrath.

> *When God waited patiently in the days of Noah, during the building of the ark, in which a few, that is, eight persons, were saved through water. And baptism, which this prefigured, now saves you–not as a removal of dirt from the body, but as an appeal to God for a good conscience, through the resurrection of Jesus Christ.* (1 Peter 3:20–21 NRSV)

Baptism is an awesome and mysterious miracle. We are baptized in the name of Father, Son, and Holy Spirit. It's equally miraculous that through the water and the Word we are baptized *into* the name of our Father, Son, and Holy Spirit. Our baptism is crossing a great threshold to enter the kingdom of heaven with all its awesome benefits.

Now, in His name and by His name we are led to walk on a narrow pathway. On this path we are free to run. In this way we come into all the benefits of our Messiah's kingdom. As we walk in the Way we are initiated into strength, peace, comfort, and victorious living. The wind of the Spirit breathes into us to restore our souls so that we may soar on wings like the eagles and not grow weary. Through the water and the Word we come to walk on this pathway and we will not grow faint.[21]

Through the miracle of baptism we become the Father's adopted sons and daughters. We are baptized into the name of the Father, Son, and Holy Spirit and we bear this name as our own. It's a powerful and awesome family name that confirms we are one with Him, and inseparable from Him. As His sons and daughters we delight to find that we begin to talk like our Father. We start to act like our Lord Jesus. His characteristics become our own. Before we know it we're walking like heavenly Father like a child who steps in their dad's footprints.

Through the water of baptism we cross a great threshold where we are sealed for the day of redemption and kept safe from God's just and righteous wrath. We come into a land of promise. We are rocks that have heard. Now we're cleansed and made into precious stones for building the house, a sanctuary where His holy name may dwell with all who are baptized into the name of the Father, Son, and Holy Spirit.

---

21. Isaiah 40:31.

Chapter 9

Baptized into His Name

Q & A

1. What is the significance of being baptized in the name of and into the name of the Father, Son, and Holy Spirit?

   _____

   _____

   _____

2. What happens to your past when you are baptized into Christ?

   _____

   _____

3. What is the significance of being called by the name of the triune God?

   _____

   _____

   _____

4. What does Noah's ark teach us about baptism?

   _____

   _____

   _____

My Journal Notes:

Count the Cost

Key Scriptures:

- "However, if you suffer as a Christian, do not be ashamed, but praise God that you bear that name. For it is time for judgment to begin with God's household; and if it begins with us, what will the outcome be for those who do not obey the gospel of God?" (1 Peter 4:16–17)

- "For I endure scorn for your sake, and shame covers my face. I am a foreigner to my own family, a stranger to my own mother's children; for zeal for your house consumes me, and the insults of those who insult you fall on me." (Psalm 69:7–9)

The Apostle Paul is our primary teacher in this study. He helps us to see the need to count the cost before we step out to serve and minister in a hostile world. His missionary experiences show us how to persevere and press on toward the goal to win the prize. We'll come to understand why Paul willingly suffered for the Gospel and continued the good work of Christ's suffering on the cross. Why did Paul, like his Savior, become persecuted for the good he accomplished in building the Church—a house for God's holy name?

Endure? Impossible on our own. Persevere? We don't have the strength. Press on to win the prize? We need the wind of the Spirit to carry us onward. As we see Paul's suffering, we'll learn that our Lord Jesus is ever-present with us and feels the pain of every stone thrown at us. This learning experience teaches us where to find the strength and power we need to go on. The following Scriptures and teaching help us to spread our wings to fly on the winds of the Spirit. Every verse serves to tap us into the source of the strength we need to carry on to the end.

Study Prayer

Give us hearts that rejoice in suffering, knowing that suffering for the cause of Christ produces perseverance, and perseverance a godly character, and godly character, hope.

A prayer according to Romans 5:3–4

Building a house with lumber and nails, bricks and mortar requires a lot of sweat, some tears, and occasionally some blood. We get blisters on our hands as they toughen up. Our back hurts from lifting buckets, blocks, and boards. At the end of every work day our whole body is bone tired. But we press on, knowing the finished home will be worth all the pain.

Until that day comes when the work of the Great Commission is finished, our calling is to apply our hands to the job until it's done. We endure the hard work our Savior has given us for the sake of the church.[1] We press on, without looking back, as we build God's eternal kingdom, stone upon precious stone. There will be painful moments, sorrowful trials, heart-rending rejections, and bruising insults as we press on to complete our work of the kingdom. But then, before we take our final breath we can look back and say, "It's been worth it all."

Before the Apostle Paul began his missionary work among the Gentiles, God made it perfectly clear to him how much he would suffer. Paul needed to count the cost.[2] With his eyes wide open, Paul willingly stepped forward to complete the work our Savior began on a cross of suffering.

> *I will show him how much he must suffer for my name.*
> (Acts 9:16)

As Paul trekked on toward Jerusalem for the last time, several prophets in the church told him about the perils he would face. Their prophetic words offered clear signs—warnings of what he would suffer at the hands of the entrenched religious establishment and the Roman government. Paul saw his friend's tears and felt their sorrow on his behalf. But he counted the cost and refused to turn back from the work of his calling.

The Apostle to the Gentiles pressed on toward Jerusalem, but not in his own strength. His own mortal strength would never be enough to meet such a great challenge.[3] With his eyes fixed on Christ Jesus, and in the power of the Spirit, he determined to push on to the goal to win the prize and fulfill his calling in the Church.[4] He unwaveringly continued to lay the foundation for those who would come after him to build a house for God's holy name.

> *Then Paul answered, "Why are you weeping and breaking my heart? I am ready not only to be bound, but also to die in Jerusalem for the name of the Lord Jesus."*
> (Acts 21:13)

---

1. Colossians 1:24.
2. Luke 14:28.
3. Zechariah 4:6.
4. Philippians 3:14.

As Jesus approached Jerusalem, He wept with a lament for the city He loved.[5] Surely, He looked back through time to see the many prophets sent to warn the people of the consequences of their sin and rebellion. Indeed, Jesus was present with every true prophet who came before Him. He felt the blows as God's people beat, stoned, and killed His messengers. Finally, He came as God's only Son to bless, teach, heal, and restore. He ministered strength to the weak and lifted their burdens.[6] Jesus blessed their children. He fed thousands with bread and fish to satisfy their hunger. He raised their dead to life. But their hearts were hard and the Son of God wasn't enough. They rejected Him, falsely accused Him, and demanded He be crucified.

The crowds that gathered in Jerusalem welcomed Jesus in His triumphal entrance. They waved palm branches and sang out with praise, "Blessed is He who comes in the name of the Lord."[7] And then, just four days later, the crowds stood before Pilate and demanded that he act on their behalf. Their leaders stirred them into a frenzy to shout out, "Crucify, crucify, crucify!"

This is what our Savior suffered as the Lamb of God. Now we are called to speak out in the name of the Lord, giving our all as we build this house.

Brothers and sisters, as an example of patience in the face of suffering, take the prophets who spoke in the name of the Lord.
(James 5:10)

When we suffer, our Lord Jesus suffers with us because we are one with Him. When we hurt, He knows and bears our pain because we are one with Him. When we are locked behind bars, He is present with us. When people incite persecutions and violence against us, He is our shield who takes the blows with us.

How can we who are called by His name do any less than suffer for the cause of Christ and the cross? When our brothers and sisters are imprisoned for their faith, we stand with them with our earnest prayers to strengthen them. Our hearts are roiled with their suffering. We visit them to bring relief from their trials. We prepare for the day when they will be free again and we can welcome them home in Jesus' name.

Continue to remember those in prison as if you were together with them in prison, and those who are mistreated as if you yourselves were suffering.
(Hebrews 13:3)

The weariness of pandemics, wars, lost loved ones, empty store shelves, mass shootings, and fear of storms and wildfires press in from every side. We

---
5. Luke 19:41–44.
6. Matthew 11:28.
7. Luke 19:38.

grieve when those who speak God's word are blamed and accused of hate speech. These dire circumstances make it evident that we have no strength of our own to endure. There is no mortal power that can carry us through an unending barrage of adversities followed by more miseries that get all kneaded together with turmoil. Endure to the end? It's impossible on our own. Our Savior's strength must be renewed in us.

In Christ we have the greatest hope even in the darkest hour. We know a Redeemer who is joy, strength, peace, and comfort and He dwells in us as we abide in Him. When we have no strength to persevere, He encompasses us with His might to carry us through. When the weight of hardships crush us, our Savior lifts our burdens and sorrows.[8] Our Lord and Messiah is more than able to carry us through and make us victors who boldly speak the word to push back the darkness that would consume us. Indeed, the Spirit of Christ renews His strength in us so that we may be overcomers who build a house to stand as a mighty fortress.

> *You have persevered and have endured hardships for my name, and have not grown weary.*
> (Revelation 2:3)

For the sake of the cross of Jesus Christ and for the Church, of whom Christ is the Head, we are called to count the cost and then step out into a hostile world to press on toward the goal to win the prize.[9] Jesus counted the cost as He approached Jerusalem. He was painfully aware that the religious elite lay in wait, wanting Him out of their way. With each step on the trek up to this holy city, Jesus could hear the crowds who prepared to welcome Him, singing out, "Hosanna." He could also hear some from the same crowd shouting out, "Crucify!" Paul walked in Jesus' footsteps as he approached Jerusalem. He counted the cost with every warning he heard, telling what waited ahead for him. But he pressed on in the strength of the Lord.

We, like Paul, are one with Christ in His suffering. We know the full cost and we press on with weeping to advance the work of building a house for our Father's name according to His perfect plan. In our Great Commission work we go out with seed to sow, water the seed with our tears, and then return with singing, carrying a bountiful harvest of souls.[10] Can we endure to the end to complete this good work? It's impossible on our own. Yet, in Christ Jesus we have the greatest hope. In all of life's darkest moments of suffering for the cause of Christ, He is present with us, strengthens us, and sends His Holy Spirit to lift us up like the wind that lifts the eagle with its wings spread wide.

8. Psalm 68:19.
9. Philippians 3:14.
10. Psalm 126:6.

Chapter 10

Count the Cost

Q & A

1. Why is it important to count the cost before witnessing for Christ in a hostile world?

2. Why did the Apostle Paul press on toward Jerusalem, even after prophets warned about what would happen to him?

3. Why did Jesus keep going on the roads that led to Jerusalem, fully aware of what awaited Him?

4. How is it possible for us to endure to the end?

My Journal Notes:

A Covenantal Name

Key Scriptures:

- "You repented and did what is right in my sight: Each of you proclaimed freedom to your own people. You even made a covenant before me in the house that bears my Name." (Jeremiah 34:15)

- "As for you, because of the blood of my covenant with you, I will free your prisoners from the waterless pit. Return to your fortress, you prisoners of hope; even now I announce that I will restore twice as much to you." (Zechariah 9:11–12)

We've all heard of double agent spies who play the game of gathering intelligence on two client nations who are adversaries. But this kind of duplicity never works for those who are in covenant with the kingdom of heaven.[1] Nothing is hidden from God's sight.[2] This study makes it clear that split loyalties don't work in God's family. We'll learn that covenantal children are called to return to God's house and come into a stronghold that makes us the best kind of captives. We are prisoners of hope.[3] This is an awesome picture of a redeemed people.

This study opens our eyes to see that people in covenant are still fallible. We're rarely satisfied with God who is all sufficient and we start looking for greener pastures. But we must ask ourselves, "If God is more than enough, why do we want more?"

This lesson leads us to understand how names and covenants are interwoven to serve as fabric that binds us together. Why is our heavenly Father's name such an integral part of this bonded relationship? We'll learn that our covenant comes at a great cost. Our Lord Jesus paid our sin debt in full so that we may be set free from the chains of darkness and live like Paul as a bondservant of Jesus Christ.[4] You'll come to know the freedom we have as we are brought into a covenant that is sealed with a promise. We will no lon-

---

1. Titus 1:16.
2. Hebrews 4:13.
3. Zechariah 9:12.
4. Romans 1:1.

ger serve, torn by duplicity, but as covenant keepers, honoring our Lord and God's holy name.

Let's come together as sons and daughters of the Most High God where our strength is renewed so we may build a house for God's holy name according to plan.

> Study Prayer
>
> *Holy Spirit, teach us your ways so that we may walk according to all truth. Unite our hearts so that we may build this house in the fear of the Lord.*
>
> A prayer inspired by Psalm 86:11

We cannot serve two masters because our God is jealously protective. It's not possible to live in covenant with Christ and also live in agreement with the kingdom of darkness. Attempting to work as a double agent will rip us apart. Saying that we live in the Light of Christ while secretly living in agreement with the kingdom of darkness is to live a lie with a false sense of security.[5] We compromise our faith when we continue to enjoy the pleasures of sin. A double life places us outside of God's protective covering and makes us vulnerable to every deception that's set to entrap us. Wandering in the world's darkness makes us vulnerable to predators. Compromising with the world around us doesn't make the world love us. They are quick to see our duplicity and mock us because they see us wearing our Sunday morning name tags while we go bar hopping.

Our problem with God's covenant is that we get the "I wants" and our heavenly Father is suddenly not enough. It's easy to become like David who became dissatisfied with his wives and stole Bathsheba away from Uriah. Jehovah God had given him the throne of Israel. The Lord established him as a mighty king in an expanding kingdom. He lived in splendor, but all his God-given trappings of success were not enough and he refused to overrule his flesh. He coveted his neighbor's wife. After David's murderous sin, the prophet Nathan spoke God's word to him, saying; "And if all this had been too little, I would have given you even more."[6]

God is all sufficient. He is more than enough. Our Lord God is everything to us, just as His name reveals. But we must find contentment and be satisfied in His abundance and not allow the world's sparkling sequins and flashing neon to drag us into pleasures that destroy us. Our deceit leads us to disaster.[7]

---

5. Isaiah 28:15.
6. 2 Samuel 12:8. ("Even more" did not include his neighbor's wife.)
7. Malachi 2:9.

All who pass by have plundered him; he has become the scorn of his neighbors.
(Psalm 89:41)

The Maker of the ever-expanding universe desires to adopt all who will come as sons and daughters. His desire is to give us His holy name as our own. Our neighbors and coworkers look to see the face of Christ Jesus in us. But what will they see? We are called to advance the honor of our Father's holy name. His honorable name and reputation ought to be the yearning of our heart and be reflected in the light of our faces, because He is our Father.

Isaiah, the prophet, made this truth clear when he wrote; "Your name and renown are the desire of our hearts."[8] God's name and His word are exalted above all things.[9] We are called to do our part to exalt His name. In original Hebrew, "name" (שֵׁם shêm) also means reputation, fame, and glory. But even when we fail to glorify God's name, He is faithful to fulfill all His covenant promises. In the forgiveness and mercy shown to us, His holy name is glorified. Our friends and colleagues see God's abundant grace at work as He forgives and cleanses us for the sake of His name. It's good to admit to our friends and family our need of Christ because of our weaknesses and offenses. When we give witness to the Father's forgiveness, grace, and mercies, we present the true face of our Savior.

*For the sake of his great name the L*ORD *will not reject his people, because the* L*ORD* *was pleased to make you his own.*
(1 Samuel 12:22)

When you sign all the paperwork and offer your endorsed down payment check, you're in covenant with the bank. When the bank official also signs the contract and puts the bank's seal on it, you know you can move into your new house. This mortgage is a covenant that binds you to the bank until every penny plus interest is paid in full. Years later, when you finally receive a clear title in the mail, you can celebrate by burning the mortgage and by hanging a plaque with the family name on the front porch as a sign of full ownership.

Your Lord Jesus paid your sin debt in full. And then He gives you His name as your own and you are bound to Him as family. This household bond is infallible and trustworthy. It's a bond of love that will last for eternity. Even through your failings, when your feet slip from His pathway, His love continues to surround you to bring you back home. Through sickness, turmoil, and troubles that surround you, His love for you is unfailing. His name is securely inscribed on your heart's door.

---

8. Isaiah 26:8.
9. Psalm 138:2.

I will maintain my love to him forever, and my covenant with him will never fail. (Psalm 89:28)

The blessing of a newborn child who becomes part of a family is incredibly awesome. Mom and Dad carefully complete the hospital's form, filling in the child's name, printing every letter perfectly. "William" is his first name, after his beloved great grandfather. They write down "Oscar" as his second name in honor of maternal granddad. Then mom poises her pen over the blank for his last name. She smiles and says it out loud as she inscribes the name given to her in their marriage covenant: "Wilcox." Then the doctor reads the name, William Oscar Wilcox, and exclaims, "Wow." He congratulates the family. He puts a pen to the paper, and signs to certify a live birth. Now this new family is bound together in covenant and sealed with daddy's name.

We serve a God of covenants. He made covenants with Adam and Eve in the garden. God made a covenant with Noah, giving him rainbows in the sky to seal His promise. Our heavenly Father made covenants with Abraham, Isaac, and Jacob who are the patriarchs of our faith. He cut a covenant with Moses who delivered Israel from bondage in Egypt. The Almighty brought the nation of Israel into a covenantal agreement before they entered the Promised Land.[10] And finally, this holy nation, the Church, is brought into the bond of a New Covenant. Every one of God's covenants has been broken by unfaithful people, but the Almighty will never fail to keep every word He has spoken, and every promise He has made because His covenant is established upon a tested stone, a precious cornerstone, and a sure foundation.[11]

I will not violate my covenant or alter what my lips have uttered. (Psalm 89:34)

When you open your car's gas cap to fill the tank, there is a clear warning: "Unleaded Fuel Only." You can't put diesel fuel in the tank instead, thinking that it contains more energy and it's more efficient. If you fill the tank with jet fuel because you want to beat your rival, drag racing your classic Chevy Malibu SS muscle car against his Plymouth GTX, your car will stall out and you'll damage your engine.

When those who minister before Christ, our High Priest, stray from ministering in spirit and according to truth, the Lord patiently warns them. Teachers and pastors who speak only to please their audience get stern warnings from the Word and the Holy Spirit to get them back on track. The job of ministry in every position of service is covenantal work, and we must keep true to our calling in Jesus Christ. Spiritual houses are not built by means of

---

10. Deuteronomy 11.
11. Isaiah 28:16.

human reasoning, mortal strength, or the skill of a craftsman. Indeed, unless God builds the house—unless the house is built by the power of the Holy Spirit—what we build is not according to plan and will crumble into ruin. The builder who tries to build a spiritual house from his own blueprint ultimately falls into disrepute and his name will be remembered for the mess he created. Instead, we must build an eternal house, stone upon precious stone, in reverence and awe of His holy name.

> *And you will know that I have sent you this warning so that my covenant with Levi may continue," says the* Lord *Almighty. "My covenant was with him, a covenant of life and peace, and I gave them to him; this called for reverence and he revered me and stood in awe of my name."*
> (Malachi 2:4–5)

Baking your daughter's birthday cake from scratch requires a recipe and all the necessary ingredients. You can't say, "I don't like baking powder, so I'll just leave it out." Throwing out the wheat flour and using cornmeal instead doesn't make a great cake. Tossing out the egg whites and using okra mucilage in its place isn't a good plan. The best way to make a cake worth celebrating is to follow the recipe.

When we believe in Jesus' name we are encompassed in Christ, who is head of the Church. We are joined together with all who are called by His name. It's a family thing. We can't honestly say we believe in God the Father if we reject His Son. Rejecting the Holy Spirit and His good gifts is to reject the Father and the Son. We can't say, "I love Jesus," and snub His family—the Church. It's impossible to be joined with Christ and not accept, love, and serve all those who are called by His holy name. A house is not built with one stone, but with many precious stones together, and it's important to follow the plan.

> *Yet to all who did receive him, to those who believed in his name, he gave the right to become children of God.*
> (John 1:12)

We are not a product of our own making. We've all heard of self-made men, but it's a myth—there is no such thing. Indeed, the mother who rocks her newborn child has in her arms the means to rock the world. Our heavenly Father beautifully and perfectly molds our personalities, shapes our lives, and sets our feet on a path that leads us into useful service in His kingdom. All family members who came before us have contributed to our strengths, or passed on weaknesses we must overcome in Christ. In Him, both our strengths and weaknesses, by the grace of God, are used for good. In our weakness He receives all the glory.

Consider David, the shepherd boy who killed Goliath with his slingshot, became a fugitive who hid out in the wilderness, and then God raised him up as Israel's king. What are the genetic roots of this great king of Israel? Rahab the prostitute is part of his lineage. His great-great grandmother, Ruth, came from Moab, a reviled descendant of Lot.[12] Does this sound like a lineage of the righteous? No, it's a lineage of the redeemed whose righteousness is of God. This is typical of all God's family who are brought into a covenantal name that makes them flourish, bear good fruit, and then send out roots deep into the springs of the Living Water.

Those who came before us and brought us to the throne of grace suffered so much for the cross of Jesus Christ. Now, through the fires of affliction, we become precious stones, building the house for His holy name according to plan.

> *Remember Jesus Christ, raised from the dead, descended from David. This is my gospel, for which I am suffering even to the point of being chained like a criminal. But God's word is not chained. Therefore I endure everything for the sake of the elect, that they too may obtain the salvation that is in Christ Jesus, with eternal glory.*
> (2 Timothy 2:8–10)

A spiritual house is strong when it's built according to covenant. This ruling directive provides a clear plan that inspires our work. Living in agreement with our heavenly Father is like holding a treasured diamond in our hands that reflects and refracts many facets of light. The light of Christ is more than we could ever have asked for or imagined possible. Every aspect of our lives, our family, and neighbors are affected by this spectacle of light. At the center of this light is the King of our lives—Father God, the Maker of all the heavens and earth.

Abraham is the father of our faith and the life he lived still teaches us today. He displayed a beautiful facet of God's refracted light when he returned from rescuing Lot, his family, and his neighbors from plundering kings who captured them. Abraham's victorious war camp overflowed with the spoils from the battle—gold, silver, jewelry, household goods, and other precious possessions. But Abraham didn't see these spoils of war as his own because he served under the rule of God his King. To honor his covenant with God, Abraham gave a tenth of his plunder to Melchizedek, the priestly king of Salem,[13] and the rest he returned as gifts to its rightful owners.

Melchizedek served as priest of the Most High God and came out to bless Abraham after his great victory. His name means "king of righteousness." He

---

12. Deuteronomy 23:3.
13. Salem is another name for Jerusalem.

served as king of Salem, which means "king of peace."[14] He had no earthly mother, father, or any earthly ancestors. He was like the Son of God—a priest forever. In keeping with the honor of his new covenantal name, Abraham paid Melchizedek a king's tithe—a tenth of all the plunder.

> *This Melchizedek was king of Salem and priest of God Most High. He met Abraham returning from the defeat of the kings and blessed him, and Abraham gave him a tenth of everything.*
> (Hebrews 7:1–2)

When we run a marathon there comes a point when every bit of strength is gone. Our aches, pain, and weariness bring us to the point of collapse. But when we turn the corner the finish line comes into view. We can see the prize. Then with a rush of adrenaline we run on to break the tape at the finish line where we will celebrate our victory.

The reality of Christian life is that we don't have enough strength of our own to endure the trials and persecutions to the end of our days. But we have a great hope who is Christ, and He is strength in us. When we become weary enough to give up, He is strength in us. When we're about to stumble and fall down exhausted, He powerfully indwells us. He renews us in His strength. His Holy Spirit is like the wind that lifts the eagles to soar on the heights. In Him we have strength to press on to the goal. In His strength we can carry on and we will not grow weary or faint.[15] This great vitality is ours because our Lord and Savior lifts us up by His name—a covenantal name that binds us together in His strength so that we may continue in the work He has called us to accomplish.

> *I know your deeds. See, I have placed before you an open door that no one can shut. I know that you have little strength, yet you have kept my word and have not denied my name.*
> (Revelation 3:8)

We must give up our double agent status and dedicate our lives to serve only in the kingdom of heaven. We can't divide our loyalties or have one foot in the kingdom of heaven and the other in the kingdom of darkness. We must turn away from the glittering distractions the world offers and walk true to our covenant. We have to quit making up our own designs and plans and build in keeping with our Father's covenant.

But we've all failed in our duties as keeper. We need to stop our work for a moment and let the Master Builder's rod measure the work we've accomplished. When it doesn't measure up, we need to repent and get back on track with the terms of our covenant with the Father, Son, and Holy Spirit.

---

14. Isaiah 9:6.
15. Isaiah 40:29–31.

In repentance and rest is your salvation, in quietness and trust is your strength. (Isaiah 30:15)

We get a great boost to our faith when we witness manifestations of faith lived out in everyday life. Covenants with God's people made past generations come to life with living names—real people who put their hands to the work of building God's kingdom. Consider Jonadab, son of Recab. This family made a covenantal vow before the Great I AM and every generation after remained true to the family covenant. God's promise to this family is awesome to consider. Those who bore their family name would never fail to have a man who served before God.[16] Indeed, even today we might expect to bump into ancestors of the Recabite family who are still faithful in serving the Lord God Almighty.

Children that your family brings into the world give you great joy. The child's first cry is a welcomed song of praise to their Creator. Your joy is even greater when you lead them to Christ who makes them into precious building stones of the kingdom. Your Savior's shed blood binds you in a covenant that affects everything around you, and makes you a sower of good seed; broadcasting it wherever you go. This blood covenant makes you the face of Christ to the world. Through you they know His name and renown. The life you live establishes what your friends, neighbors, and coworkers know about the name you serve. Our Redeemer doesn't appear in person on a public stage to broadcast powerful speeches that inspire us to action. No! He spoke through the Holy Scriptures and anoints, gifts, and empowers His followers to be His voice in today's world. Jesus won't come to us as a man to proclaim the Good News. No! The Spirit of Christ empowers Christians to be His hand extended to offer forgiveness, mercy, and His healing touch. This is our covenantal work—because of His name.

Think of it in this light: The name Churchill brings up images of resoluteness, resilient leadership, and great oratory that inspired a nation in time of war. Consider the name of Corrie ten Boom. Her name is synonymous with self-sacrifice, forgiveness, and for providing safe hiding places during the threats of war.

Now consider what the Lord's name means to your next-door neighbors. Building a covenantal house for God's holy name means that those who are in covenant with our heavenly Father speak, act, and do what brings honor and glory to God's name. Saying Yahweh's name according to historical accuracy is not the point here. Speaking Yehovah's name in correct Paleo Hebrew does not serve a purpose as you build this house. The way you serve, minister to

---

16. Jeremiah 35:19.

your neighbor, and gather to worship in spirit and truth is the way to bring honor and renown to the Great I AM's holy name so you may build a house according to His beautiful covenantal name.

Chapter 11
A Covenantal Name
Q & A

1. Why is it important to follow the Bible's recipe?

___

2. How does a covenant strengthen a spiritual house?

___

3. Why are divided loyalties so harmful to those who build the house for our Father's name?

___

4. What do the Rechabites teach us about the significance of covenantal names?

___

My Journal Notes:

Part 4:
A Beautiful House

All the flocks of Kedar shall be gathered to you; the rams of Nebaioth shall minister to you; they shall come up with acceptance on my altar, and I will beautify my beautiful house.

(Isaiah 60:7 ESV)

A Name that Reveals

Key Scriptures:

- "I will give you hidden treasures, riches stored in secret places, so that you may know that I am the Lord, the God of Israel, who summons you by name." (Isaiah 45:3)

- "Now this is eternal life: that they know you, the only true God, and Jesus[1] Christ, whom you have sent." (John 17:3)

Without revelation, the people perish.[2] Our heavenly Father reveals Himself to show us the hidden treasures in His holy and awesome name. This study leads us, Scripture by Scripture, so we may come to know the awe-inspiring beauty and glory of our Father's majestic name. Every Scripture opens our understanding to see the powerful family connection we have because of the new family name we bear. Verse by verse we are lifted up like the feet of a deer climbing to the heights of Mount Zion.[3] Our eyes will open to see God's creation revealing the wonders and glory of our Father's holy name. We'll look upon His Son in His awesome holiness as a conquering, victorious King who will put all things under His feet.[4] The name of the Father, Son, and Holy Spirit reveals to us the perfect plan for this house we are called to build for His holy name.

> Study Prayer
>
> *Lord Jesus, our Savior, make us to serve in the light of Christ and reflect your glorious light so that those in need of a Redeemer will see Christ in us and glorify our Father in heaven.*
>
> A prayer according to Matthew 5:16

Christians are given a name that is boastworthy.[5] Our God is Creator of all the vast heavens and He alone established the foundations of the earth. Our Savior's name is above all other names. At the sound of His name every

---

1. Jesus' Greek name, Ἰησοῦς, *iēsous*, originates from Hebrew, יְהוֹשׁוּעַ Yᵉhôwshûwaʻ, meaning "Yehovah is Salvation."
2. Proverbs 29:18.
3. Psalm 18:33, Hebrews 12:22.
4. 1 Corinthians 15:25.
5. 2 Corinthians 10:17.

knee bends low and heads bow down. The proclamation of His name compels voices in every language to acknowledge that our Redeemer lives, and Jesus Christ is Lord, to the glory of our heavenly Father.[6] His name is exalted and His splendor is manifested above all heaven and earth.[7]

As Jesus pressed on, working His way toward Jerusalem where He would be crucified, He proclaimed: "Father, glorify your name!"[8] Indeed, the Father's name is glorified in His Son who was obedient to the cross. Then, His is glorified again and again in all His adopted sons and daughters who are brought into Christ, His suffering, death, burial, and resurrection. It's an awesome truth that this highly exalted name is conferred upon us as our own—a family name that reveals our family characteristics of kindness, justice, righteousness, and love.

> *"Let the one who boasts boast about this: that they have the understanding to know me, that I am the LORD, who exercises kindness, justice and righteousness on earth, for in these I delight," declares the LORD.*
> (Jeremiah 9:24)

Jesus' name is Immanuel, that is, God with us. This awesome name reveals the nature of our Savior, who gave up the glory of heavenly places to be born of the flesh and then placed in a crude cow's trough in a stable. He didn't come as a king riding on a war horse. He gained the victory as a servant who gave His body to be broken and His blood shed on a cruel Roman cross, to pay the debt of our sin.[9] Through His vicarious sacrifice He won a great victory over sin, Satan, and death for the glory of His name. Now we are captives in His train to whom He sends His Holy Spirit to give us good gifts for the good of the Church and the blessings of eternal life in Christ Jesus our Lord.[10]

> *The Word became flesh and made his dwelling among us. We have seen his glory, the glory of the one and only Son, who came from the Father, full of grace and truth.*
> (John 1:14)

The Creator's awesome name is painted in brilliant colors on the horizon of every sunrise and sunset. The bright morning star rises above the skyline to greet the new day as a faithful witness. The shining light of the sun, moon, and stars brighten the night skies and give witness to the Almighty's majesty.

---

6. Philippians 2:9–11.
7. Psalm 148:13.
8. John 12:28.
9. Romans 6:23. Also see chapter 25 in author's book *The Greatest Love*. This chapter provides a detailed Scriptural guide to God's saving grace through Jesus Christ.
10. Psalm 68:18, Ephesians 4:8. These verses reflect Abraham's victory when he recaptured Lot, his family, and neighbors and then brought them back as "captives" and gave them good gifts from the spoils.

We are surrounded by the glory of God's creation and we cannot deny the faithful witness they offer of an awesome Creator. Everything He established in the beginning continues on because of His faithfulness. His created wonders speak in universal expressions, like sign language everyone understands. The hearts of those who see and hear this witness turn to seek God. He gathers them in His loving arms, adopts them as His sons and daughters, and gives them His name as their own.

> *The heavens declare the glory of God; the skies proclaim the work of his hands. Day after day they pour forth speech; night after night they reveal knowledge. They have no speech, they use no words; no sound is heard from them. Yet their voice goes out into all the earth, their words to the ends of the world. In the heavens God has pitched a tent for the sun. It is like a bridegroom coming out of his chamber, like a champion rejoicing to run his course. It rises at one end of the heavens and makes its circuit to the other; nothing is deprived of its warmth.*
> (Psalm 19:1–6)

It's amazing how hard some people work to deny Christ Jesus. Some progressive Bible scholars don't believe He was anything more than an ancient prophet and teacher. But the reality of Christ as "God with us" is undeniable. Matthew, Mark, and John are three first-hand eyewitnesses to the Gospel's truth. Luke researched and wrote a verifiable historic record as a witness. But hardened hearts will not hear that Jesus is Immanuel, God with us. He fed five thousand men and their families, walked on the water, cast out demons, raised the dead, healed the sick, taught truth and righteousness—all this as a witness that He came as Messiah, the only Son of God. But the religious leaders of the day denied all this irrefutable evidence and demanded a clear statement, saying, "If you are the Messiah, tell us plainly."[11] When Jesus spoke clearly and said, "I and the Father are one,"[12] they picked up stones to kill Him.

Our Savior came in the flesh to walk among us. He spoke only what He heard the Father speaking. He reached out to touch all those whom the Father desired to touch. He came among us in the Father's name to reveal to us the heart and nature of Creator God. Jesus' name reveals to us who He is and His eternal plan and purpose. His name means "God is Salvation."

> *Jesus answered, "I did tell you, but you do not believe. The works I do in my Father's name testify about me."*
> (John 10:25)

---

11. John 10:24.
12. John 10:30.

Our victorious Redeemer is seated on a white horse and totally prepared for battle. First, He came in peace, riding on a donkey's colt, but now He will come as a conquering king over all the earth. He will secure the crowns of every nation as His own. Our Savior's eyes blaze with the fire of piercing insight; nothing in the heavens or earth can be hidden from Him. On Him is written an awesome and holy name that no mortal can fully perceive but only Himself. He wears a robe washed in blood. Out of His mouth comes a double-edged sword that is called faithful and true. He raises up a battle standard, and He is mighty in battle. He is victorious over the nations, and rules over rebellious leaders with an iron scepter.

Can any mortal mind perceive the wonders of the name that is given without merit to all sons and daughters of the Most High God? And yet, this mighty name reveals the power, love, joy, strength, and all of Jesus' mighty attributes with which He indwells us in keeping with His name.

His eyes are like blazing fire, and on his head are many crowns. He has a name written on him that no one knows but he himself. He is dressed in a robe dipped in blood, and his name is the Word of God.
(Revelation 19:12–13)

Jesus' awesome name is above every name. There is no other name under heaven by which we can be saved from the dungeons of darkness and the chains of our sin. Our victorious Messiah wears a sash, like a breastplate, over His robe inscribed with all who are in His name as a declaration of His victory over all the tyrants who oppressed the nations. He is, indeed, our victorious King who is above all kings and Lord over all lords. In His final victory we will stand with the twenty-four elders who cast their crowns before Him, saying, "You are worthy, our Lord and God, to receive glory and honor and power."[13]

His name reveals that His judgments are just and righteous. By His name we know He has overcome on our behalf so He may usher us into His eternal kingdom of light where we will rest in Him forever in peace, comfort, and joyful worship. His holy name assures His promise. There will be no cause for tears, no source of sorrow.[14] All who are called by His name will bask in the Light of Christ forever and ever. Amen!

On his robe and on his thigh he has this name written: KING OF KINGS AND LORD OF LORDS.
(Revelation 19:16)

---

13. Revelation 4:10-11.
14. Revelation 21:4.

The sound of the Almighty's name comes like peals of thunder. At the sound of His voice every knee bends low and every head bows down. The Father, Son, and Holy Spirit's name and titles reveal His kind, just, righteousness, and loving nature. It reveals heaven's light that breaks through the world's darkness.

Every particle and element of creation illumines His holy name. The sun, moon, and stars are His faithful witnesses, declaring the might and power of His holy name. God sent His only Son as the Light of the World. He came with many signs and wonders; miracles to reveal Himself as Immanuel, who is God with us. But Jesus threatened the status quo of the entrenched religious elite of His day. The teachers of the Law hardened their hearts, stopped up their ears, and refused to believe in their promised Messiah.

This same Jesus comes to us today with the same Gospel message preached through his followers. Through His servants He speaks forgiveness and healing, revealing His loving nature and His saving grace. But what will we do with the revelation of Jesus Christ we are given? There is no other name under heaven by which we might be saved.[15]

When those who are called by the name of the Father, Son, and Holy Spirit meditate on the name, His attributes and titles, the revelation of His name opens our eyes to see the plan of the house we are called to build for His holy name.

---

15. Acts 4:12.

Chapter 12

A Name that Reveals

Q & A

1. In your own words describe the awesome beauty and glory of your Father's name.

   _____

   _____

   _____

2. What is the connection we enjoy because of our new family name?

   _____

   _____

   _____

3. Jesus' name is awesome above every name. Why did He come riding into Jerusalem on a donkey instead of a war horse?

   _____

   _____

   _____

4. Why is it necessary for us to be separated to Christ as we do the good work of building a house for the Father's holy name?

   _____

   _____

   _____

5. What will you do with the revelation you are given?

   _____

   _____

   _____

My Journal Notes:

A House for Gathering

Key Scriptures:

- "Save us, Lord our God, and gather us from the nations, that we may give thanks to your holy name and glory in your praise." (Psalm 106:47)

- "There is more than enough room in my Father's home. If this were not so, would I have told you that I am going to prepare a place for you?" (John 14:2 NLT)

This study leads us to a bountiful kingdom where the doors are thrown open to all who will come. We are blessed to see God's realm expand to make room for those who answer the call to come to the great wedding banquet. The invitations are sent out and the tables prepared with a bountiful feast. Those who received the first invitations tossed them in the trash. The second invited guests were too busy and refused the invitations. Finally, messengers went out to invite the down and out, the good and the bad, the vagrants and wanderers who agreed to come. They were ushered into the Father's garden of delights forgiven and cleansed; dressed and made ready. They came with joy and entered through a beautiful gate emblazoned with His banner of love. But when a wedding crasher tried to sneak in without proper wedding attire provided by the Father, he was thrown out.[1]

> *So the servants went out into the streets and gathered all the people they could find, the bad as well as the good, and the wedding hall was filled with guests.* (Matthew 22:10)

As we pass through the door that opens God's kingdom to us we'll learn that the house we build is a family dwelling with a very large table where we gather together in Jesus' name. At this table, those who the world considers the least among us are welcomed and given places of honor. The following Scriptures teach us that the house we build for His holy name is a place of favor where the family of God gathers as His Church—a blessed household. We are given the job of building even though we are weak and unable, but then as we separate ourselves from all the distractions of the world, we are strengthened in the Spirit of Christ to accomplish this good work.

---

[1]. Isaiah 61:10, Matthew 22:1–14.

> Study Prayer
>
> *Our Father, fill us with expectation as we look forward to the city with sure foundations whose architect and builder is God. Keep our eyes looking forward to the new heaven and earth where you dwell in righteousness.*
>
> A prayer according to Hebrews 11:10 and 2 Peter 3:13

Why do we build a house for God's name instead of simply saying it is a place where our Lord and God dwells with us? The answer is a beautiful and simple truth. We build a house that is true to plan where Father, Son, and Holy Spirit may come and dwell with all who bear His name. In this dwelling His awesome name embraces and encompasses every gathered and redeemed soul. All adopted sons and daughters of the Most High God are embodied in this house our God inhabits. We build a family dwelling where every member of the family is called by His name. This is a place where all who are in Christ are gathered to be joined as one with the Lord Almighty.

Come, let us dwell together under His banner of love and the covering of His name. We are like many rooms joined together in the Father's house as a household with an awesome family name engraved on the doorpost.[2]

> *Bring my sons from afar and my daughters from the ends of the earth–everyone who is called by my name, whom I created for my glory, whom I formed and made.* (Isaiah 43:6–7)

You're sitting in the dregs of the mess you've made for yourself and you feel barely alive. Dirt and rubble tangle around your feet. Your eyes look up and you see dark clouds ready to drop icy rain on your back. You have nothing to show for all your years of hard labor. Your eyes burn, your stomach growls, your throat is parched, and the shivering cold penetrates to your bones.

Then, in your abject condition, you hear a kind and gentle voice. He hands you an invitation with your name written on the envelope. You're invited to a wedding banquet. "Huh?" you ask. "Why would anyone invite an old bum like me to a wedding feast? My clothes stink. I can't sing. I can't dance. I have no gift to bring." But then you open the envelope and decide to give it a shot.

Your soggy socks and worn-out shoes slog along to take you to the garden party. You see a narrow gateway with a banner emblazoned over it and a sense of being loved floods over you. You're welcomed at the gate and shown the way to prepare yourself for the great banquet. There's a cleansing bath that washes away your filth. As you are raised up from the cleansing flow you feel like a brand-new person with all the past burdens lifted from your shoulders.

---

2. John 14:2.

You're given bracelets for your arms, new sandals for your feet, a white wedding robe to wear, a crown of beauty for your head,[3] and beautiful jewels to adorn your neck.

Then you hear the sweetest words ever spoken. With outstretched hands He says, "Come unto me."[4]

> *Let him lead me to the banquet hall, and let his banner over me be love.*
> (Song of Songs 2:4)

The family of God, the Church, is the blessed household where the Father dwells. This home has deep roots in an Abraham kind of faith. Consider what he did as evidence of his great faith. In obedience to God's call he separated himself from the land where his forefathers had put down their roots. Abram told Sarah, "Pack up, we're moving on."

When Sarah asked, "Where are we going?" he may have replied, "I don't know. God told me we'll see it when we get there."

Then he set out with all that they had, and brought his father and his nephew Lot with him. With every step he took on this long journey his eyes searched the horizon, looking forward to a city with foundations whose builder and Maker is God Almighty.[5] Abraham blazed a trail of faith for all who would look forward to a new heaven and new earth—a home of righteousness.[6]

Abram held onto God's promise of a son, and finally when he was almost a hundred years old the Lord came to him to strengthen and encourage him to continue walking in the way of truth and righteousness.

> *When Abram was ninety-nine years old, the LORD appeared to him and said, "I am God Almighty;[7] walk before me faithfully and be blameless.*
> (Genesis 17:1)

All of Jesus' followers could benefit from the experience of working as a shepherd. A herder learns that goats and sheep don't do well in the same flock. Goats are head-strong, stubborn, and can be mean. They look for opportunities to escape and lead other animals astray. Some goats are quite clever and try to blend in with the sheep and put on a sheepish act. But they end up leading some of the sheep away from the fold.

When these "goats" come to help us build a house for the name of the Father, Son, and Holy Spirit, they stand back and tell you what you're doing wrong. They're not leaders except to lead you astray. They disrupt the work

---

3. Isaiah 61:3.
4. Matthew 11:28.
5. Hebrews 11:10.
6. 2 Peter 3:13.
7. אֵל שַׁדַּי, 'êl Shaddai

with their misleading advice. Those smelly goats try to convince you that they are well-meaning, but their purpose is to discourage you.

You need to be kept safe from the goats so that you can be faithful and continue the good work of building a gathering house for the name above all names.

> *In the name of the Lord Jesus Christ, we command you, brothers and sisters, to keep away from every believer who is idle and disruptive and does not live according to the teaching you received from us.*
> (2 Thessalonians 3:6)

The work of building is not an easy task. In fact, it's quite impossible for mortal beings. We must not allow those who come with seemingly good intentions to "assist" us in the work. Their purpose is to get an "in" with us so they can work from within to discourage us and bring the good work to a halt. They're thieves and robbers who steal away our strength and zeal. They are Sanballats who mock, ridicule, and accuse us.[8] They scoff at the work we've accomplished, calling it weak and inadequate.[9] Their intention is to divide us.

But we are protected and shielded with God's armor. We take the offensive with the sword of the Spirit. We are safeguarded with a shield of faith. A helmet of salvation protects our mind and thoughts. We march out strong wearing Gospel shoes to compel us forward. Our hearts are protected with a breastplate of righteousness. Our strength is in the Lord and we cannot give up the work. We are made willing and ready for the work and for battle.

> *So we rebuilt the wall till all of it reached half its height, for the people worked with all their heart.*
> (Nehemiah 4:6)

In any battle, those who defend home and family are the fiercest warriors. They fight vigorously to defend their children and their homestead. The warriors strengthen themselves with visions of home, wife, and family as they charge to the front line of battle. They fight with all their strength to overthrow the invading destroyers who intend to plunder them.

Soldiers of the cross are warriors who fight to defend and advance the kingdom of heaven—our homeland. We don't settle for crumbled bulwarks, half-built walls, or the ruin of God's house. Instead, we press on to "take hold of that for which Christ Jesus took hold of" on our behalf.[10] The enemy roars like a lion. He rages out with fearsome threats. He exploits our weaknesses and tempts us to give in and give up gathering together. But our enemy is only a paper tiger.

---

8. Nehemiah 2:19.
9. Nehemiah 4:3.
10. Philippians 3:12.

We stand strong in God's mighty fortress. We are covered in the shadow of our Savior's wings. The Lord our God is mighty in battle and we stand at His side, fully protected in His armor. We know the enemy will not prevail against those who gather in this house we build. We have nothing to fear.[11]

> *Don't be afraid of them. Remember the Lord, who is great and awesome, and fight for your families, your sons and your daughters, your wives and your homes.* (Nehemiah 4:14)

In the kingdom of heaven's right-side-up economy the least of us are made the greatest. The person who sits at the foot of the table is honored to be seated at the head of the table. This is the plan for the house Jesus prepares with many rooms where we are joined together as one. This is the blueprint for building a family household for a name that is above all names. His name is written on the hearts and foreheads of all who are gathered in His name. Our Father's name is engraved on the doorpost of this holy dwelling place.

In the dregs of our own mess and in our darkest hour a bright and beautiful light comes into our lives in the form of an invitation to a wedding banquet. Why would anyone want a bedraggled nobody to come to a wedding? We have nothing to offer. But the words on the invitation tug at our hearts and we step out and go. Our hearts leap with anticipation and our eyes fill with tears as we come to a narrow gate emblazoned with a banner called love. Then we hear the most precious words ever spoken: "Come unto me and I will give you rest."[12]

Jesus' extended hand leads us through this gateway. We're forgiven. We get cleaned up. We're given fresh clean clothes to wear. Then we are blessed to be prepared for a job that's been waiting for us. We are set free to run on a narrow path. But there are hazards along the way. There are many who would disguise themselves in sheep's clothing and stand to our side to deceive and distract us from the work of the kingdom. But, in Christ, we are made strong. We are prepared for the day of battle by our Lord who is mighty in battle. Our hands are strengthened so we may serve our risen Savior and build a house where God's people may gather in the name of the Father, Son, and Holy Spirit.

---

11. Matthew 16:18.
12. Matthew 11:28.

Chapter 13

A House for Gathering

Q & A

1. Which is better, to sit at the foot of the table or the head?

2. What will you do with your wedding invitation? How are you prepared for the banquet?

3. Why are Sanballats not welcomed to help us build the house for our Father's holy name?

4. Why are builders also called to serve as soldiers?

My Journal Notes:

Authority to Build

Key Scriptures:

- "While he was teaching, the chief priests and the elders of the people came to him. 'By what authority are you doing these things?' they asked. 'And who gave you this authority?'" (Matthew 21:23)
- "Who has gone up to heaven and come down? Whose hands have gathered up the wind? Who has wrapped up the waters in a cloak? Who has established all the ends of the earth? What is his name, and what is the name of his son? Surely you know!" (Proverbs 30:4)

Anyone who has ever designed and built a house for their family ends up with built-in mistakes. When we finally move in, we find things that should have been done differently. We could eliminate a lot of errors if we could watch someone else build a house like ours and learn from their mistakes. This topic on authority helps us look to the generations who have built before us to learn from their weaknesses and failings. After observing them, we'll realize that we have to unlearn bad habits and relearn a lot of skills necessary for building a house for God's holy name.

This lesson helps us see the errors and consequences of builders who grumble. We'll learn that it doesn't work for a construction worker to look back and criticize the jobs done before him. But a worker who builds according to plan and in keeping with the covenant builds a house that is strong as a fortress. The house he builds will withstand every storm and tempest that comes against it.

The teaching here helps us to see that we are commanded to build, and by this command we have authority to build. By this charge we are strengthened and empowered in the Spirit. The whole crew prayerfully and confidently puts their hands to the work and we press on to build this house in accord with Jesus' holy name. We'll learn why it's important for each builder to follow the plan and work within the parameters of the authority given to them so they can construct a house that stands for eternity.

> ### Study Prayer
>
> *Father in heaven, may your name be exalted in all the earth.*
>
> *Strengthen our weak hands and steady our knees for the work of building this great house.*
>
> *Drive all fear from our hearts to make us bold and strong. Give us confidence to work under Christ's command and authority. Cover us in the safety of your wings.*
>
> A prayer according to Isaiah 35:3–4

The Bible offers us a history of our faith to help us learn from others' mistakes. Their failures teach us not to fall into the same traps. But it's human nature to forget our history and repeat the very grave errors inherent in all humankind. It's easy to just live in the moment and focus on ourselves, thinking, "What has God done for *me* lately?"

We must learn lessons from the past generations of our faith. The people of Israel were first hand witnesses as the Great I AM delivered them from servitude in Egypt. He unleashed His wrath against Pharaoh and the land that enslaved His people. They watched as the plagues devastated the land of their suffering. They walked through the parted waters of the Red Sea and then witnessed Egypt's army get crushed under the waters that swept over them. As a free people they sang and danced together to celebrate the Almighty's awesome victory.

Then their hearts turned to grumbling in their tents: "What is this stuff we have to pick up off the ground to eat every day? It all tastes the same—so boring." They blamed Moses because they missed the fresh fish they used to catch in the Nile. They growled at Moses, "And those fresh cucumbers we grew tasted so good." Their taste buds yearned for the melons, fine onions, leeks, and garlic they had enjoyed as part of their Egyptian cuisine.[1]

They tested Yehovah God with their constant complaining. But God is faithful, even when we are not. For the sake of His name, by which His people became known, and for the honor of His name He continued to save them. Because of this, the nations around the tribes of Israel trembled at the sound of His name. He made His might and power well known and He would not let His name be disgraced. The Great I AM raised up Moses to speak and act by the authority of His holy name and to intercede for the people.

> *When our ancestors were in Egypt, they gave no thought to your miracles; they did not remember your many kindnesses, and they rebelled by the sea, the Red Sea. Yet he saved them for his name's sake, to make his mighty power known.* (Psalm 106:7-8)

---

1. Numbers 11:4–6.

The Creator of all the heavens and earth stirs up mighty, thundering waves in the great seas around the world, and He is able to calm the waves to a whisper.[2] Every act of His mighty arm and the wind of the Spirit serves His purpose and fulfills His plans. Even as mighty ships laden with cargo pass through the seas, their crews rarely consider all the good things God has created. Their ocean-going vessels leave a wake in their paths through the sea that quickly fades away. From the deck of a grand ship it's easy to forget the Creator who lifts up the waves with a mighty voice. When the wind-driven waves come with a crash, sailors are quick to remember and acknowledge their creator. They cry out to God Almighty when the pounding waves lift up their voices.[3]

Life's storms pummel us in every season. Because of these tempests, the house we build must have its foundation firmly set upon the Rock who is Christ Jesus, and upon His Apostles and Prophets. The Master Builder watches over us to strengthen us as we build this house. It's like a lighthouse with its foundations set in the bedrock of the jetty. What we build for His name serves as a mighty fortress against the pounding waves of the sea, and brings glory and honor to His name; the Almighty One.[4] By His command and sealed with His name, we have the strength and authority to build this house that will withstand the pounding waves of all life's storms.[5]

For I am the LORD your God, who stirs up the sea so that its waves roar–the LORD Almighty is his name.
(Isaiah 51:15)

What kind of house will you build and how will you build it? What kind of foundation will you build it on? What will this house be known for? Those who are called by His holy name build upon the Rock who is Christ Jesus. Stone upon precious stone this house is built within the spacious boundaries of the kingdom of light. What we build under authority is strong enough to withstand every assault. Surrounding this home is a garden of delight, a peaceful and restful place that abounds with fruitfulness in every season. This is all made possible by the power and authority of the Father's holy name.

Those who build their house on the sands of time in the kingdom of darkness suffer a much different destiny. Their gardens are overwhelmed with parched desert sands. The storms of life pummel their house until they crumble into ruin. There is no peace, no rest for their souls because they reject the name of God their Creator and His Son who came to save us. They build by means of their own strength, for their own name, and by their own authority.

---

2. Psalm 107:29.
3. Psalm 93:3-4.
4. Yehovah, צָבָא tsâbâ'.
5. Zechariah 8:9, 13.

> *Yet their Redeemer is strong; the* Lord *Almighty is his name. He will vigorously defend their cause so that he may bring rest to their land, but unrest to those who live in Babylon.*
> (Jeremiah 50:34)

Answer the call and come to the mountain of the Lord! Hear the word of the Lord that beckons you to bow your knees in the presence of the Lord Almighty. Listen to the yearning that is planted in your heart and call out His mighty name to come save you from the chains of your sin and the prison of your depravity. Confess your sin, failings, and weaknesses before God who can save you, and He will come to meet with you. He is faithful and just. He forgives you all—yes, ALL your sins. And it gets even better, because He cleanses you of all your past sins and from every stain that remained. By the blood of Lamb of God you are washed cleaner and whiter than fresh fallen snow.[6]

The greatest miracle of all miracles is a redeemed soul. This is only possible by the power of the name of our Lord and God. He searches for every lost and wandering lamb and then rescues you from the clutches of sin, anoints you with healing oil, holds you close to His heart, and brings you into His house with great celebration—all by the power of His name, the authority of His name, and for the sake of His holy name.

> *And everyone who calls on the name of the* Lord *will be saved; for on Mount Zion and in Jerusalem there will be deliverance, as the* Lord *has said, even among the survivors whom the* Lord *calls.*
> (Joel 2:32)

When you start a new construction project in most jurisdictions, a building permit is required. The document from county building and zoning gives you or your contractor the authorization to start building your home. Before you start you have to put a post in the ground with a tube for the plans and permit. Then the work can begin in earnest.

After seventy years of exile there came a time for God's chosen people to go home and rebuild the temple in Jerusalem. But the plans required God's command and the king's stamp of authority.[7] The prophet Zechariah records that by God's authority Joshua was anointed as high priest and king to lead the people in righteousness and to govern over them with justice. He wore two crowns, one of gold and one of silver. These two laurels gave him authority to build the temple for worship and govern the nation. His crowns offered living proof of the promise of Messiah who would come as High Priest and King to build His Church. The Prophet Zechariah wrote to foretell the

---
6. Psalm 51:7, John 1:29.
7. Nehemiah 2:4-5.

victory of Christ. It's as if this prophet stood in the ruins of Jerusalem and looked forward through the centuries to see the anointed One who would come to serve as High Priest and King and to rule over His people with righteousness and justice as the foundation of His throne.[8] Our Savior came with the authority of the Root of Jesse to redeem His people who are called to serve as the precious building stones of His kingdom.[9]

> *Tell him this is what the LORD Almighty says: "Here is the man whose name is the Branch, and he will branch out from his place and build the temple of the LORD."*
> (Zechariah 6:12)

All those who are "in Christ" have the authority and strength to overcome any threat that might harm those who are called by His name. This authority is ours by means of God's command through the Word. Our strength comes by the anointing oil of the Spirit of Christ. Victory is ours by the power of our Savior's holy name.

We have authority by His command, but never by our own initiative. Every act and deed is accomplished in Jesus' name and under the authority of His holy name. We can't stick our bare foot in a rattlesnake den just because we're a Christian. We'll get a lot of snake bites, for sure. But by the command of the Word and the anointing of the Spirit of Christ we have the authority and strength to trample under our feet everything that comes against us as we do the work of rebuilding the Church stone upon stone.

> *I have given you authority to trample on snakes and scorpions and to overcome all the power of the enemy; nothing will harm you.*
> (Luke 10:19)

In the following verse Jesus' promise of "whatever" removes a lot of barriers. When He says "anything," we are ushered into an infinite realm. The essence of what Jesus taught is that through the power of prayer and intercession He opens the kingdom of heaven and all its vast treasures to us. This is a "no limits" kind of promise to all who abide in His holy name and ask according to what is in His name.

We've all heard the Christian cliché, "Be careful what you ask for, you might get it." There is Biblical precedent for that statement. The tribes of Israel grumbled and complained until God sent them meat. But then His anger rose up against them and their dinner got stuck in their throats.[10] Why didn't they just ask instead of muttering in their mush?

---

8. Psalm 89:14.
9. Isaiah 11:10, 1 Peter 2:5.
10. Psalm 78:30–31.

How do we know what to ask for? To answer this question, we need to focus in for a closer perspective. Jesus spoke clearly when He said, "anything in my name." What He means is that boundary lines of what we ask for are established within the kingdom of God. When we pray, "Your kingdom come," this establishes our requests within heaven's infinite borderlines.

Now we can see why it's important to intimately know Jesus, our Savior's name, and everything that is in His name. In His name there is forgiveness and healing. Now we know to pray for our sick family, friends, and neighbors. In His holy name there is righteousness and justice. This encourages us to pray for our friend who is wrongfully accused. Because His name is Provider we can confidently ask for the new work shoes we need. Indeed, we could fill a whole book with His titles and holy names that reveal Him in all His glory. By means of His authority, we set our prayers and petitions before Him. We pray in agreement with His holy name knowing it will be given to us. This written guarantee gives us the confidence we need to press on and pray on as we build a house for His holy name.

> *And I will do whatever you ask in my name, so that the Father may be glorified in the Son. You may ask me for anything in my name, and I will do it.*
> (John 14:13-14)

When Jesus prayed His High Priest's prayer, did the Father hear and answer? Beyond any doubt everything Jesus asked for will be done on our behalf. He prayed in perfect harmony with every element of the kingdom of heaven. We have great confidence knowing that we are still safeguarded by the wings of His prayer.[11] We are covered by the power of our Savior's holy name. By His name we are held safe in His mighty fortress. His name covers us in the shadow of His wings. In His name we are led beside still waters to refresh us. Our souls are restored when we hear His name. We abide safely in the house built for His name. By His name we are assured that if we wander away, He will bring us back home in His loving arms. He will never leave us nor forsake us.[12] The beauty and majesty of His name compels us to build this glorious house.

> *While I was with them, I protected them and kept them safe by that name you gave me. None has been lost except the one doomed to destruction so that Scripture would be fulfilled.*
> (John 17:12)

---

11. An in-depth teaching on the "wings" of Jesus' High Priest's prayer can be found in the author's book, *The Greatest Love*, Chapter 11.
12. Deuteronomy 31:6.

As the early Church came into being, the religious establishment feared the power in Jesus' name. They became upset that the Apostles healed a crippled man while proclaiming faith in the name of Christ Jesus and the power of His resurrection. Men who ruled in the Sanhedrin were alarmed when they heard Jesus' name and had the disciples arrested and locked in jail until the whole ruling body could meet the following morning.

Then, with all their eyes glaring daggers at Peter and John, Israel's high priest and the religious elite demanded to know the name that gave them the power and authority to heal the lame man. Speaking by the Holy Spirit, the disciples boldly proclaimed the name of Jesus Christ of Nazareth. They were witnesses of the Cornerstone whom the religious rulers had interrogated, spurned, and crucified.

We need to be reminded that the power of The Name has not diminished in the last two thousand years. There is still power and authority in the name of Jesus, who continues to serve as High Priest of the Church. Even today, especially today, in this chaotic, creeping darkness that engulfs all the nations, we remain a holy people, a royal priesthood, who must, by faith, stand up and speak out with the authority of His name. By faith in the name, we reach out our hands to touch all those whom our Lord and God is touching. In His name we are His hand extended to a world steeped in darkness and bound by the chains of sin. In His name we heal wounded souls and bring them to the throne of grace where they are made into precious, eternal building stones for this house.

> *They had Peter and John brought before them and began to question them: "By what power or what name did you do this?" Then Peter, filled with the Holy Spirit, said to them: "Rulers and elders of the people! If we are being called to account today for an act of kindness shown to a man who was lame and are being asked how he was healed, then know this, you and all the people of Israel: It is by the name of Jesus Christ of Nazareth, whom you crucified but whom God raised from the dead, that this man stands before you healed".*
> (Acts 4:7–10)

When you get promoted to project manager, you get a new job description that outlines the parameters for the job. The priorities spelled out on this company document give you authority to hire qualified people, train workers, maintain staff levels, and, when necessary, dismiss those who cannot or will not perform their jobs. By means of an authorized signature on this work profile you have the authority to hand out daily job assignments. As long as you work within the established boundaries, and under this authority, you'll find success and get the job done. With this example in mind, we can begin to understand the greater workings of the superior authority of the name of Christ Jesus our resurrected Savior.

We are a people endued with the authority of a resurrected Christ. We minister, serve, and worship by means of resurrection power. By means of Christ's resurrection we live victorious in the eighth day of creation. The words we speak have an eternal impact on people's lives because the resurrected Christ ascended to the Father and sent His Holy Spirit to indwell, gift, and empower His Church. By this same power Christ Jesus is raised up over all rulers, strongholds, and every other name.[13] He has given us His name and by the authority of His name we step out with boldness. By His name all things in heaven and earth are to be placed under His feet and therefore, under our feet.[14] In Christ we are promoted to a position of authority, and we serve within the realm of His holy name to build a house for the honor and glory of His name.

> *That power is the same as the mighty strength he exerted when he raised Christ from the dead and seated him at his right hand in the heavenly realms, far above all rule and authority, power and dominion, and every name that is invoked, not only in the present age but also in the one to come. And God placed all things under his feet and appointed him to be head over everything for the church, which is his body, the fullness of him who fills everything in every way.*
> (Ephesians 1:19–23)

People who get their education from the College of Hard Knocks are the most resilient workers in the kingdom of heaven. Those who learn from others' mistakes are the smartest laborers in the harvest field. Tried, tested, and wise builders are the least likely to get dragged down by grumblers. Astute workers separate themselves from complainers in the work crew, because they want to get the job done. Never give up if you're working with a crew of whiners and grouches because God is faithful, even when His people are not.

Jesus came and ministered among the people, teaching with authority from above. He came from the Branch of Jesse to sit on David's eternal throne and He is given all authority. The Master Builder's command is our signet of authority that gives us the power to build this house for the name of Father, Son, and Holy Spirit.[15] Christ Jesus, who was raised from the dead, is seated at the right hand of the Father in heavenly places. He is far above every name in this age and in the age to come. All things are placed under His feet and He is head of the Church, which is His body. We are the fullness

---

13. δύναμις dýnamis.
14. Romans 16:20.
15. Haggai 2:23.

of Christ,[16] and by His command we have the authority to build this house for the name of our Lord and God.

By our Savior's authority and under His authority, we have strength to overcome every obstacle. By the power and authority of Jesus' holy name we are made victorious workers in God's kingdom. When Jesus says we can ask for; "whatever" and "anything" that is in His name, this opens to us a kingdom with vast, uncountable treasures. We simply need to know what to ask for within the boundaries of the kingdom and grasp hold of the authority of Jesus' holy name.

Chapter 14

Authority to Build

Q & A

1. What is the source of our authority to build a house for God's holy name?

_____
_____
_____

2. How can we build a house that will stand as a mighty fortress forever?

_____
_____
_____

3. How do we overcome every mountain sized obstacle that stands in the way to keep us from the work of building?

_____
_____
_____

4. How do we come to know what is within the boundaries of the kingdom and serve under the authority of Jesus' name?

_____
_____
_____

---

16. Ephesians 1:20–23.

My Journal Notes:

A Cup of Cold Water

Key Scriptures:

- "And if anyone gives even a cup of cold water to one of these little ones who is my disciple, truly I tell you, that person will certainly not lose their reward." (Matthew 10:42)

- "For I was hungry and you gave me something to eat, I was thirsty and you gave me something to drink, I was a stranger and you invited me in, I needed clothes and you clothed me, I was sick and you looked after me, I was in prison and you came to visit me." (Matthew 25:35–36)

This topic helps us avoid the infamous "bait and switch" games. They're as old as Earth itself, but people still fall for them. Adam and Eve teach us by their mistake; getting duped by a misleading promise. Fruit from the tree looked so good, but it was bitter to the core. We must beware because people haven't changed much since the beginning of time.

In some Christian circles today we find it easier and more self-satisfying to offer water from our own wells, rather than water from the Spring of Living water. Well, why not? Our own product may fit better with our interpretation of the Good News Gospel. But we only fool ourselves. In this study we'll learn the dangers of working from our own resources, offering water from the well we dug for ourselves and with our own label.

Abraham's servant teaches us a valuable life lesson when he asks Rebekah for a drink of water. We'll learn how her response reveals the very core of what makes her tick as a person. The servant needed to know if she qualified as a builder for the house of Abraham and his question teaches us a valuable life lesson.

> Study Prayer
>
> *O Lord of our salvation, make us thirst for the water our Lord Jesus offers us so that we will never thirst again. Lead us to drink from the spring of water that wells up to eternal life.*
>
> A Prayer according to John 4:14

Remember the time you bit into a doughnut with your taste buds expecting mmm-good apple fritter flavors? Instead of sweet apple filling you got a taste of something else; an unsweetened healthy zucchini fritter. Your taste in doughnuts does not like to be fooled. What if you were bone dry thirsty and someone offered you what you thought was a bottle of fresh cold spring water, but the first sip assaulted your senses with lukewarm quinine water? The jolt would be revolting; not at all refreshing.

This bait and switch game has been played since the snake in the garden told Eve: "Eat it and your eyes will be opened.[1] Just take one bite and you'll see." Sham revelations became common among ancient Israel's false prophets. It still happens in today's churches more often than we can imagine. The prophet Jeremiah described this deceit as abandoning the Spring of Living Water and digging our own water wells in its place. It's like offering a bottle of water with our private label on it, claiming that it will fully satisfy. We offer this instead of offering Christ the Living Water. But fake living water only fools the senses and doesn't quench our thirst even for a moment.

Too often, a church calls out to lost and wandering sheep, saying, "Come drink our fresh, cool water, and be satisfied." But what is offered is only a poor substitute for truth and righteousness. We call a wandering soul to join us in worship that is not spiritual and real. Instead, we worship according to made up rules, traditions, and the preferences of the congregation.[2] We say all the right things in our gatherings. Our songs have words right out of the Bible. But our songs of praise are inspired by our personal desires, customs, and preferences. We worship for what we get out of it. The prophet Zechariah's words echo in our churches today to warn us that we worship for yourselves.[3] Our songs are not stirred up by the Spirit of Christ, nor does our praise flow out from our spirit. We proclaim a savior that is custom made in our own likeness, rather than leading a lost soul into the fullness of Christ.

> *My people have committed two sins: They have forsaken me, the spring of living water, and have dug their own cisterns, broken cisterns that cannot hold water.* (Jeremiah 2:13)

How is it possible to know the real deal, a true offer? Can you discern others' attitudes and personal traits, even before spending time in friendly conversation? Is it possible to make wise choices about who to befriend before you get too entangled in a relationship? It's possible to do this by just listening with unbiased ears for clues to the attitudes of their heart. Don't listen to the flattery they lavish on you; instead listen carefully to what they say about

---
1. Genesis 3:5.
2. Isaiah 29:13.
3. Zechariah 7:6

other people.[4] Words that come out of their mouth reveal their heart. You can observe their actions with impartial eyes to see what makes them tick. But watch out, because if you have deceived yourself with a lie, or if you are living a lie, your prejudices and partiality will draw you into a deceiver's web.

One great chapter in the Bible records the story of Abraham's servant who was sent to find a bride for Isaac. The story continues as the servant arrives in His master's old homeland and then prays to the God of Abraham. "Before he finished praying, Rebekah showed up with her jar on her shoulder." With great wisdom the servant worked out a beautifully simple test to help him find the right bride for Isaac. He would ask for a drink of water and see how she responded. Rebekah responded beautifully. Not only did she offer him a drink of water from her jar, she also watered his thirsty camels until they were satisfied—and thirsty camels drink a lot of water.[5] She had a good heart—the heart of a servant—and she proved it by her acts of kindness. Her heart and soul became evident with a simple request for one cup of cool water. The servant's wisdom kept him from being deceived. The girl's response proved she would be a strong builder in the house of Abraham.

> *The servant hurried to meet her and said, "Please give me a little water from your jar."*
> (Genesis 24:17)

Young men and girls who look forward to getting married need to know what they're getting into. They'll have children together that they'll have to live with for the rest of their lives. The kids need two godly parents who will teach, nurture, and admonish them in the Lord. A momentary attraction that makes the heart flutter rarely lasts for fifty years. It's a good idea to test a person's character before getting involved with them. To do this you need intellectual honesty and an upright life to help you avoid being deceived. Good and wise questions pave the way to solid and lasting relationships. The answers to your honest and intelligent inquiries open a person's soul to you.

When Jesus traveled through Samaria on His way to Jerusalem, he stopped where an ostracized woman came out to get water from the community well. He asked her the same question that Abraham's servant asked Rebekah, and with this question He knew her heart. She argued with Jesus, but her words revealed a sure sign of brokenness. It isn't recorded that Jesus ever got his cup of water from the well, but she did become a witness of Christ Jesus who gave her Living Water. She became a living, redeemed jewel, a precious stone in the house we build for His holy name.

---

4. Psalm 41:6.
5. A camel can drink up to 200 liters, or 53 gallons of water in about three minutes.

A well-stated question can lead to well-placed building stones for a great house.

When a Samaritan woman came to draw water, Jesus said to her, "Will you give me a drink?"
(John 4:7)

If you eat salty potato chips, you're going to get thirsty. After you munch on salted nuts you know you're going to need a glass of water to satisfy your thirst. The words of the Bible have an even greater effect on your soul and spirit. When you hear the truths of the Gospel right out of the Scriptures, they make you thirsty for springs of Living Water. The bride of Christ (that's all of God's sons and daughters) proclaims the word by means of the Spirit's power. We call out to those who are caught in darkness, "Come to the Waters of Life." The Holy Spirit works through the Scriptures and Christians that speak out to make people thirsty. In fact, they get so thirsty that they call out in desperation; "What shall we do?"[6] That is the moment you've been waiting for. Hold a cup of refreshing water—the Water of Life—out to them. It will turn into a mighty river.

The Spirit and the bride say, "Come!" And let the one who hears say, "Come!" Let the one who is thirsty come; and let the one who wishes take the free gift of the water of life.
(Revelation 22:17)

The bait and switch game has been going on since the beginning and it still works to deceive people today. Don't fall for it! In the spiritual realm it's a game that has serious eternal consequences. These plots attempt to change a person's eternal destiny. What happens when a church puts their own label on their own water and then offers it as the real thing? The end result is devastated lives. Those who drink it always get thirsty for more—they're never fully satisfied.

We play into this bait and switch game when we welcome people to worship in a way that is not spiritual and real. Too often, we invite our friends to come praise the Lord with us, but our worship gathering only satisfies ourselves, and only for a moment.

How do we know what is real and what is not? Is it possible to discern what is true and right? It's impossible for us, but totally possible in the Spirit. We pray for godly discernment and then ask questions guided by the Holy Spirit. In the spirit we can test the waters. Abraham's servant and Jesus both used a request for water to test and discern a person's heart. They asked for a drink of water and then waited to hear and see the person's heart and soul.

---

6. Acts 2:37.

Rebekah revealed her servant's heart. The woman at the well revealed her thirst for Christ.

When a friend who is thirsty comes to you asking for Living Water, give them Christ our Savior. He offers them water to eternally satisfy their thirst. He holds out a cup of water that begins with a sip and then floods a person's soul with an ever-expanding river that gets deeper and wider until it washes completely through them. The Holy Spirit moves upon these waters to pour out spiritual gifts on His sons and daughters to anoint, gift, and empower Jesus' servants to flood the Earth with the Water of Life.

A fountain will flow out of the Lord's house.
(Joel 3:18)

Chapter 15
A Cup of Cold Water
Q & A

1. What is the best way to avoid getting trapped by bait and switch games?

___

2. What is the significance of a church that abandons the Spring of Living Water and digs its own well?

___

3. How is it possible to discern what is real and true and what is a lie?

___

4. What does Abraham's servant teach us about how to know a person's heart?

___

My Journal Notes:

16

Praise and Glorify

Key Scriptures:

- "As they make music they will sing, 'All my fountains are in you.'" (Psalm 87:7)

- "Sing to God, sing in praise of his name, extol him who rides on the clouds; rejoice before him—his name is the LORD."[1] (Psalm 68:4)

- "Let them praise his name with dancing and make music to him with timbrel and harp." (Psalm 149:3)

Word upon word, verse after verse, this study leads us to see the victory that is ours by means of that cruel Roman cross prepared for our Savior. Jesus knew what lay ahead, but trekked along the dusty roads on His ascent to Jerusalem. He pressed on, knowing that an illegal trial, mockery, hateful accusations, a cat-of-nine-tails, a crown of thorns, nails for His hands and feet, a crude wooden cross, and certain death all awaited Him. With his heart so troubled Jesus asked, "What shall I say?" Without hesitation he resolved, "Father, glorify your name!"[2]

In this lesson we'll come to see ourselves as builders who also serve as soldiers of the cross who press on to fulfill our high calling in Christ Jesus for the honor and glory of our Redeemer's holy name. The truths of God's word will cause our hearts to overflow with grateful praise. In triumph, we'll write our Deliverer's name on our hands. By faith we know that our names are written on the palm of our Father's hand. This joyful knowledge permeates our being and inspires us to lift up holy hands in the assembly to sing His praises. We know that we once wandered, but now we are found. The carpenter from Nazareth came among us as Immanuel to bring us home to dwell in His house of prayer, praise, and worship. Come, join with this mighty army to prepare ourselves, singing praises so we may build a house for the glory of our Father's holy name.

---

1. יָהּ Yâhh.
2. John 12:28.

> **Study Prayer**
>
> *O Lord, let our light shine before others, that they may see our good deeds and glorify our Father in heaven.*
>
> A prayer according to Matthew 5:16

As Jesus approached Jerusalem, He warned the disciples of the suffering and death He must face. He pressed on, knowing the agony that lay ahead, but He was determined to fulfill His purpose. He prayed openly in their presence: "Now my soul is troubled, and what shall I say? Father, save me from this hour? No, it was for this very reason I came to this hour."[3]

The child was laid in a manger. The Magi presented a toddler with gifts. A young boy deliberated with the scribes in Jerusalem's temple courts. He learned the carpenter trade from Joseph. When He was raised up from the waters of baptism, God spoke, saying, "This is my Son, whom I love; with him I am well pleased."[4] At every moment of Jesus' life, suffering loomed on the horizon. With every word of forgiveness He spoke and with every healing touch He worked His way toward Jerusalem where He would offer Himself as the Lamb of God—the Paschal Lamb. Casting out demons and walking on the waters of Galilee served as steps toward His final victory over sin, Satan, and death. Every step Jesus took on Israel's dusty roads led up to the sacred city. Each stride kept Him painfully aware of what was in store for Him. He knew they would arrest, accuse, and mock Him. He was agonizingly mindful of the crown of thorns they would press on His head, the cat-of-nine-tails prepared to thrash His back, and the nails ready to drive through His hands and feet. As the city came into view, He wept.[5] He wept over their ruin even though He knew the agony that would grip Him when the Father turned away from His only Son as He took upon Himself the sins of the world.[6]

With each stride up the dusty road toward the gates of the city where so many prophets had died, Jesus set His face like flint to fulfill the very reason He came; all for the glory of the Father's holy name. He did all this for us to prepare the way for us to carry our cross and follow in His footsteps as builders of the kingdom of heaven.

"Father, glorify your name!"
Then a voice came from heaven, "I have glorified it, and will glorify it again."
(John 12:28)

---

3. John 12:27.
4. Matthew 3:17.
5. Luke 19:41.
6. Psalm 22:1, 1 Peter 2:24.

The thunderous footsteps of a mighty army echo on the hillsides as the soldiers march forward. The troops step out in unison, united under Christ's banner. Their strength is in the Almighty, and their hearts are set on pilgrimage.[7] They are armored with God's armor, led forward into battle with shouts of joy and songs of victory.[8] They sing out with a new refrain; the song of our triumphant Redeemer. Their voices resonate with salvation's songs.[9]

This troop marches in agreement with their mighty purpose—to spread the Good News of the Gospel; the Gospel of peace.[10] Step by step the soldiers press on toward the prize of their high calling in Christ Jesus.[11] They're strong, tested, refined, and proven living stones for building a mighty fortress. With shouts of praise to strengthen them, they build a strong house for the glory of The Name that is above all names.

May the God who gives endurance and encouragement give you the same attitude of mind toward each other that Christ Jesus had, so that with one mind and one voice you may glorify the God and Father of our Lord Jesus Christ.
(Romans 15:5–6)

The Name of our Lord and Master is written on our hands.[12] His glorious name is written on our heart's door. The name of God, Creator of all the heavens and earth, is written on our foreheads.[13] The new name given to us in Christ is inscribed on the palm of our heavenly Father.[14] By the power and authority of our Savior we press on to build this house of worship.

Because of His name, our hearts are inspired to gather together and sing out the praises of our Master Builder, Jesus Christ. The heavens shout out with rejoicing because our names are written down in glory, and we are a people who bear the Almighty's name. The earth bursts out with song as the dew of righteousness descends to refresh our gardens.

I will declare your name to my brothers and sisters; in the assembly I will sing your praises.
(Hebrews 2:12)

We offer a joyful sacrifice, opening our mouths to shout out with praise. Our hands reach out with exaltation while our mouths are filled with thanksgiving. What is the inspiration for our praise? Consider that we were once orphaned, banished and rejected, lonely and forgotten; but now we are adopted

---
7. Psalm 84:5.
8. Psalm 118:15.
9. Psalm 40:3, 98:1.
10. Ephesians 6:15.
11. Philippians 3:14.
12. Isaiah 44:5.
13. Revelation 22:4.
14. Isaiah 42:16.

as sons and daughters and made part of the family of God. We are established in a land with pleasant boundaries and we have a bountiful heritage.[15]

We once wandered around in darkness but now we have been led into His glorious light. The light of Christ burns bright within us and compels us to shout out with glory and honor. We overflow with worship for the Father, Son, and Holy Spirit in all His majesty because we bear His name. The walls of the house we build with living stones constantly echoes with the resounding praise of God's victorious people.

Through Jesus, therefore, let us continually offer to God a sacrifice of praise–the fruit of lips that openly profess his name.
(Hebrews 13:15)

With our eyes fixed on the goal, put one step in front of the other and march forward. Agony racks our bodies. Our hearts are troubled. Our soul is in turmoil, but we keep our eyes on the goal to win the prize, the crown of victory. In our own strength, weariness takes over our body and we fall down. Our own eyes grow weak and the goal becomes a hazy prospect that lies beyond our reach. But we have a great hope. The Holy Spirit lifts us up to triumph over every weakness and obstacle that stands in our way.

Jesus pressed on to fulfill His eternal purpose. The destruction of sin, Satan, and death rested in His hands. He was determined to die in our place, for our sins, and the sins of the world. His heart was troubled and His soul in turmoil, and yet He called out to His heavenly Father for His name to be glorified. Jesus won a mighty victory on the cross. Because of this we can now march out as a mighty army of kingdom builders under Christ's banner to advance the Gospel of Peace.

We have every reason to praise and glorify our Father, Son, and Holy Spirit. We were once lost like sheep that wandered from the fold. We got ourselves tangled up in the world's thorny traps. But the Good Shepherd came searching for us. He found us and brought us home carrying us close to His heart. Then He called for the angels in heaven to celebrate with Him. We were once lost, but now we are found. He raises us up as builders of a house of worship. We put our hands to do the work, strengthened with praise and glory sung out to our Father who is in heaven.

---

15. Psalm 16:6.

Chapter 16

Praise and Glorify

Q & A

1. Describe how every moment of Jesus' life led Him forward to fulfill His purpose.

2. What is the remedy when our soul is in turmoil and our heart deeply troubled?

3. How does worship serve to advance the building of this house of prayer and praise?

4. What inspires you to praise and glorify your father in heaven?

My Journal Notes:

17

Make Way for His Exalted Name

Key Scripture:

- "Let them praise the name of the LORD, for his name alone is exalted; his splendor is above the earth and the heavens. And he has raised up for his people a horn,[1] the praise of all his faithful servants, of Israel, the people close to his heart." (Psalm 148:13–14)

This study helps us tackle some of life's hard choices. We'll learn that at every intersection of life we must choose between one way that is decorated with sequins, glitter, and glamor; or another way that is a narrow, hard, and rocky pathway. This teaching helps us to see that the end of each pathway isn't obvious at first. The signpost that points to the left is so appealing to our senses, and the marker pointing to the right doesn't appeal to our human desires.

The choices we make aren't always big, clear-cut decisions. Instead, they're like nibbling on finger food before dinner is served. We'll learn that life decisions come in small morsels that we grab on the go. This collection of Scriptures leads us to choose between the world's flashing neon lights and heaven's narrow path.

We'll discover that it's humbling to take a path that requires constant prayer to keep our feet from slipping. We like to be in control of every aspect of our destiny and in command of every step we take as we seek fame and fortune.

Mary, the mother of Jesus, teaches us the way of humility. She chose an obedient path, fully aware that an unwed mother could be stoned to death. Her humble submission instructs us with godly wisdom so we may choose what is right and good even as we face impending dangers. Looking back on Mary's life shows us how her humility and submission to God's call is a great benefit to all Christians today. Mary's humble spirit inspires us to choose a path that leads us to gather in joyful assembly where we join our voices to exalt God's holy name in the house we are building for His holy name.

---

1. "Horn" Hebrew קֶרֶן qeren, in this verse means a mighty, powerful leader.

> ### Study Prayer
>
> *Teach me your way, L*ORD*, that I may rely on your faithfulness;*
> *give me an undivided heart, that I may fear your name.*
>
> A prayer according to Psalm 86:11

Many times through the seasons of life you'll come to an intersection and have to decide which way to turn. If you grew up on a farm you learned about making choices by watching the animals you care for. When a playful young heifer sees a barn door left open, she has to choose: Will she run free or go out to graze on lush green pastures in the safety of the herd? Will she choose new adventures with unknown dangers or safe and familiar meadows?

When you come to a crossroads in your life it's good to ask yourself: "What road will I take? The choices you make can be life changing. You have to stop and ask yourself, what gate will you enter through? What house will you dwell in? Where will you take up residence? There are clear and simple sign posts at intersections pointing different ways. But in real life, the choices you make are not always as easy as choosing Homestead Way or Adventure Road. In reality, the big mistakes you make start with bite sized compromises. The world's attractions constantly assault you. You are confronted with two pathways, two different gates, two distinct doorways. Will you choose contempt or reverence, the burning heat of the sun or its healing rays, scarcity or abundance, the kingdom of darkness or the kingdom of light?

The long and dusty trail you've been slogging on finally comes to a crossroads with one pointer showing the way to a land of promise, and another directing you to a desert wasteland. But the signs don't make it easy to decide. The placard with an arrow toward the desert is well lit with bright, flashing neon. It's very appealing to the eye and it leads to a well-worn path. The indicator for the land of promise is weather beaten and faded. It's obvious not many people go that way.

You can't see what is at the end of either path. Go left on that wide pathway and there's a promise of glamor and glitter. There's a chance for fun in the shadows, and no one will ever know. The path on the right is saturated with light. It's so well-lit that every bit of dirt in your life is exposed. There's the promise of a better life, but it's a rocky road where you must leave behind the load of personal possessions you prize, but weigh you down. Going that way will test you and make you give up the things you hold so dear. This path requires that you stop and let Jesus unload your life's burdens so you can take in hand the tools of a builder.

You strain your eyes to see what each path leads to, but you can barely see the promise each way offers. Which direction will you choose? What name will you exalt? Will you answer the call to follow the path where you will build your house on the Rock or go left to build on shifting sand?

> *"Surely the day is coming; it will burn like a furnace. All the arrogant and every evildoer will be stubble, and the day that is coming will set them on fire," says the LORD Almighty. "Not a root or a branch will be left to them. But for you who revere my name, the sun of righteousness will rise with healing in its rays. And you will go out and frolic like well-fed calves."*
> (Malachi 4:1–2)

Jesus taught us to begin our prayers with an exaltation of the Father's holy name. We prayerfully enter the kingdom's gates with thanksgiving and into this house of prayer with praise on our lips. We exalt the name of the Great I AM and in Christ all His sons and daughters are lifted up with Him.

The way of light and liberty is a challenging path.[2] Along this narrow way there are hazards and distractions. Attractive detours try to lead us astray. There are deceptions to trip us up on each side of the road. It's not as if we made a choice to follow this narrow road and it's all smooth cruising. We're constantly tempted to go back to the ways of glitter and glamor. Our every step must be surrounded with prayer to keep us on the path. The way of the kingdom of light is an impossible way that is cleared for us by Jesus' High Priest's prayer and our continual prayers in agreement. We exalt the Father who is more than able to make the way straight ahead of us. We're a small remnant on a path less trod and the enemy's front lines of battle press in from both sides. We are builders who remain strong, singing as we do kingdom work, exalting the Father's glorious name. Jesus intercedes for us to make the way straight so we may build as victorious pilgrims.[3]

> *This, then, is how you should pray: "Our Father in heaven, hallowed be your name."*
> (Matthew 6:9)

Mary, mother of Jesus, chose to humble herself and walk in the way of humility and submission before God Almighty. She walked on this pathway, singing out with a prophetic song to exalt the holy name of the Almighty One. Her heart overflowed with joy, knowing that Isaiah's prophecy of a virgin birth was conceived in her, and she exalted the name of the Lord.[4] She traveled to visit her cousin Elizabeth. When her cousin heard the sound of Mary's voice, her own child leaped for joy in her womb.

---
2. John 16:33.
3. Isaiah 11:16.
4. Isaiah 7:14.

Mary gracefully submitted to God's call when the angel Gabriel came to her with a message. Then, at the moment of greeting, both Mary and Elizabeth overflowed with joyful song by the inspiration of the Spirit. They sang out with prophetic verse proclaiming what God had done. Mary knew the child she bore would come as Savior, and she sang out, "My soul glorifies the Lord and my spirit rejoices in God my Savior."[5]

Now, every generation celebrates Mary's blessings in every season of the year. We delight to retell the glorious story of Immanuel, born of the virgin Mary. We rejoice to know He came humbly as a newborn child to be our Redeemer, Deliverer, and Savior who would die in our place and for our sins, and pay the full penalty for our sins.

Indeed, the Almighty One has done great things for us and we too exalt His name that is above all names.

From now on all generations will call me blessed, for the Mighty One has done great things for me–holy is his name.
(Luke 1:48–49)

Sunday is a good day for new beginnings. We begin our week by gathering together to worship, minister, and serve as a community of faith. It's good to start our week receiving forgiveness and taking a refreshing dip in the Spring of Living water. In our house of prayer we celebrate the Gospel message and proclaim this Good News with spiritual songs and hymns. We listen and learn so we can know our heavenly Father and live in harmony with Him. Surrounded with friends, family, and welcomed guests we serve each other; prayerfully ministering according to the Spirit's gifts and strength. In the light of the Word and the power of the Spirit we lift up those who are suffering and weak. We pray for our nation and leaders so we may live in peace.[6] Farmers are covered as we pray for our daily bread. We intercede for our soldiers who serve to protect our nation. Our prayers provide a covering for first responders who serve to protect us.

All God's bountiful blessings are poured out upon us in our worship gatherings and then flow out with us as we go to our homes and workplaces. It's as if we come into our house of worship with a cup ready to receive and depart with an enlarged and overflowing cup of blessings and thanksgiving. Then, on Monday morning we pick up our brimming cup and carry it with us. We don't need to go to the coffee shop to get it refilled because it's already spilling over. This flood affects all those we rub elbows with during the week. When Christ spills out from our cup this provides daily, living proof of the blessings

---
5. Luke 1:46–47.
6. 1 Timothy 2:2.

of our Savior who satisfies all who hunger and thirst.[7] Now, fully satisfied and totally covered, we have the strength we need to build a house for our Father's exalted name.

> *And whatever you do, whether in word or deed, do it all in the name of the Lord Jesus, giving thanks to God the Father through him.*
> (Colossians 3:17)

To exalt God's name also means to uphold our Father's reputation. When our friends, neighbors, and coworkers hear us talk about our Savior, will they scoff because our lives misrepresent His name? Can we speak Jesus' words with one breath, and then use His name as a curse when we hit our thumb with a hammer? People notice our confusion when we try to walk on two diverging pathways.

Please understand, there's no need to come across to our coworkers as perfect images of Jesus. The reality is that we are fallible people who are forgiven and cleaned up. We don't do crazy, stupid stuff just to show how Jesus forgives us.[8] Instead, we do our best to live in agreement with Christ who indwells us, and when we fail, we turn to our Savior with a repentant heart.

When people know we're Christians, they watch us carefully to catch us slipping up so they can say, "Aha!" But when they see our failings, it's our job to tell them how we admit our wrongs and are then forgiven. With this kind of testimony, we exalt the name of Christ and proclaim a genuine Gospel.

> *Therefore God exalted him to the highest place and gave him the name that is above every name, that at the name of Jesus every knee should bow, in heaven and on earth and under the earth.*
> (Philippians 2:9–10)

In gatherings for worship we exalt the Lord with our teaching, preaching, hymns and spiritual songs. We sing out with words of our Redeemer who speaks in the moment to comfort His people. By the authority of The Name we extend our hands to touch those in need with the hand of Christ. Prophetic words are voiced to reveal Christ who is, and was, and is to come.[9] Jesus, our High Priest, ministers to us, coming like a mighty flood to reveal His living and active presence to all who gather in His holy name.

Together, in our worship gatherings, exalting His holy name strengthens our soul and spirit so that we may press on and prevail in every hardship and then march on to victory. As a congregation we are armored up as soldiers of

---

7. Matthew 5:6.
8. Romans 6:1–2.
9. Revelation 1:8. (For a complete teaching on the spiritual gift of prophecy see author's book, *A Jewel of the Kingdom.*)

the cross.[10] In the Presence of Christ our burdens are lifted from our shoulders. Every facet of light revealed in His awesome name lifts us up so that we may "run with perseverance the race marked out for us."[11]

As we glorify His name in our worshipful assemblies, we serve as builders of a great house. We endure together as we are refined and polished to serve as tried and tested stones for building a house worthy of His exalted name.

> *You have persevered and have endured hardships for my name and have not grown weary.*
> (Revelation 2:3)

Green light, yellow light, red light, turn light; why are there so many intersections on the way home? Life constantly confronts us with intersections where we have to stop and ask ourselves: "What road will we take?" We live in a world that constantly assaults us with false goodies if we take that left turn. Life's road signs don't make it easy to decide. Will we answer the call to follow the right path where we will build a house on the Rock, Christ Jesus? Or, will we turn onto the wide thoroughfare that leads us to build our house on shifting sands?

We've chosen to take the narrow path, but temptations pop up on both sides. We're constantly faced with distractions, attractive detours, and the world's glitter and glamor to sidetrack us. To keep on the path we need the Word to light our way, constant prayer to keep us safe, and the Holy Spirit to keep our feet from slipping.

Mary, mother of Jesus, teaches us with a beautiful example of walking humbly before God. She gracefully submitted to God's call to serve, fully aware of the hazards of her day for an unmarried woman who became pregnant. She showed us the way of courage and strength as she exalted the Father's holy name for all He had done for her.

We are called to exalt our Father's name by living our lives in a way that upholds His reputation and the glory of His name. When we walk on two diverging pathways, we bring dishonor to His name. We are called to choose the right way. Tried and tested builders of this house choose to exalt our heavenly Father's holy and awesome name by the work of their hands, no matter how difficult the path.

---

10. Ephesians 6:13.
11. Hebrews 12:1.

Chapter 17

Make Way for an Exalted Name

Q & A

1. Why do the road signs at all of life's intersections make it so hard to decide which way to go?

   _____
   _____
   _____

2. When we walk on Jesus' narrow path, what are the roadside hazards that we need to watch out for?

   _____
   _____
   _____

3. What does Mary, mother of Jesus, teach us about walking before God?

   _____
   _____
   _____

4. How many ways can we exalt God and uphold the great repute of His holy name?

   _____
   _____
   _____

My Journal Notes:

18

Blessings of the Name

Key Scriptures:

- "May the LORD answer you when you are in distress; may the name of the God of Jacob protect you. May he send you help from the sanctuary and grant you support from Zion. May he remember all your sacrifices and accept your burnt offerings. May he give you the desire of your heart and make all your plans succeed. May we shout for joy over your victory and lift up our banners in the name of our God. May the LORD grant all your requests." (Psalm 20:1–5)

- "They feast on the abundance of your house; you give them drink from your river of delights." (Psalm 36:8)

Jimmy trudged up the steps, dragging his muddy boots to his front door. He looked at his reflection in the door glass and smirked at his freckled face. They looked like orange dots on his pale skin. With one tug on his hoodie string he tucked away his mop of carrot red hair. He'd had enough of bullies harassing him about it. He heaved a breath of relief as he reached for the door knob, knowing home was his safe harbor.

Before Mom could greet him, he mumbled, "I wish I wasn't adopted and had blonde hair like you."

Mom responded with a hug. "You're better than adopted. We chose you. And now you're a full-fledged Martin."

Jimmy's troubles melted away as he breathed in the aromas of Mom's lasagna. He looked over their dining room table; all set for dinner. For just a second his thoughts took him to cloud nine where he saw a table set with dishes called Help, Support, Protection, Plenty, Goodness, Mercy, Favor, Success, Victory, and with cups filled with Love.

"Are you okay, Jimmy?" Mom asked, untying his hoodie.

"All of a sudden I'm real hungry," he said with a chuckle.

This study opens our understanding to know the abundant blessings that are ours as we feast on the abundance of our Lord's bountiful table. We are adopted sons and daughters brought into a house that overflows with many good things. We are brought into a house, a home that is a safe harbor where we find forgiveness and healing for our wounded souls.

Every Scripture that follows is part of a Christian's benefit statement, and it's so much better than the one you got when you started your new job. All these good things are yours, and by the conclusion of this study, you'll see that it costs you nothing. You won't have to max out your credit card.

> Study Prayer
>
> *Give us godly wisdom as we build this house, and understanding so it may be established in us. May this house for your name be filled with rare, beautiful, and eternal treasures.*
>
> A pray according to Proverbs 24:3–4

All those who are called by our heavenly Father's holy name are welcomed to dwell with Him in a house that overflows with abundance. A river of delights flows from this house. This is a place of safety, a dwelling where our heart's desire is fulfilled beyond our wildest dreams. In this home we are nurtured so we can grow and flourish. This dwelling offers a great table where we may dine with our Lord and Savior. The rafters of this lodging resonate with continuous laughter, shouts of joy and victory.

In the bountiful gardens of this abode we are nourished. We blossom like a rose bud that opens to the sunlight. In this shelter we can rest and take in the full fragrance and beauty of our Savior's name. In this household we come into the knowledge of His name so we may know the security of His name. In this abode we seek first our Lord and His righteousness, and he brings us into the security of His loving arms.[1]

Those who know your name trust in you, for you, LORD, have never forsaken those who seek you.
(Psalm 9:10)

Before time began the Creator knew your name and wrote it down on heaven's scrolls. He made a way for you to come into His house to dwell with Him in His rest. The Creator did this with the first words spoken to bring order out of earth's chaos. You are one of the many who are called, and among the few who are chosen to abide with Him in a house that overflows with blessings.[2]

The courtyards of this house are like peaceful and bountiful gardens. As you enter you are given new clothes so you can dress with the finest fare

---
1. Isaiah 55:6.
2. Matthew 22:14.

and with precious jewels—gifts from the Bridegroom. The Father's sons and daughters are welcomed to gather in the courtyard of His house. Gentle winds spread the aromas of fig trees, myrrh, aloes, and spices—fragrances for the bride. We browse among the lilies of the garden and then carry this sweet perfume into His temple, shouting out with exaltations of joyful worship.

> *Blessed are those you choose and bring near to live in your courts! We are filled with the good things of your house, of your holy temple.*
> (Psalm 65:4)

The people whom our heavenly Father gathers into the Good Shepherd's fold are an unlikely flock. We come as orphans, widows, and the downtrodden. We're a dubious bunch. We're like David's mighty men who came to him distressed, running from debt, and discontented.[3] Very few of the sheep of God's pasture are wise by the world's standards. Rarely are we of noble birth. It's quite seldom that any of us are counted among the world's power brokers.[4] But we are lifted up from the dregs of our filth, forgiven, washed in the cleansing blood of the Lamb of God. Then He sets our feet upon the Rock, who is Christ Jesus. On this Rock we are made into useful building stones—integral parts of the house we build for His holy name.

When God called us we were loners, mavericks, and malcontents. Some were locked behind prison bars. But we found that His desire for us is to set us free to run on the pathway of His commands.[5] He adopts us as His own and makes us part of His family. Now we have many brothers and sisters in Christ. The abandoned become brides who are prepared and adorned for their Bridegroom. The barren and childless are settled in God's dwelling place as the mother of children.[6] We are abundantly blessed to be brought out of a drought scorched wilderness into God's Garden of delights that surround us in His holy dwelling place. Our hearts are wrenched with grief for those who refuse to answer God's call because their names are written in the dust of the earth.[7]

> *A father to the fatherless, a defender of widows, is God in his holy dwelling. God sets the lonely in families, he leads out the prisoners with singing; but the rebellious live in a sun-scorched land.*
> (Psalm 68:5–6)

The following verse inspires an image of a young girl standing in the open doorway of her father's house, straining her eyes to look down the long road

---

3. 1 Samuel 22:2.
4. 1 Corinthians 1:29.
5. Psalm 119:32.
6. Psalm 113:9.
7. Jeremiah 17:13.

that leads to her family's front gate. She whispers a prayer for her beloved, while her heart races with expectation. She is ready to cry out with a song at the first sight of her betrothed. She's been busy preparing the house with a table that overflows with good things. She steps back into the house to double check and be sure everything is in order when she hears a knock at the door.

"Come in! Please come in," she calls out as she runs to the door. She takes his coat and offers refreshment from his travels on dusty roads. Then they join the family in the fellowship of a bountiful table. The mutuality in this house and its plentiful fare, the laughter, and candor draw their hearts together in a greater bond of love.

Isaiah reveals God's house of prayer as a place where blessings overflow. In this temple we are given a new name that is better than any other family name. This dwelling we are ushered into is a place of true and real worship. This is a place where all that is holy and common are kept separate and in their places. In righteousness we gather on His holy mountain.[8] In the Father's house of prayer the congregation overflows with acceptable offerings given with great joy.[9]

> *Blessed is he who comes in the name of the LORD. From the house of the LORD we bless you.*
> (Psalm 118:26)

Through sleepless dark hours of the night our sorrows tend to grow. Our restless, spinning minds are in a whirl, and our troubles mount up to weigh us down. Finally, with a sigh and a prayer we put our bare feet on the cold floor, hoping for some relief. Our feet shuffle to the window as we utter a prayer with our eyes barely open. When we open the shutters the morning light comes flooding in. The warmth of the sunrise floods over us as a witness for the everlasting light of Christ, and the burden of the night's restless worries lifts from our shoulders.

A reverence for God is to stand in awe and acknowledge the good work He has done among all those who bear His holy name. The Son of righteousness is the Light of the World and His light shines on us to lift life's burdens of our hearts. His light is the light of justice, mercy, lovingkindness, forgiveness, and healing. All these benefits are ours because of the promise of His holy name—the name for whom we build a house.

> *But for you who revere my name, the sun of righteousness will rise with healing in its rays.*
> (Malachi 4:2)

---
8. Hebrews 12:22–24.
9. Isaiah 56:4–8.

Psalm 103 is a Christian's benefit statement, like the one you received when you started your new job. But unlike the benefit pamphlet from the HR department that tells you about your individual 401(k) account, the Psalmist's statement encompasses the community of faith as a whole—all of us together as one.

Isaiah prophesied in agreement with the Psalmist and foretold of our Lord Jesus' wounds, bruising, and scourging that would be inflicted on Him. Isaiah looked forward in time to the Messiah who would suffer in our place and for our sins.[10] The Apostle Peter affirms the truth of these benefits, writing in his epistle: "By His wounds you have been healed."[11] The guarantee of these benefits is written in Jesus' blood that He shed to redeem us from our debt of sin.

Let's dig into this truth with an in-depth perspective. The Psalmist praised the Lord who "heals all your diseases." Isaiah penned inspired words on his scroll: "By His stripes, we are healed." Then Peter upheld this truth when he penned the words: "By His wounds you have been healed." When Isaiah wrote "we" and Peter wrote "you" they included all of us together—we all and you all as one. The truth this teaches us is that Jesus' broken body makes His body, the Church, whole. This means, all of us are made one whole, functioning, and healthy body—the body of Christ. This truth brings all of us together in one house called "Church" made strong and whole without any building stones broken, fractured, or missing. This is the victory of Christ. The Church, the body of Christ, is healed and made whole by His suffering, death, burial, and resurrection.

Join together to answer Jesus' call to enter through the gate into this holy sanctuary. Open your eyes. Open your heart. Open your mind. Now, what do you see as you enter through the gate? You see the glory of His holy presence in His dwelling place. Now that you have found a safe place in His abode, you come into the blessings of forgiveness, healing, and wholeness for you personally. This includes your mortal body. Indeed, every part of Christ's body, every functioning servant in the Church is made whole in this tabernacle built for His holy name. As you come to rest in this house, you find mercy, your health returns, your wounds are healed, and your soul is restored. All to the glory of the Father, the Son, and the Holy Spirit.

In this house we lift up our prayers: "Your kingdom come, your will be done, on earth as it is in heaven."[12]

---

10. Isaiah 53:5.
11. 1 Peter 2:24.
12. Matthew 6:10.

> *Praise the L*ORD*, my soul; all my inmost being, praise his holy name. Praise the L*ORD*, my soul, and forget not all his benefits—who forgives all your sins and heals all your diseases, who redeems your life from the pit and crowns you with love and compassion, who satisfies your desires with good things so that your youth is renewed like the eagle's.*
> (Psalm 103:1–5)

When all the groceries are bagged up and put back in your cart, the cashier holds up the paper tape and says, "That will be three hundred and seventy-five dollars." A few bottles of water, cereal, milk, bread, and a bottle of wine are expensive nowadays. As you push your cart through the parking lot you hear a still, small voice speaking in your heart, compelling you to come and partake of heaven's Spring of Living water, milk and meat of the word, and the Spirit's new wine without cost. Why didn't you hear this voice before you went into the store where you maxed out your credit card?

The Father's blessings cost more than all of earth's wealth. He sent His only Son to die in your place, for your sins, and to pay the price for your freedom. Now, in Christ, all His blessings are free. So, when you are thirsty, come and load up your grocery cart with the abundance of heaven's blessings. They're already paid for.

> *Come, all you who are thirsty, come to the waters; and you who have no money, come, buy and eat! Come, buy wine and milk without money and without cost.*
> (Isaiah 55:1)

Precious gems from every nation on earth are brought together to serve as building stones of a house for the Name who is above all names. The Great I AM sent His messengers to prepare the way before Him. He gathers all those He has stirred up to seek Him. The foundations for rebuilding this temple are established upon the groundwork of repentance. We must turn from the sin that led us to dig our own wells and abandon the Spring of Living water. But now we see our sin and our need of Christ. Now that we are forgiven and cleansed, we are ready to build. We are prepared to throw open the gates and open the doors so the King of Glory may enter in all His majesty.

As children of promise we serve to build a spiritual house—a mighty fortress. We are diligent in the work because this is a house for all who are called by His name. In this house we look forward to the day our Redeemer comes back for us. We build on the Rock, who is Christ Jesus. We remain in this house so that when all the nations are in turmoil, we are held safe. We will not be shaken.[13] This house will remain unbroken as we work toward the day when every nation will cry out for the blessing of His saving grace. We yearn

---
13. Hebrews 12:27.

for the day when the power and authority of the wicked will be thrown down and Christ's ruling authority will be forever established.

The scepter will not depart from Judah, nor the ruler's staff from his descendants, until the coming of the one to whom it belongs, the one whom all nations will honor. (Genesis 49:10 NLT)

Now is the time to rebuild the Church and we need a sure foundation, a Rock to build on. We can't use new wallpaper and simply cover over what is long past. Gluing new paneling on the wall won't conceal a weak structure. The stain of sin always soaks through that new coat of paint. We can't go back to try the same old things that didn't work many years ago.[14] Jesus taught that we can't put new wine in old wineskins.[15] His teaching shows us that we can't go forward by going back to what never could save us. No, we must enter into the fullness of Christ and delight in His living and active presence in the present. We are called to repent of our sin and failures and also for the sins of the whole Church. This means that we must repent of our own failings and for the wrongdoing of other Christians as well because we're all together in the same house. This repentance brings us back to Christ who is our sure foundation.

When the Rock, Christ Jesus, is set in place as our foundation and we begin the work of building, the glory of the Lord returns to His temple—our temples—temples gathered in His name. Then the blessings of our New Covenant in Christ are poured out like a flood.

Consider our abject spiritual condition before we repented and returned to the fullness of Christ. We constantly came up empty. We gather together according to rules taught by men.[16] Too often we gathered to do church according to our own likes and dislikes and then went away with little to show for the hour we gave up from our weekend. We worship for ourselves, confusing what is holy and what is common.

There is only one way to rebuild, and the groundwork begins with repentance. First, we confess our own sin and then the sins of the whole Church, because even one Christian's sin stains us all. When any one of the Father's sons or daughters act immorally, we have tarnished the name He gave to us. But we have a great hope because our Father acts on behalf of His people for the sake of His name. When contrite hearts come to the throne of grace, from that day on we open the door into the full blessings of our promised Lord and Savior. All the promises of the New Covenant are ours to make us flourish and be fruitful in God's kingdom.

---

14. Romans 8:3–4, Hebrews 10:1–4.
15. Mark 2:22.
16. Matthew 15:9.

> *"Now give careful thought to this from this day on–consider how things were before one stone was laid on another in the Lord's temple. When anyone came to a heap of twenty measures, there were only ten. When anyone went to a wine vat to draw fifty measures, there were only twenty. I struck all the work of your hands with blight, mildew and hail, yet you did not return to me," declares the Lord. "From this day on, from this twenty-fourth day of the ninth month, give careful thought to the day when the foundation of the Lord's temple was laid. Give careful thought: Is there yet any seed left in the barn? Until now, the vine and the fig tree, the pomegranate and the olive tree have not borne fruit. From this day on I will bless you."'*
(Haggai 2:15–19)

As we present our invitation, we hear those precious words: "Welcome to the banquet hall. Please be seated at our Father's bountiful table." We're awed by the celebrative gathering where all may partake together of God's bounty. This is a house of abundance, surrounded with a garden of delights. As we enter we are given a new robe with fine embroidered linen, ornamented with precious jewels as gifts from our Bridegroom.

We came to the door of this house as broken wretches. We were desperate, weighed down with our sin, and desperate to be forgiven so we might forget our past sins. In God's forgiveness and mercy we are lifted up, made whole, given a new name, and offered a job in God's kingdom.

We are blessed in waiting. We're a bride who sings out with delightful anticipation of her Bridegroom who is coming for her. As a bride in waiting, we enjoy many benefits—kingdom blessings in abundance. We hold onto these good things, knowing they are guaranteed because they are written in our Savior's blood. These treasures are held secure for us in His nail scarred hands. They cost Him everything and they cost us nothing.

As we wait, we stand secure in this fortress strong house. We came to the Throne of Grace with contrite hearts and now the bountiful blessings of our Lord and Savior are ours as we are seated at His bountiful table of delights.

Chapter 18

Blessings of the Name

Q & A

1. What are each of us given as we enter the Father's banquet hall?

___

___

___

2. Describe your life before Christ and your life with your new family name.

___

___

___

3. What is the guarantee of the blessings and benefits of God's kingdom?

___

___

___

4. What is the significance of Jesus' body that was broken for His body the Church?

___

___

___

My Journal Notes:

Forgiveness and Mercy

Key Scriptures:

- "For the sake of your name, LORD, forgive my iniquity, though it is great." (Psalm 25:11)

- "If we confess our sins, he is faithful and just and will forgive us our sins and purify us from all unrighteousness." (1 John 1:9)

Jesus holds out His nail scarred hands to us. In one hand He offers forgiveness, and in the other He extends mercy. This lesson focuses on two of the most awesome promises we receive that prepare us to gather around the bountiful table of our Lord and King. Because of God's abundant mercy, His forgiveness is quick and complete. We'll learn that in forgiveness we are set free to run on His narrow pathway, but not to run amok. This study opens our understanding to see that without forgiveness and mercy, life is a dead-end street. Indeed, God forgives us according to the way we forgive others. He restores us to the abundant blessings in the house we build for His holy name. By the power of the Word and the ministry of the Holy Spirit we come into abundant forgiveness that is ours in keeping with the promise of His holy name.

> Study Prayer
>
> *O Father of grace, mercy, and forgiveness,*
> *"Create in me a clean heart, O God, and renew a right spirit within me."*
>
> A prayer according to Psalm 51:10 ESV

Our heavenly Father is longsuffering with us, abundant in mercy and quick to forgive His sons and daughters for the sake of His name. While forgiveness is abundant, we must also consider the truth that forgiveness doesn't preclude consequences. Before we yield to temptations that tug at our sleeves, catch our eyes, and shout out at every turn, we must think about how our sin affects the people around us. Consider the mess we leave in our wake. We can't sow our wild oats and then pray for crop failure. For that reason, let's turn from our sin and receive God's forgiveness and cleansing with pure hearts, and then live in keeping with repentance.[1]

---
1. Matthew 3:8.

The nation of Israel constantly wandered away from true worship in God's house. They forgot about separating holy from common. We must learn from their mistakes. They wanted to be like the nations around them rather than serving as a unique nation set apart to a holy God. In their greed they refused to allow the land to rest as prescribed by the wisdom of the Law. In their contempt for the great I AM they threw open the city gates to merchants so they could buy and sell on the Sabbath. They married foreign wives and then worshiped their wooden and stone gods all week before going to God's temple on the Sabbath. Over and over, they violated their covenant with the Father.

But God was longsuffering with His people. He sent many prophets to warn them and teach them truth and righteousness. Finally, when the weight of their sin tipped the balance against them, the consequences of their sin swept them away from homes, from the sanctuary stronghold—the object of their pride.[2] Their seventy-year exile served a good purpose. The land finally had a rest. The agony of captivity in a foreign land served to restrain their sin.

In captivity they yearned for true worship in the Promised Land. They desired the God of Israel, their Deliverer. Finally, a redeemed people returned to Israel to rebuild the temple. Once again, they could enter into true and real worship and fellowship with God their Maker in His holy sanctuary. They came home to rebuild the house for the Father's holy name where they could sing the songs of Zion with joyful hearts.

Christ Jesus, our Lord and Savior, offers us a new and better covenant. We're no longer bound or condemned by the Law. Instead, we are liberated in Christ who fulfilled the Law. He gave us freedom to run free on His pathway of truth, righteousness, love, justice, and mercy.[3] Now we are liberated to worship, serve, and minister in the power of the Holy Spirit. Instead of having the Law to restrain and condemn us, we can overrule the yearnings of the flesh. By the power of the Word and the Holy Spirit we can live as victors in Christ. Even so, our flesh still needs the fear of the Lord. We need to be alarmed about the consequences of our sin. We must learn from our predecessors' mistakes.

> *Seventy "sevens" are decreed for your people and your holy city to finish transgression, to put an end to sin, to atone for wickedness, to bring in everlasting righteousness, to seal up vision and prophecy and to anoint the Most Holy Place.* (Daniel 9:24)

---

2. Ezekiel 24:20-21.
3. Psalm 119:32.

Without forgiveness and mercy life is a dead-end street with a gaping precipice waiting to swallow us up at the end. But there is no cause for despair. Look to Jesus as our example. When He reached out to touch and heal the sick, He spoke forgiveness first. Then by His word He healed them and sent them on their way fully restored, saying, "Go and sin no more."[4] A repentant heart and a pardon for sin are the beginning of restoration so that we may once again be made whole, rest in the Lord, and enjoy the full fruit and blessings of the kingdom of heaven.

Consider what your life used to be like. Were you violated by another person's filth? Have you been the target of hatred's bloody violence? Has your livelihood been ripped away by others' greed? Look up, for your redemption is at hand.[5] In forgiveness and mercy you are restored. In your heavenly Father's eyes you are once again unblemished and undefiled. Under you Father's care, He provides. Giving up your claim to revenge prepares the way for all to be set right on your behalf. The cleansing fire of the Holy Spirit will blaze out to purify and restore all those who have forgiveness in their hearts.

> *In that day the Branch of the LORD will be beautiful and glorious, and the fruit of the land will be the pride and glory of the survivors in Israel. Those who are left in Zion, who remain in Jerusalem, will be called holy, all who are recorded among the living in Jerusalem. The LORD will wash away the filth of the women of Zion; he will cleanse the bloodstains from Jerusalem by a spirit of judgment and a spirit of fire.*
> (Isaiah 4:2–4)

How is it possible that someone would even consider dying in our place to pay the penalty of all our sin and depravity? This truth is beyond human ability to grasp. We hear testimonies of God redeeming His sons and daughters. Hearing their words is beyond any human ability to comprehend. Then, by the power of the Holy Spirit our ears wake up to hear the Word speak to us words of saving grace, forgiveness, and mercy. God calls us by name and the seed of faith is planted in our hearts. Now we can hear, believe, and receive the Good News Gospel of Jesus Christ. Yes! Amen! There is forgiveness in His name.

> *All the prophets testify about him that everyone who believes in him receives forgiveness of sins through his name.*
> (Acts 10:43)

Our heavenly Father wants His name to be known as a name that offers forgiveness and mercy. His desire is for His holy name to draw all who are thirsty to come to the Spring of Living Water. The sound of His name ought

---

4. John 8:11 NLT.
5. Luke 21:28.

to strike fear into the hearts of those who stand opposed to His Son, our Savior. Our Redeemer's enemies are struck down and they cannot prevent Him from extending His saving grace to all those who will receive.

Forgiveness is not like the sudden flash of a lightning strike. Forgiveness brings us into a cleansing and healing flow. This happens in a moment and then its healing work may take some time. Old Testament Law makes this truth evident.[6] After a person was "unclean" they were required to wait seven days before going back to the temple to worship. This served as a time for contemplation and meditation, to think about sin's effect on their lives and on the world around them. This is consistent with Paul who taught us to examine ourselves to know if we are truly in the faith.[7] After we are convicted of our moral failings and confess our sin, we gladly receive God's forgiveness. When we stand forgiven, we ought to take time to further examine ourselves and consider the effects of our sin on our lives, our family, neighbors, and our church.

The nation of Israel spent seventy years in exile because the weight of their sins tipped the scales of justice against them. Many years were necessary for the Land of Promise to heal and for the people to have time for healing, reflection, and restoration. Indeed, the consequences of our sin serves as a means to restrain sin and instill the fear of the Lord in our hearts.

Because His name is holy, the Father forgives the sins of His people and brings them back home to rebuild the house of worship—all for the glory and honor of His name.

I am writing to you, dear children, because your sins have been forgiven on account of his name.
(1 John 2:12)

Our heavenly Father is quick to forgive for the sake of His holy name—the name He has given to all His adopted sons and daughters. As forgiven children we ought to live our lives in "the fear of the Lord," because forgiveness doesn't preclude consequences. God is longsuffering with us, but when we persist in going our own way, and unrepentant in our sins, there comes a time when our misdeeds tip the scales of justice against us and the consequences are severe. But our Lord God is faithful. Imposed consequences are designed to serve a good purpose—to restrain sin in us.

Consider the history of God's holy nation. Their sin built up until the weight tipped against them and God sent them into exile in Babylon for seventy years. When the years of their consequences finally tipped the scales back, their God, Yehovah, brought them back to Jerusalem to rebuild the city

---
6. 2 Timothy 3:16.
7. 2 Corinthians 13:5.

and its temple. Forgiveness and mercy restored God's people so they could rebuild the house for His holy name.

What was your life like before you were brought to Jesus to drink from His living water? You made a mess of it. But now all of the damage done to you and by you is washed away. You are made into a new creation in Christ with your feet set firmly upon the Rock who is your Redeemer. From the least sin to the greatest sins, your past wrongs are eradicated forever.

In repentance you came to the throne of grace where you received the miraculous work of forgiveness, cleansing, and redemption. Grasping hold of the Good News is only possible by the power of the Holy Spirit at work in you. When you hear God's word, the Spirit of Christ plants the seed of faith and the Gospel message takes root in your heart. Now that you are forgiven and totally made new, consider the miracle child that you are. You are totally free of the burden of your sins. You are set free to run on our Savior's narrow pathway.[8]

---

8. Psalm 119:32.

Chapter 19

Forgiveness and Mercy

Q & A

1. Does God's forgiveness mean that you won't suffer any consequences for your sin?

   _____
   _____
   _____

2. What good purpose do consequences accomplish in our lives?

   _____
   _____
   _____

3. What are the effects of God's forgiveness and mercy?

   _____
   _____
   _____

4. Why is it important to take some time to consider the damage your sin has left behind you?

   _____
   _____
   _____

5. Describe your life before and after forgiveness.

   _____
   _____
   _____

My Journal Notes:

20

A Wise Builder

Key Scriptures:

- "The fear of the LORD is the beginning of wisdom; all who follow his precepts have good understanding. To him belongs eternal praise." (Psalm 111:10)

- "By wisdom a house is built, and through understanding it is established." (Proverbs 24:3)

If you put a novice to work building your house, and he doesn't understand the value of a blueprint, you may end up with a building that isn't square, tips to one side, won't keep out the rain, and gradually sinks into the ground because it doesn't have a proper foundation. In this study we'll focus on Christ who is Wisdom and who comes to serve as our Master Builder. He'll join us at the work table where the design plan of God's Word is rolled out as our standard. We'll learn to build in the fear of the Lord because this is the beginning of wisdom that serves as a wellspring of strength for all builders.

This lesson opens our eyes to value the Good Shepherd's measuring rod. He uses it to make sure we build according to His plan and not our own. We'll see the importance of working according to plan with constant prayer to keep ourselves on track. There will be many distractors who oppose us in the work; but who will we fear? Will we bow to the detractors or submit to the Master Builder's measuring rod? The learner will come to appreciate the Carpenter's laser tape that inspires us to do the best job possible. Our boss is a very experienced carpenter himself, and in His guiding presence we put our hands to the work of building a house for our heavenly Father's holy name—a Rock-solid house.

Study Prayer

Oh Lord God of majesty, raise up teachers who will show us the plan for your temple so that we may turn away from working according to our own design and purpose. Give us wisdom so that we may be faithful to build according to your purpose and plan.

A prayer according to Ezekiel 43:10–11

The straw boss looks at his watch and puts down his empty coffee mug with a thump. "Okay, guys. Strap on your tool belts and let's get to work." He rolls out the blueprint on the sawhorse table, turns a couple pages, and says with a scoff, "I've got a better plan. Listen up, guys. We're going to do this my way."

Too often we have to learn by hard knocks. It never works to throw out the blueprint. We must resist the desire to do things by our own design. As we begin the task of building a House for the Father's name, it's important to follow the blueprint and constantly measure what we have built to be sure everything is square, plumb, and true to plan. We must build on the solid Rock who is Christ Jesus so the house will stand firm. The consequences of creating any structure on a poor foundation is disaster. In the spiritual realm our own plan leads to moral failings that bring consequences, both natural and imposed. The aftereffects of our sin encourage us to think before we act. Our mortal flesh needs the fear of the Lord to keep us in close fellowship with the Father. Our soul and spirit are strengthened in the Word. The Holy Spirit indwells us so we may resist the tug of the flesh. Our desire to obey is love-driven—compelled by our desire to be in communion with the Father who loved us first.

In the everyday work world we build offices, houses, and bridges according to plan because we know that if they fall down, we're in deep trouble. Accomplishing the task of building God's kingdom requires wisdom from above. In the spiritual realm we build in the fear of the Lord knowing that what we build according to wisdom will never crumble. God instructed Ezekiel to describe the temple to the people. The true worship ordained for the temple brought them to shame because of their idolatrous worship. Those with contrite hearts could be shown the design of the temple.[1] A love-driven desire for true worship causes faithful builders to delight in the plan and put all their heart and soul into the work to build for eternity.

> *And now, Israel, what does the L*ORD *your God ask of you but to fear the L*ORD *your God, to walk in obedience to him, to love him, to serve the L*ORD *your God with all your heart and with all your soul.*
> (Deuteronomy 10:12)

The living stones of the City of God hear the voice of our Savior calling out. All astute builders turn their ears to His call. He is the Word who comes with a measuring rod to be sure we are building according to His blueprint—the Bible. We watch with trepidation as He carefully measures everything we have constructed. Anything that doesn't keep what is holy separate from what is common doesn't measure up. He will order it torn down so we can start over.

---

1. Ezekiel 43:10–11.

The rod Jesus wields is the rod of the Good Shepherd. His staff is the whole counsel of Scripture. We need this measuring rod because our human tendency is to build using only the "pleasant" parts of the Bible that make us feel good about ourselves. We prefer positive promises but ignore the correction of God's Word. Examining ourselves and what we build is sometimes too painful because we must face the truth. We want to build only with promises that say, "I have plans to prosper you."[2] We tend to forget that self-directed builders need to hear the prophet's warning: "Though they build houses, they will not live in them."[3] This warning is necessary for men who prefer their own plan. It serves to turn us around so we may prosper according to the Master Builder's good purpose. Wisdom calls us to value the measuring rod and build according to plan.[4]

> *Listen! The LORD is calling to the city–and to fear your name is wisdom–"Heed the rod and the One who appointed it.*
> (Micah 6:9)

Agreeing to walk together in the fear of the Lord brings us into harmony so we can march arm in arm in unity and purpose. Prayers inspired by the wind of the Spirit, intercessions lifted up in harmony with the Word, and petitions offered up in agreement as a community of faith are awesome and powerful. This is like getting all the tools lined up in your tool belt, the pockets full of nails and fasteners, and your gun's magazine full of nails.

These earnest and effective prayers sent up in the fear of the Lord and according to His name are received as precious incense in the heavens. These prayers are embraced with joy because of the dynamic effect of praying together in the spirit, by the leading of the Holy Spirit and the Word. These dynamic prayers are recorded in glory—stored up as incense in golden bowls.[5] Prayers, intercessions, petitions, and servitude in a community of faith are essential tools for a wise builder.

> *Then those who feared the LORD talked with each other, and the LORD listened and heard. A scroll of remembrance was written in his presence concerning those who feared the LORD and honored his name.*
> (Malachi 3:16)

Every created being on earth has a natural instinct for self preservation. A bird flutters away to draw a predator away from her nest eggs. A mother deer hides her fawn and dashes deeper into the forest. The natural human reaction

---

2. Jeremiah 29:11.
3. Zephaniah 1:13..
4. It's important to note that Jeremiah first warned the people against their sin, and then through God's forgiveness and mercy proclaimed His blessings.
5. Revelation 5:8.

to a threat is fight of flight. But there is a greater fear instinct than distress about our personal safety. A quick review of the heroes of our Christian faith reveals many prophets, priests, missionaries, and everyday folks overcame this natural instinct and put their lives on the line to serve the cause of the Gospel of Jesus Christ. They gave greater value to helping, serving, and proclaiming the Good News. It's as if they put on their hard hats and safety glasses and then committed their safety and well-being into God's hands. They refused to fear threats of violence from those who served in the strongholds of darkness. Their view of life extended beyond this temporal world. Instead, they built a house to stand for eternity in the fear of the Lord that leads into all wisdom.

> *And do not fear those who kill the body but cannot kill the soul. Rather fear him who can destroy both soul and body in hell.*
> (Matthew 10:28 ESV)

A person puts themselves in danger when they make false claims about acting or speaking in the name of Jesus Christ. Using the name of the Christ to promote a self-inspired ministry is to misuse His name. If we insist that we are called by Jesus' holy name and declare that we are part of the family of God as a false cover for our own agendas, this claim puts us on dangerous ground.

The honor of true service within the realm of the kingdom of heaven is only granted to those who submit to serve under the authority of the name, Christ Jesus. We can only speak with the authority of the name by being subject to His name. True service and ministry are only possible in the Spirit of Christ. The work of the Church is eternally effective when it is in harmony with the Gospel's commands. Attempting any work apart from the authority of His name, no matter how good it sounds, puts us in harm's way.

> *When this became known to the Jews and Greeks living in Ephesus, they were all seized with fear, and the name of the Lord Jesus was held in high honor.*
> (Acts 19:17)

By His power and might, God pulls down every stronghold that is raised up against Him.[6] We build with confidence knowing the Master Builder watches over every wise builder who puts their hands to the work. We apply ourselves with great concern for building a strong house that meets the standard of eternity. The laborers step up to the work in awe of the Carpenter from Nazareth who works at our side. The workers build in the presence of our God Almighty who is King above every king. Every detail of the work must measure up, glorify His holy name, be in agreement with the Spirit and all truth, and separate what is holy from what is common. We shudder to think of our own failings in this great work. Then, in forgiveness and mercy

---
6. 2 Corinthians 10:3–5.

we are strengthened to accomplish the work that is impossible apart from the anointing, gifting, and empowering work of the Spirit of Christ. We rejoice as we press on. We are in awe as we see wisdom build this house where the Great I AM's name is honored and glorified.

> *Great and marvelous are your deeds, Lord God Almighty. Just and true are your ways, King of the nations. Who will not fear you, Lord, and bring glory to your name? For you alone are holy. All nations will come and worship before you, for your righteous acts have been revealed.*
> (Revelation 15:3–4)

When you begin the task of building a house for the Father's holy name, it's important to resist the temptation that whispers in your ear, saying, "Your idea, and your plan is so much better." Wise builders understand how critical it is to work according to God's plan. They know that what they build must stand forever. They resist the desire to do things their way. Instead, they keep themselves on track, delighting in the fear of the Lord.

Constructing a safe edifice that is right and true is a love-driven desire of the heart. Every wise builder knows that what they construct must measure up to the standards of the Master Builder's measuring rod. Every worker keeps the goal in sight; a house for the Father's name that will stand through every storm, every test of time, and endure for eternity.

We take up this good work with the essential tools in our belt. Prayer is a vital tool for every astute builder. Prayers and intercessions are necessary because we need the Lord's strength to stand up against the threats and hostilities stirred up against us. Our safety and well-being on the job depend on prayer to keep us safe in God's hands and keep us from being distracted from this good work.

As workers in God's kingdom, we submit ourselves to work under the authority of the Carpenter from Nazareth. We have no authority to do this work apart from Him. Under the covering of His name we know we're kept safe under the watchful eye of our Father in heaven. The work of building a house for the Father's holy name can only be accomplished in submission to the Master Builder. We work in agreement with the Spirit and according to all truth so that the house we build is according to the blueprint—a plan that holds separate what is holy and what is common.

Chapter 20

A Wise Builder

Q & A

1. How can you overcome the temptation to look at the blueprint and say, "My plan is so much better"?

   _____

   _____

   _____

2. Describe your love-driven desire to build a house for the Father's name that is true to plan.

   _____

   _____

   _____

3. What is the first job for a wise builder?

   _____

   _____

   _____

4. Why is submission to the Master Builder an essential element in building this house?

   _____

   _____

   _____

My Journal Notes:

21

A Worker's Songs

Key Scriptures:

- "I will praise you, LORD, with all my heart; before the 'gods' I will sing your praise." (Psalm 138:1)

- "On what were its [earth's] footings set, or who laid its cornerstone—while the morning stars sang together and all the angels shouted for joy?" (Job 38:6–7)

Singing or whistling while we do our job tends to lighten the load and make everything zip along smoothly. When soldiers march out in formation they sing, "Over hill, over dale, we will hit the dusty trail."[7] A restaurant server who sings for her guests adds a touch of fun to her work and delightful flavors to her guest's meals. A preschool teacher might sing her way through her lesson plan to brighten her classroom and help the children learn their ABCs.

The workers in God's kingdom build a spiritual house that resonates with songs of praise and reverent worship. In this study we'll learn the joy of shouting out with praise as we build this house. We build a dwelling place that cannot be shaken. The foundation of this sanctuary is Rock-solid. The Cornerstone of this temple will never be moved. The rafters echo with notes of praise as we sing with the angels and rejoice in accord with the bright Morning Star. When people gather to worship in spirit and truth, and in agreement with Jesus' name, their shouts of exaltation shake the ramparts. God's covenant people overflow with praise in harmony with the Almighty's voice that makes the mountains skip like rams and the hills like lambs.

In this study our work crews join with Moses and Miriam to celebrate with songs of victory and praise. We'll look upon the work of many generations who have built on the Rock, Christ Jesus. We'll stand up with them to shout out because of what the Lord, our God, has accomplished through us. This survey of the Scriptures opens our eyes to Christ who is victorious over the enemy. The destroyer left behind him a devastated, drought-ruined, and sun scorched-land. Our Redeemer strengthens us to rebuild the ruins into

---
7. Sousa, John Philip, and H. F Odell. *U.S. Field Artillery March*. Carl Fischer, New York, 1918. Notated Music. https://www.loc.gov/item/sousa.200028220/.

pleasant streets with dwellings.[8] We'll recognize that our Savior refines us as living building stones of the great city whose Builder and Maker is God.

> Study Prayer
>
> *Lead us to shout out with glorious praise at the presence of the Lord, at the presence of the God of Jacob, who turned the rock into a pool, the hard rock into springs of water.*
>
> Prayer inspired by Psalm 114:7–8

The Great I AM won a mighty victory as He led Israel's tribes safely through the Red Sea. Then He destroyed their captors' armies with crushing waves. With God's chosen nation on the other side, the walls of water swept over the horses and chariots that pursued them. By this mighty act The Great I AM made the power of His name known to all the nations. And they shuddered in fear.[9] With Israel gathered safely on the banks of the Sea, they sang a joyful song of praise along with Moses who led them across: "The LORD is my strength and my defense; he has become my salvation. He is my God, and I will praise him, my father's God, and I will exalt him."[10] Miriam echoed their song, continuing in prophetic praises for the Most High God. Their songs established Yehovah's name forever as Deliverer and Protector of all the people He called as His own.

Our Lord and King is worthy of all praise for His mighty acts performed on behalf of His name and for all who are called by His holy name. He sent His only Son to walk among us, to teach us according to truth and righteousness, to heal our sick and raise the dead, and then give His body to be broken, His blood to be shed to deliver us from the enslaving clutches of sin, Satan, and death. Our heavenly Father is worthy of all praise. So let us gather together to sing His praise, and dance before the triumphant One with our hands and voices lifted up with exaltations.

> *Then Miriam the prophetess, the sister of Aaron, took a tambourine in her hand, and all the women went out after her with tambourines and dancing. And Miriam sang to them: "Sing to the LORD, for he has triumphed gloriously; the horse and his rider he has thrown into the sea."*
> (Exodus 15:20–21)

The rafters of the sanctuary ring with shouts of "GLORY!" The foundations of this house of prayer resonate with rejoicing as we build, living stone upon precious stone. The Cornerstone leads us in a new chorus, the song of

---

8. Isaiah 58:11-12.
9. Exodus 15:14, Isaiah 64:2.
10. Exodus 15:2.

the Lamb.[11] Joyful voices sing out into all the earth to glorify the Lord of all the heavens and earth. We rejoice because He shows His arm is strong on our behalf. He has performed awesome deeds for His people. His honor and glory inhabit His people who revere His holy name.

At the sound of the Almighty's name our enemies shrink back, trembling in fear. With our eyes we have seen His glory. His mighty acts are celebrated from generation to generation. All men, women, and children who are called by His name lift up the Word of God as a sword and proclaim victory in His holy name. His enemies are subdued under His feet. Those who oppose Him are vanquished and the God's people are set free to worship in spirit and in all truth before Christ victorious.

> *Shout for joy to God, all the earth; sing the glory of his name; give to him glorious praise! Say to God, "How awesome are your deeds! So great is your power that your enemies come cringing to you. All the earth worships you and sings praises to you; they sing praises to your name."*
> (Psalm 66:1–4 ESV)

All through the darkness of night, storms blow and parched desert sands sift to engulf bountiful fields and meadows, turning them into a dry and thirsty land. In the dead of night, the Destroyer attempts to steal away what our God has provided for every creature on earth. The enemy overthrows once prosperous cities and imprisons them as captives.[12] He leaves broken lives and chaos in his wake.

But we have a great hope. Our Deliverer rose victorious, defeating death and the grave. He gathers His people and leads us in joyful songs. Our voices echo from the hills. The saints shout with joy and watch as invasive sands of darkness are driven back. The morning sun crests the horizon and the congregation sings out: "Rise up, LORD! May your enemies be scattered."[13] With one bold voice we sing out victorious. Our eyes overflow with wellsprings of joy as we see God's mighty arm making a way through the wilderness. Parched gullies spring forth with fresh water. A land once scorched with drought and fire is refreshed and comforted. The desert blossoms into a bountiful garden. Fire-scorched ruins are rebuilt with tested and refined stones. With gratitude and delight our hearts ring out as a harmonious choir to exalt our Father, Son, and Holy Spirit, for He has won a mighty victory on behalf of His people. Indeed, the beating heart of every Christian's life is the song we sing in the unity of faith.

---

11. Revelation 15:3.
12. Isaiah 14:17.
13. Numbers 10:35, Psalm 68:1.

> *Sing to God, sing praises to his name; lift up a song to him who rides through the deserts; his name is the LORD; exult before him!*
> (Psalm 68:4 ESV)

Why should people look at Christians as desolate and then wonder, "Where is their God?"[14] The world around us sees the devastation of our backsliding ways and our meaningless gatherings. They see vineyards unkempt and unfruitful. The sheep of God's pasture have wandered away from the Good Shepherd's flock. We have turned worshipful gatherings into a show of personal talents. We worship for our own gratification. Our leaders have denied spiritual gifts to God's people. We no longer worship in spirit or in accord with all truth. But take heart. We are offered a great hope. In repentance we take hold of Christ Jesus who is our hope.

The Great I AM has an appointed time when He will strengthen the remnant of His people to complete the building of the house for His name.[15] We press in, interceding for all God's people to strengthen us for the task. The prayers of the saints lift us up to Mount Zion, the city of the living God.[16] We build this holy dwelling, singing with the angels united in a joyful work. We rebuild what has fallen down and we can look forward to see the work completed. When we fall down on the job, our Savior and Redeemer forgives us, picks us up, and dusts us off so we can continue this good work and see it through to the end.

> *When the LORD restored the fortunes of Zion, we were like those who dreamed. Our mouths were filled with laughter, our tongues with songs of joy. Then it was said among the nations, "The LORD has done great things for them."*
> (Psalm 126:1–2)

Calloused hands dig into the work. Backs are bent from hard labor. But their weary bodies find rest and strength in His holy presence. At the sound of the shofar[17] every worker pauses to look up. They put their tools aside for a moment and lift up holy hands with mighty shouts of praise. Their unified voices minister words of exaltation that drive back forces of darkness. This mighty troop stands back to examine their progress. They see the Light of World pushing back the forces of darkness. They can see that the night is nearly over. They raise up their voices with a great and victorious shout.

The blessings of Zion encompass the laborers in this great work. This mighty army flourishes in the light of God's kingdom. By means of the Word and the Holy Spirit workers are made strong in the power of His might. Like

---
14. Psalm 79:10.
15. Habakkuk 2:3.
16. Hebrews 12:22-24.
17. Trumpet made from a ram's horn.

the mighty armies of old, the songs of the saints go before all those who are armed for battle. Tens of thousands of voices sing out, "Give thanks to the LORD, for His love endures forever."[18] Our foes are defeated and the work goes forward. This good work's completion is in sight.

> *Praise the LORD, all you servants of the LORD who minister by night in the house of the LORD. Lift up your hands in the sanctuary and praise the LORD. May the LORD bless you from Zion, he who is the Maker of heaven and earth.*
> (Psalm 134:1–3)

Living stones cry out, and they will not be silenced. The religious elite of Jesus' day objected to the little children shouting "Hosanna to the Son of David."[19] But the little ones would not be hushed. Jesus answered the Pharisee's protests, saying; "if they keep quiet, the stones will cry out."[20]

As we press forward in the work of the kingdom of heaven, we build the walls of the City of God with living stones.[21] With every step of our pilgrimage, we cry out with jubilant praise, "Hosanna in the highest." A mighty army marches on with shouts of "hallelu Yah." We press on as a mighty troop and shout out with songs of exaltation.

> *And the crowds that went before him and that followed him were shouting, "Hosanna to the Son of David! Blessed is he who comes in the name of the Lord! Hosanna in the highest!"*
> (Matthew 21:9 ESV)

A song always lightens the load we carry. Look to our soldiers as an example. They carry packs as heavy as 150 pounds of body armor and gear, and they ease their burden with a marching song. A new mother who is a few weeks away from her due date can lighten her load by singing to her unborn child.

Builders of the house for our Father's holy name lighten their load, singing out with praise and exaltations to the God of salvation. They rejoice because of the mighty works of His strong arm. The work crews join with Moses and Miriam to sing songs of victory. The congregation shouts out with, "Glory!" as they see this good work progress. We all sing out together because we serve an awesome God. Our hearts burst out with song because of our Father's mighty work among His people. Indeed, at the sound of His name, His enemies shrink back, trembling with fear.

We, the Church, have failed to build what is true and according to plan. The world around us looks at what we've built and they wonder, "Where is

---

18. 2 Chronicles 20:20-22.
19. Matthew 21:15.
20. Luke 19:40.
21. Psalm 51:10.

their God?" It's no wonder because we build in our own strength and by our own design, and what we build is like a false front that soon tips over. But in repentance we have a great hope. The Great I AM will come upon those with contrite hearts like a tsunami. He will lift us up and set our feet on the Rock, Christ Jesus. His Holy Spirit will teach us and equip us for the work we are called to do, building a house for His holy name.

The walls of this house echo with shouts of victory as a mighty chorus. As we put our hands to the task of building, we can see the night driven back by the Light of Life.

> *The night is nearly over; the day is almost here. So let us put aside the deeds of darkness and put on the armor of light.*
> (Romans 13:12)

Chapter 21

A Worker's Song

Q & A

1. Why does a song lighten our load as we do our work?

   _____
   _____
   _____

2. Describe the joy of working with and singing along with the Carpenter from Nazareth.

   _____
   _____
   _____

3. Why do songs of God's glory and majesty cause God's enemies to shrink back and tremble?

   _____
   _____
   _____

4. What songs will you sing as you take your tools in hand and begin this good work?

   _____
   _____
   _____

My Journal Notes:

No Other Name

Key Scriptures:

- "You shall have no other gods before me." (Exodus 20:3)
- "I am the LORD, and there is no other; apart from me there is no God." (Isaiah 45:5)

Step through the gate into the pleasant boundaries of God's kingdom where the sound of singing is better than anything you have ever heard. In this space you are encompassed with the fearsome, awesome wonders of creation; reverberations of our heavenly Father's holy name. This lesson resonates with God's all-encompassing name that changes our lives forever, because His holy name is written upon every element of our being.

We'll learn that when we speak in Jesus' name, we are not speaking according to our own intuitions, ideas, or thoughts about what true worship ought to be. No doubt, we've all failed and acted on our own, but when we repent and turn from our sin, there is forgiveness, cleansing, and then a right spirit is renewed in us.

This lesson makes it clear that we can't feast at tables set in the kingdom of darkness and the kingdom of light. We come to the Lord's table where we are forgiven, washed clean, and strengthened in Christ. At this table we honor His holy name and in turn, He makes our names great. Join us in a great feast where there is security and comfort in knowing our God watches over us just as He watches over the sparrow.[1]

Study Prayer

Father, we have brought shame upon your holy name by our divisive hearts. We confess our sin against you and you alone. Forgive us, cleanse us, and change our hearts. Renew a right spirit within us and cleanse us from all our unrighteous acts.

A prayer according to Psalm 51:10 and 1 John 1:9

---

1. Matthew 10:31.

We bow, bending our knees in awe of God in all His splendor and majesty. Children of hope proclaim His name with reverence. The awesome sound of His name fills us with trepidation and we shudder in His holy presence. Yes, we tremble with fearsome wonder as we take up His name on our lips. Children of the resurrection marvel at the miraculous mystery of the Name He has bestowed upon His people. By His name we are made a holy nation, a royal priesthood. In His name we gather to minister before Him. He has revealed Himself to us in His name so that we may walk according to all truth and righteousness.

God has not changed. His name is from generation to generation through all time. We are called by His name and we do the work of the kingdom in His name. In our worship gatherings we lift up holy hands to exalt His name. The congregation must worship no other god. We must not call on any other name, relying on man-made traditions or our own ways. There is only one Throne of Grace where we can find forgiveness, mercy, cleansing, and restoration in His name.

> *I am the Lord; that is my name! I will not yield my glory to another or my praise to idols.*
> (Isaiah 42:8)

All those who are in Christ are called by the Name that is above all names. We proclaim the most awesome Name so we may tell a sin-bent world of His forgiveness, healing, and saving grace. The Almighty gave us His name so we may subdue the earth even to the farthest corner of this fallen world. In His name we proclaim Christ who was crucified. We are witnesses of a Savior who shed His lifeblood for the sins of the world. His name is inscribed on our hearts, written on our foreheads, and His name encompasses every word we speak as witnesses of His power and might to save. As His called and chosen servants, the lives we live, the words we speak, and the work of our hands are drenched with the Name so we may be living illustrations, witnesses of His power to redeem lost souls. We begin each day with prayer and intercessions in His name. We commit the work of our hand and every word we speak to the honor of His name. We stand tall, strengthened in His name to do our work covered by the blessings of His name.

> *"You are my witnesses,"* declares the Lord, *"and my servant whom I have chosen, so that you may know and believe me and understand that I am he. Before me no god was formed, nor will there be one after me. I, even I, am the Lord, and apart from me there is no savior."*
> (Isaiah 43:10–11)

If you want to make fresh baked bread you have to use the right ingredients. The cook can't use sawdust instead of flour, nor can he use talcum powder in place of baking powder. A true baker uses true ingredients so they can feed real, growing, and healthy children.

The following verse gives double emphasis to the phrase, "one true God." It's a warning to "whoever" will speak on God's behalf to bless their friends and neighbors. They must do so in His name alone. This Scripture cautions all of us to be sure that when we make a vow it is in keeping with the one true God, as He has revealed Himself. We can't offer a true blessing if we speak in the name of a custom-made Jesus who only fits our private view of religion. Our pledge or vow is of no effect if our promise is in the name of a god we have made in our own image. To speak what is right we must come to know the one true God, His only Son, and the true Spirit of wisdom, understanding, and knowledge.[2] We must not be like Job's three friends who came to help with misguided but good intentions.[3] Their words spewed out from their religious traditions, speaking out from their human reasoning. We are called to say only what Jesus is saying so we can proclaim true words of admonition or blessing. As we abide in Christ, just as He has revealed Himself, we can be assured of every promise because there is power in His name.

We have all failed to keep our promises. We have blessed where our heavenly Father has not blessed. Like Job's friends, we speak out by our own initiative and by our own intuitions. But in repentance we have a great hope. When we see our sin and turn away from it, God is faithful and just to forgive us our sins. He completes the good work of forgiveness by cleansing us and renewing a right spirit in our heart of hearts.[4]

> *Whoever invokes a blessing in the land will do so by the one true God; whoever takes an oath in the land will swear by the one true God. For the past troubles will be forgotten and hidden from my eyes.*
> (Isaiah 65:16)

If you accept an invitation to join a devious rich man at the white linen-draped table in his mansion, you may end up choking on the food.[5] Sons and daughters of the Most High God cannot feast on the bread of wickedness and the Bread of Life as well.[6] The wine of violence doesn't mix with the cup we partake of at the Lord's Table.[7] We cannot serve both the kingdom of light and the kingdom of darkness. Any attempt at such duplicity would

---

2. Isaiah 11:2.
3. Job 42:7.
4. Psalm 51:10, 1 John 1:9.
5. Proverbs 23:1-3.
6. 1 Corinthians 10:21.
7. Proverbs 4:17.

be like a woman marrying into God's holy nation who hyphenated her new family name as Baal-Israel.[8]

Indeed, we partake of Christ at an abundant table that fully satisfies. We have no need of any other table. When we commune with Christ each one receives their portion according to His promise. As we come to the Lord's Table we are encompassed with every promise in the Word. Each one who comes in His name is fully satisfied in keeping with His promise. Indeed, our God owns the cattle on a thousand hills. He is more than able to place before us a table of abundance.[9] Our portion is in Christ who strengthens us for the task of building a house for His holy name where He spreads a bountiful table before us.

> *No one is like you, LORD; you are great, and your name is mighty in power. ... He who is the Portion of Jacob is not like these, for he is the Maker of all things, including Israel, the people of his inheritance–the LORD Almighty is his name.* (Jeremiah 10:6,16)

Try to imagine your calendar filled with appointments for every sunrise and sunset, every new moon and crescent moon, the positions in the heavens for Orion and Pleiades, and for all the storms upon earth's great seas. But that's not all. The Lord Almighty appoints the footsteps for His sons and daughters in between dawn and dusk, evening and morning. He knows every timely word we will speak in His name. Consider that the most powerful quantum computer could never find or track all the springs in the great oceans. Does the National Weather Service's supercomputer know where lightning will strike or what homes are in the path of the storm? Our God's "cloud" does even more than simply protect the weak and helpless who are in danger. He keeps track of every bird of the air so He can care for them.[10] Indeed, His watchfulness over us is far greater than a new mother holding her child and tenderly counting the hairs on her head where she'll tie the pink bow with her name on it.[11]

All His love, mercies, and His plan of redemption are guaranteed by His sovereign and holy name. The sun, moon, and stars keep to their appointed times as God's faithful witnesses in the sky. Earth's appointed seasons come faithfully: Springtime for planting, Summer for tending the garden, Autumn for harvesting, and Winter when orchards, fields, and forest rest—all according to the Creator's appointed times.[12] Is there any engineered technology that can help us build a house for such an awesome name?

---

8. Baal is a false deity worshiped by the Canaanites and Phoenicians.
9. Psalm 23:5, 50:10.
10. Matthew 6:26.
11. Luke 12:7.
12. Genesis 8:22.

This is what the LORD says, he who appoints the sun to shine by day, who decrees the moon and stars to shine by night, who stirs up the sea so that its waves roar— the LORD Almighty is his name:
(Jeremiah 31:35)

In post-modern American culture, we all want to make a name for ourselves. We long for that day when we see our name in credits; our moment of fame. At old-time theaters a worker on a step-ladder put big plastic letters on the marquees to announce a new movie and its famous actors and actresses. In our current culture of fame, it's as if thousands of people trip over each other, trying to get their name on the billboards before the next guy comes along to replace it with his name. We end up with a tangle of meaningless names, all competing to be the most popular idol.

In our quest for fame and fortune we forget the Lord God who makes our names great.[13] We don't consider that the King of all the earth exalts one while throwing down another.[14] Our fallible minds fail to consider that our heavenly Father has given us His name, and He will make our name—which is His name—great. We will see our new name illuminated in the light of Christ, shining out from the house we build for the Father's holy name.

The LORD will be king over the whole earth. On that day there will be one LORD, and his name the only name.
(Zechariah 14:9)

A Deliverer and Redeemer is revealed to us in God's holy name. There is no hope of saving grace apart from the name of His only begotten Son of God who takes away the sin of the world. In His name our sin debt is paid in full. We are set free. He gives us His name as our own, and we are made whole new creations in Christ. When our eyes are opened to Christ Jesus we see our need of redemption, our hearts are brought to repentance, and we are brought into a cleansing flow that began with drops of blood as they crucified Jesus on a cruel Roman cross.

Now all those who are redeemed in Christ rise up as a mighty army. The Spirit of Christ gifts and empowers us to give us the tools we need for the work of the kingdom of heaven. Together we build a house for His holy name and no other name.

Salvation is found in no one else, for there is no other name under heaven given to mankind by which we must be saved.
(Acts 4:12)

---

13. Genesis 12:2.
14. Psalm 75:7.

We were born into a sin bent world. We came into this world indebted, like a child born to parents owned by a slaveholder. In our enslaved and impoverished state we cannot free ourselves. We have no means of our own to buy our freedom. Our taskmaster lays claim to everything we touch. We are not our own and we have no way to break the chains that bind us.

With our backs bent under the whip of a slave driver, we hear the call—a call of hope. Our hearts thrill to hear our name called out. We stand up under the weight of the great burden on our shoulders. Then a gentle voice beckons us, again calling our name. He welcomes us into His loving arms, where we hear words we never dreamed possible: "I paid the price for your freedom. Come walk with me." He gives us a new name, His own name, and we are washed clean of our sin stained past that bound us.

> *For there is one God and one mediator between God and mankind, the man Christ Jesus, who gave himself as a ransom for all people.*
> (1 Timothy 2:5–6)

Our heavenly Father will not yield His glory to any other name. We can rest in knowing that He jealously guards all those who are called by His name. When we speak out in Jesus' name, we speak only what we hear Him speaking. As His holy priesthood we serve in submission to our High Priest, Jesus Christ.

All those who are baptized into Christ are called by His holy name. We are made witnesses of our Savior who shed His blood for the remission of our sin and the sins of the world. There is no other name in all the heavens and earth by which we can be redeemed from the weight of our sin and then cleansed from its stain

The Father's sons and daughters are called to speak in His name alone, and not by our own intuitions nor out of wishful thinking. In order to do this, we need to know the one true God; Father, Son, and Holy Spirit. We must see Christ in the fullness of His majesty.[15]

We can't dine at both the table of wickedness and the table of righteousness. We must not partake of the Bread of Life, drink from the Lord's cup, and then turn right around and eat the bread of wickedness and drink the wine of violence.[16] We have all failed to remain true to His name, but when we see our sin and turn from it, God is faithful to forgive us and cleanse us. He renews a right spirit in our hearts and restores the joy of our salvation.

We live in a celebrity culture where we trip over each other trying to get

---

15. Colossians 2:9.
16. Proverbs 4:17.

our names in lights. We're desperate to find our moment of fame. But the marquis ends up with a jumble of meaningless names; all in competition to be the next pop idol. We're quick to forget the Lord God who makes our name great. We must constantly remind ourselves by searching out the truths of Scripture so we can be mindful of our Lord Jesus who paid the price to buy our freedom, so we are now called by His holy name. We are a holy people who will be called by no other name.

> *Teach me your way, LORD, that I may rely on your faithfulness; give me an undivided heart, that I may fear your name.*
> (Psalm 86:11)

Chapter 22

No Other Name

Q & A

1. Why is submission to our High Priest so vital as we speak out in ministry?

___

2. What is it important to put aside our own intuitions and personal impressions and speak only by the leading of the Spirit, in Jesus' name?

___

3. We've all failed to speak only what we hear the Spirit speaking. Is there any hope for us?

___

4. How is it that our Lord God makes our name great?

___

My Journal Notes:

Part 5:
A Glorious House

"The glory of this present house will be greater than the glory of the former house," says the LORD *Almighty. "And in this place I will grant peace," declares the* LORD *Almighty.*

(Haggai 2:9)

23

Blessed Be the Name

Key Scriptures:

- "Then Job arose and tore his robe and shaved his head and fell on the ground and worshiped. And he said, 'Naked I came from my mother's womb, and naked shall I return. The LORD gave, and the LORD has taken away; blessed be the name of the LORD.'" (Job 1:20–21 ESV)

- "Though the fig tree does not bud and there are no grapes on the vines, though the olive crop fails and the fields produce no food, though there are no sheep in the pen and no cattle in the stalls, yet I will rejoice in the LORD, I will be joyful in God my Savior." (Habakkuk 3:17–18)

The first inspired book of the Bible, written approximately 1520 BC, is a narrative about an incredible and enduring faith in God our Redeemer. This kind of faith opens our eyes to see with an eternal perspective. We've all heard the cliché that proclaims: "The patience of Job." But in reality, that's a serious understatement. It took more than patience for him to remain strong through the searing pain of boils that covered his body from head to foot. We grieve with Job as we watch him scrape at his wounds with pieces of broken pottery while sitting in an ash heap.

In this study we are strengthened as we learn from Job who lived three seasons of life. First, he lived in prosperity under the Lord's protective covering. Then he endured what must have felt like an eternity of testing and trials of his faith. He was tested as he endured many months of loss and searing pain. Then in the later part of his life, he was restored with even greater blessings than at first. He enjoyed his children and grandchildren to the fourth generation.

In the first part of his life, Job focused on piety, fear of the Lord, generosity, and right living. The later part of his life didn't leave any of these important things behind, but the blinders came off so he could see the fullness of God through all His awesome works and dealings with humankind. In reality, Job's focus changed from a limited view of a temporal world to see greater revelation. He saw his Redeemer extend His hand and open his eyes to his eternal home.

Job is our teacher in this study. He helps us see the fallacy of the postmodern day Church that has banished the word adversity from our vocabulary. The Scriptures in this study open our understanding to the need we have for restraints on our lives. Indeed, adversity serves to open our eyes and redirect our footsteps.

> Study Prayer
>
> *Oh Lord, may our mouths be like wellsprings that overflow with blessing and praise for your holy name.*
>
> A prayer inspired by Psalm 119:171

Post-modern American Christians have banished the word "adversity" from our vocabulary. It's shunned like a four-letter curse. Hardships are only for the lowest-caste Christians in India, right? Isn't adversity meant for dissenters who fight to right society's wrongs? Too often we think misfortune is for "those people," not for worthy Christians. Our favorite sermons promise positive things like nice bank accounts and luxury SUVs in the garage of our McMansion. We enjoy hearing that God will prosper every job we apply our hands to, and please do not mention Job's name.

Consider how high fallible mortal beings might elevate themselves with their egotistical strivings if everything in life was smooth sailing. If no adversities existed to trip them up while they step on people on their climb up the ladder to success. Who could stop them? Without restraints, celebrity pastors might steal all the sheep from thousands of small hometown churches that serve local communities.

Human nature requires checks and balances. We're not very good at monitoring ourselves. We require safeguards and equalizers. Our tendency is to fudge a bit, offering ourselves an abundance of grace when examining our own words and actions. We're experts at minimizing the harm we've done while emphasizing others faults. We make excuses for our words and actions. After all, it's their fault, right?

Adversity serves a good purpose for imperfect Christians who live in a sin bent world. Caring for the weak and helpless brings us into God's kingdom realm of goodness and mercy. Raising up a child in Christ who is physically challenged fortifies us with an enduring strength. Suffering for the cause of Christ and the work of the cross helps us to stay true, having the mind of Christ, the heart of our Savior, and a servant's attitude like our Redeemer. Indeed, we ought to rejoice in suffering because it restrains us in our weaknesses and produces a great hope in us.[1]

---

1. Romans 5:3–5.

Shall we indeed accept good from God, and shall we not accept adversity? (Job 2:10 NKJV)

In life's darkest hours it's easy to slide into bitterness. Revenge is our default mode. But the purpose of adversity is not to make miserable people more miserable. Life's troubles serve a greater good than simply refilling that prescription of bitter pills we must swallow. Lingering in suffering does more than extend our days of misery. But it's so hard to see freedom on the other side of our troubles when we're drowning in a tsunami of trauma.

How does a child grow up who never experiences the adversity of discipline? Their family life turns into chaos, and their adult lives are roiled with turmoil. Our heavenly Father chastens those he loves. He makes us strong in our faith through adversity. His correction is like the North Winds that make an oak tree strong. Our loving Abba tests our faith, allowing troubles to come our way to prove our devotion to Him and show us how strong He has made us.

Don't sweep life's troubles under the rug. Embrace them! When the undercurrents of life try to sweep us off your feet and drown us; look up for redemption is near.[2] When piercing pain seers through our body, hold fast to the Promised One. He knows our pain. He has suffered even greater pain and sorrow to gain a mighty victory on our behalf. He is preparing a place for us where there is no pain, no more tears, no more sorrow.

Through adversity, temptations, testing, and trials our Lord God has strengthened us to "hold fast the confession of our hope without wavering, for He who promised is always faithful."[3] Through His faithfulness we are made into tried and tested stones for building a house for His holy name.

Why is light given to those in misery, and life to the bitter of soul, to those who long for death that does not come, who search for it more than for hidden treasure. (Job 3:20–21)

The weight of our sorrows is unbearable. We have no strength of our own to endure to the end. One by one our troubles and sorrows add weight to the scale until it feels like injustice tips against us and we're left devastated. In our deepest and darkest moments, we succumb to our weaknesses and groan out with sorrowful words we wish to take back.

Oh Lord, may the wellsprings of our hearts flow out with blessing and praise. Whether God gives or takes away, may the song of our heart be: "Blessed be the Name of the Lord." When life's sorrows overwhelm us, let our words speak out with good things. May we be refined, made like pure gold

---

2. Luke 21:28.
3. Hebrews 10:23.

and silver to be useful building stones for the kingdom of heaven. May we be the stones that cry out when distresses might try to silence us.

> *If only my anguish could be weighed and all my misery be placed on the scales! It would surely outweigh the sand of the seas—no wonder my words have been impetuous.*
> (Job 6:2–3)

A newborn baby comes into the world looking so beautiful and innocent. A new mother gasps with delight at the first sight of the life she now holds to feed at her breast. The special aromas of a newborn child are the fragrance of a miracle—the miracle of life. The ultimate delight is children who are born into a family of faith. They grow up in security and comfort, knowing they are dearly loved children in the family of God.

And yet we ought to be mindful that we bring a child into a fallen world. Because we live in a corrupted world, they are born into sin and in need of redemption. Parents of any two-year-old will tell you that children are self-centered terrorists in need a parent's loving discipline to guide and instruct them in the Lord.[4]

We are not born innocent. There will never be enough evidence for us to take our case before God our righteous Judge to prove our innocence. There is only one way for us to come before the Great I AM, and that is in Christ and in the covering of His righteousness. In His name, and by the power and promise of His name, we may come cleansed and blameless before our heavenly Father. Our Lord Jesus has given us a white stone with our new name inscribed on it and we hold it out as proof that we are blameless in Christ.[5] Through adversity of correction we see our need of Christ and in Him our hands are washed clean.[6] In Him we are declared innocent.

> *But how can mere mortals prove their innocence before God?*
> (Job 9:2)

In the throes of our agony, we cry out. "I'm crushed!" Storm waters swirl around us, determined to sweep us away. We can't catch our breath as we drown in our misery. Our own words condemn us. Because of our crushing pain we despise our life and yearn for that last breath to bring us into His comforting presence. The days on the calendar drag on and the dread of our suffering seems to go on forever.

In our distress we cry out for someone who will stand with us to strengthen us so we may endure. Is there anyone who will take these punishing blows in our stead? Will a Mediator speak up on our behalf? The wall that protects

---
4. Ephesians 6:4.
5. Revelation 2:17.
6. Psalm 24:4, James 4:8.

us is torn down; who will stand in the gap? Blessed be the name of the Lord. Our Father sent His only Son to take the battering on our behalf. He is our Advocate before the throne of grace.

> *If only there were someone to mediate between us, someone to bring us together, someone to remove God's rod from me, so that his terror would frighten me no more.*
> (Job 9:33–34)

Every mortal born on earth is given a special gift in the form of compulsions, weaknesses, inclinations, obsessions, or physical handicaps. Some must overcome a weakness for addictive behaviors. Others must overcome a family's bad reputation.

When our parents counted our fingers and toes they declared us flawless, but we are not born perfect. Indeed, each of us must overcome some personal obstacle during our lives. Each of these life hurdles are a special gift. Consider those who have overcome extreme personal challenges. They are the ones who live their lives displaying the greatest strength of character. When they are pummeled with life's storms, they are like the mighty oak tree that stands strong in the storm. When the road gets rough Gospel shoes step on the gas.

Powerful rulers rise up throughout the world's cycles of history. Many empires and their terrifying leaders attempted to destroy the weak and helpless that burdened them. Wicked motives drove their massacres. One sure reason for ridding themselves of the disadvantaged is that the weak are unable to serve their heads of state. They forget that serving people with physical and mental challenges provides us with a great gift: humility.

> *He humbles those who dwell on high, he lays the lofty city low; he levels it to the ground and casts it down to the dust. Feet trample it down–the feet of the oppressed, the footsteps of the poor.*
> (Isaiah 26:5–6)

In his sufferings Job cried out for an Advocate, a Mediator, and a Savior. With the searing pain of boils all over his body, he tried to find some relief by scraping at them with a potsherd. He listened to his friends accuse him of moral failings and he cried out for someone who would stand up for him. In his troubles his eyes were opened to see his need of a Redeemer. He looked ahead to see the cross of Jesus Christ and the power of His resurrection. His eyes opened to see the sacrifice the Savior made on his behalf.

> *Even now my witness is in heaven; my advocate is on high. My intercessor is my friend as my eyes pour out tears to God.*
> (Job 16:19–21)

With his eyes opened and his spirit enlightened, Job rose above his friend's accusative and dismissive platitudes and spoke some of the most powerful words any man ever spoke. He lifted up his eyes beyond his torn skin to see his Redeemer. At that moment he put his life in the Almighty's hands. He threw aside the broken pottery in his hand and rose up from the ash heap. In his broken condition he opened his mouth to declare a living and ever-present Savior. No matter his suffering in this wretched world, he stood before His God and Lord in the safety and covering of his Advocate and he looked forward to that day to come, saying, "Blessed be the Name of the Lord."

Job refused his wife's advice to curse God and die. Instead, Job stood shoulder to shoulder with Daniel's three friends; champions of faith who faced the fiery furnace and declared, "The God we serve is able to deliver us from it." And then without flinching they proclaimed their trust in the Almighty, saying "But even if He does not we will not serve your gods."[7] Shadrach, Meshach, and Abednego served as tried and tested building stones in the House we build for His holy name.

> *I know that my redeemer lives, and that in the end he will stand on the earth. And after my skin has been destroyed, yet in my flesh I will see God; I myself will see him with my own eyes–I, and not another. How my heart yearns within me!* (Job 19:25–27)

Will we put aside our pride so we can learn even from humble little plants that grow in our garden? Can we be taught if we refuse to listen to instructions from the four-legged furry friends God created? Do we stop and rest long enough to gain knowledge from the migrating birds and butterflies who neither sow nor reap? Is it possible for us to lower ourselves to listen to the earth beneath our feet to hear its teaching? Is there anything that the great salmon can teach us as we observe them fighting their way up a torrential waterfall?

Everything the Creator formed on earth by His Word is so beautifully and wonderfully made. Every newborn in the wild, whether elephant or giraffe, are wonders of creation. The puppy we cuddle with its eyes still closed, or a child taking her first breath; they are wonders of God's handiwork. As we observe the habits and ways of creatures living on the earth, we can learn of great wonders that reveal the breath of the Spirit that sustains all life on land and sea.

> *If it were his intention and he withdrew his spirit and breath, all humanity would perish together and mankind would return to the dust.* (Job 34:14–15)

---

7. Daniel 3:16–18.

In his early life, Job knew about his Maker but lived his life under a shroud. He couldn't see the full revelation of his Redeemer. His faith was strong, but untested. He was generous and spoke with words of healing and wisdom to his neighbors. He acknowledged his Creator on every path where he walked. No man on earth was more righteous than Job. But he was unrefined gold. He was like silver still tainted with earthy dross.

Three of his friends came to comfort him with wisdom inspired by their human reasoning. They spoke platitudes from their religious traditions. Their speeches went on and on forever, until the Almighty spoke and silenced their superfluous words. With a few words the God of their fathers destroyed all their earthbound wisdom. Their seemingly intelligent counsel fell apart; totally frustrated.[8]

My ears had heard of you but now my eyes have seen you.
(Job 42:5)

A tried and tested faith is an unshakeable faith. In times of trial we have to remind ourselves that life's troubles offer great benefits if we'll just hang in there. This refining process produces good character and instills a great hope in us. And this is an eternal hope with Christ Jesus' name as our guarantee. He will never disappoint us.

Listening to the drama created by the advice of Job's three friends is an arduous experience, because they offer the worst possible consolations along with implied accusations. While caught in the searing pain of his suffering, Job didn't get it all right either. But he longed for an Advocate. In the depth of his troubles, he presented evidence of his own righteous acts of service. Surely, he knew in his heart of hearts that he presented a weak case because he yearned for a Mediator who could stand in his stead. He got himself stuck in the rut of trusting in his own good deeds rather than entrusting his right-standing to God.

When the Almighty One spoke, Job heard the Words of His thunderous voice. His eyes opened and his ears finally heard the truth. He tried to stand in his own strength in an attempt to make his case before the Lord. Then God's thunderous voice made his knees buckle, humbling him, and opening his eyes to see the Creator's Glory, Power, and Righteousness.
The weight of Job's calamities and all his questions melted away and became of little consequence when the Almighty spoke. We, like Job, are called to live above and look beyond our own righteousness and bless the name of the Lord with exaltation and praise, because He is our righteousness. Through life's troubles we learn to overcome the weaknesses of the flesh and live in the righteousness of Jesus Christ, with our eyes focused on eternity.

---
8. 1 Corinthians 1:19.

People are like rose bushes, some with more thorns than others. If roses go untrimmed, they soon stop producing the prize rose blossoms that win awards at the country fair. Fallible humans on planet Earth are also like vines in a garden. A plant that doesn't get pruned goes wild and only produces a little fruit for the birds. Those who resist pruning might say, "I don't deserve this kind of painful discipline." But they rid themselves of the Lord's beneficial refining work. It's easy to forget that our own righteousness needs to be put aside so we can produce the abundant fruit of His righteousness.

Throughout the world's history there are many kings, presidents, and rulers who have risen up and exalted themselves. But before long they're overthrown. A nation's leaders, like all people, must be trimmed down to size throughout the course of time. Leaders and bureaucrats, great and small, tend to consolidate their realm of power and influence. They take great pride as they observe their great works and say: "Look what I have built by my mighty power and for the glory of my majesty."[9] But their arrogance leads to their downfall.

> *All the trees of the forest will know that I the L<small>ORD</small> bring down the tall tree and make the low tree grow tall. I dry up the green tree and make the dry tree flourish. "I the L<small>ORD</small> have spoken, and I will do it."*
> (Ezekiel 17:24)

When it comes to building a house for the most holy name ever lifted up, we cannot build this house by means of our own strength or our own righteousness. The walls of the house built with our own sacred stones will collapse around us.[10] There's a big difference between knowing *about* the need for building a solid house and gaining first-hand knowledge that is applicable to actually building that house. Job lived many years of his life knowing about God and he honored his Lord with his good life. But it wasn't until he finally heard the Word of the Lord speak that his eyes opened to truly know the One true God in all His glory and majesty.

Job's righteousness wasn't sufficient, but his heart was still teachable. He pleaded with God, "Teach me what I cannot see."[11] He needed an Advocate, a Mediator who would come in righteousness far above his own. He knew about this Redeemer and after hearing God speak, Job could truly look forward to see his Savior who would stand with him as he came before the Father to declare, "I see my Redeemer who lives."

---

9. Daniel 4:30.
10. Isaiah 30:12–14, Hosea 10:2.
11. Job 34:32.

As a tried and tested stone, Job lived the later part of his life as a solid builder for an eternal house. He lived to see for four generations of his family become house builders for the name of the Lord.

Chapter 23

Blessed Be the Name

Q & A

1. Why is the word adversity significant in a Christian's life today?

___

___

___

2. What is the good result of testing and trials in our walk of faith?

___

___

___

3. Why is serving the weak and poor such a vital part of being a faithful servant?

___

___

___

4. How does overcoming life's unique obstacles serve to strengthen our character?

___

___

___

My Journal Notes:

Restoring the Temple

Key Scriptures:

- "If my people, who are called by my name, will humble themselves and pray and seek my face and turn from their wicked ways, then I will hear from heaven, and I will forgive their sin and will heal their land. Now my eyes will be open and my ears attentive to the prayers offered in this place." (2 Chronicles 7:14–15)

- "There are many dwelling places in my Father's house. Otherwise, I would have told you, because I am going away to make ready a place for you." (John 14:2 NET)

In this study we will take a comprehensive view of the Scripture that teaches us: "By His stripes we are healed."[1] Under the old covenant, Israel served as the Church of their day. But they were not faithful to their covenant and the walls they built crumbled into ruin. Then God took away the delight of their eyes.[2] But at just the right time, a Savior came as light in a valley of darkness. He came to a Church in ruins. To redeem His people, He gave His body to be broken so that His body, the Church, could be made whole. In a revived Church, there is healing for body, soul, and spirit. All those who are in Christ and in His body, the Church, can be made entirely whole.

One often quoted Scripture in evangelical Church circles is 2 Chronicles 7:14–15 that calls God's people to humble themselves, pray, seek His face, and to turn from sin. We speak it out boldly as if we would humble ourselves and turn away from our own pathway. But what we really mean is that the other churches need to get humble and repent because they're not doing church the right way, like we do. We often proclaim this Scripture as a call to repentance for "those other sinners" who despoil this nation. But what about our own sin?

In reality, it's rare for churches of any denomination to fully worship in spirit and truth. Our worship is too often clouded by rules taught by men.[3] But

---
1. 1 Peter 2:24 NKJV.
2. Ezekiel 24:25.
3. Isaiah 29:13, Matthew 15:9.

how do we get out of this trap when few of us have known a church that enters into the fullness of Christ? Will we allow the Holy Spirit to lead us into worship that is spiritual and real? Will we allow the Holy Spirit to lead us to separate what is holy from what is common?[4] This lesson encourages us to apply ourselves to the work of restoration. This truth is crucial because the house we build is for our Father's holy name. What we build exalts Him in high honor.

> Study Prayer
>
> *Father, strengthen your sons and daughters*
> *so we may do the work of rebuilding the house for your holy name.*
>
> A prayer inspired by Nehemiah 6:9

A troop of Assyrian invaders stormed out to plunder Israel. They left a trail of heart-breaking trauma in every town they raided. A young girl, playing peacefully with her little friends, was suddenly grabbed by the nape of her neck, bound with a rope, and dragged barefoot on the long road back to Aram. She never saw her home, family, or friends again. Naaman forced this little girl into the service of his wife. But the bitter turn in this young girl's life could not destroy her faith. When her master, Naaman, suffered from leprosy, she said to her mistress, "If only my master would see the prophet who is in Samaria! He would cure him of his leprosy."[5]

This little girl from the Northern tribes had a supersized faith in the God of Israel. Even when subjected to servitude in a foreign land, by faith she spoke up to proclaim God who heals. As a lone remnant from God's people, she stood up strong. We don't know her name, but her words and actions still set her apart as a hero of our faith.

Ezra and Nehemiah also had this kind of faith. When they heard the word of the Lord they knew it was time to rebuild Jerusalem and the temple. They gathered a remnant who had a little girl's kind of faith. Ezra, Nehemiah, and a company of willing people left Babylon behind and returned to their promised homeland. The devastation of Jerusalem's overthrow, seventy years before, left behind heaps of ruin because their ancestors had built with malice and bloodshed.[6] But out of this rubble the remnant rebuilt the city and the temple for God's holy name. The work of their hands was beautiful to behold. Indeed, the scorched earth blossomed with new life. With the burden of past sins lifted, their guilt forever washed away, this mighty remnant worked in joy of the Lord's presence. All they needed was a "little girl" kind of faith.

---

4. For an explanation separating holy from common see index, page 257. The author's book, *Great Separations*, offers an in-depth study on this topic.
5. 2 Kings 5:2–3.
6. Micah 3:9–10.

> LORD, *the God of Israel, you are righteous! We are left this day as a remnant. Here we are before you in our guilt, though because of it not one of us can stand in your presence.*
> (Ezra 9:15)

Because of Judah's constant rebellion and sin they were conquered and forced into exile for seventy years. Jerusalem and the temple laid in the ruins of fire and smoke tarnished stonework lay heaped in disheveled mounds. But in the piles of broken stones they found great hope, because the Almighty's purpose in judgment is always to restore to what is right and good. As fallible beings, we take great hope in this because we know that our heavenly Father is ready to forgive repentant hearts. He is quick to restore our right-standing before Him.[7] God disciplines those He loves so that we may rebuild His house on the Rock with refined precious stones.[8]

What happened to the Jewish people thousands of years ago may seem remote to modern day people. But the reality is that human nature hasn't changed. We are still fallible people who need the Almighty's loving discipline. His correction serves to restrain further sin.[9] When we slip up and trip up in our walk with the Lord, we require correction, forgiveness, and restoration. We need to be brought back to the right path so we can rebuild from the ruins of our sin.

> *He has granted us new life to rebuild the house of our God and repair its ruins, and he has given us a wall of protection.*
> (Ezra 9:9)

When surveying the mountainous piles of our life's ruins our knees get weak and we slump down into the slag pile and ashes. We have no strength of our own for the task that confronts us. Our hands are soiled with soot. Our faces streaked with the ashen tears of our past failures. We sink down as if melding in with the rubble.

But there is One who is mighty to save. We have a Redeemer whose arm is strong. He reaches down into the debris, takes us into His loving, nail scarred hands, and He sets us on our feet. He heard our weak cry for help as we collapsed into defeat. He never left us and He's close by to hear our penitent plea. Our weaknesses overwhelm us. Only in the Spirit of Christ can we find strength for the task of rebuilding. In the joy of the Lord we find the power to tackle the task of rebuilding a house for His holy name.

---

7. Isaiah 1:26–27.
8. Proverbs 3:11–12.
9. Psalm 76:10, Daniel 9:24.

> *Surely the arm of the LORD is not too short to save, nor his ear too dull to hear.*
> (Isaiah 59:1)

Before time began the Creator of all heaven and earth knew your name. His eyes looked upon you as He orchested every detail that led up to your birth and life. You answered His call and came to saving faith, as He knew you would, and He is ever-present with you to watch over you and protect you. He is so close to you that He can hear the slightest whimper of fear, every painful moan from your body, and every sigh of despair. He knows the nightmares that trouble your sleep. Our heavenly Father sees every tear and knows every sorrow of all those who are called by His holy name.

> *For the eyes of the Lord are on the righteous and his ears are attentive to their prayer, but the face of the Lord is against those who do evil.*
> (1 Peter 3:12)

It's important to remind ourselves that people of faith are still fallible. It seems like our neighbors who have never stepped foot in church have the nicest cars, boats, quads, and camper trailers. All our friends on social media are enjoying luxury vacations while we feel lucky to fill our tank at the gas station without maxing out our credit card. Before long we are tempted with feelings that God just isn't enough for us.

It's so easy to compromise just a little so we can grab a bit of the glitter and glamor the world offers. We make a bargain with life's dark side so we can gather the good things this life has to offer. We're quick to forget that in doing so we let go of greater things that build for eternity. But God is faithful even when we are not. He seeks out His wandering sheep. The Good Shepherd searches for those who get lost along the way. He brings us back, forgives us, cleanses us, and heals our wounds. Then He restores us to the work prepared for us—even restoring the years our sin has devoured.[10] When we get back on track, forgiven and cleansed, our heavenly Father once again blesses us with a job so we can do our part in building a house, a temple for His holy name.

> *"Return, faithless people; I will cure you of backsliding." "Yes, we will come to you, for you are the LORD our God."*
> (Jeremiah 3:22)

The following verse brings to mind a picture of the Almighty observing the ruin of our lives. We caused the destruction, but our Father looks upon us with abundant mercy. He is a loving Father who constantly looks far down the road, yearning for us to return home. In His love, He sends the Good

---
10. Joel 2:25.

Shepherd to reach out to us even in our wandering ways. The Father longs for us to come back into the sweet fellowship with Him in His Church.

Our Lord and Savior is more than able to lead us home where we find restoration, comfort, a refreshed joy in our Salvation, and new strength to continue the work we have been given to accomplish. Once again, we are cleaned up and refined so that we can be a precious building stone in this eternal house, just as God planned from the beginning.

> *"I have seen what they do, but I will heal them anyway! I will lead them. I will comfort those who mourn, bringing words of praise to their lips. May they have abundant peace, both near and far," says the* LORD, *who heals them.*
> (Isaiah 57:18–19)

Try to imagine the scene that took place in every family tent as Israel camped near Mount Sinai. Every family member got involved as they excitedly prepared for the next day. After supper Mom rummaged through their baggage and exclaimed: "Oh, look at this. The craftsmen can surely use this jewelry for the temple." And then in the morning thousands of people lined up to deliver their treasures to the workers for the Tent of the Congregation. They held out their hands offering gold chains and valuables, saying, "Can you use this to make the candlesticks for the temple?" A daughter from the tribe of Benjamin asked, "Can you use this precious metal to make the gold filigree to mount the jewels in the priest's breastplate?" The next person in line eagerly holds out his offering: "This is the finest linen. Can you use it for the priest's robes?"

Their zeal went viral. They couldn't do enough or give enough goods for building the temple; the house where God would dwell among them. The Egyptians had given them many valuables in the days before they marched away from their slavery in Egypt. Now the freed slaves offered the plunder for building a house of worship.

> *They received from Moses all the offerings the Israelites had brought to carry out the work of constructing the sanctuary. And the people continued to bring freewill offerings morning after morning. So all the skilled workers who were doing all the work on the sanctuary left what they were doing and said to Moses, "The people are bringing more than enough for doing the work the* LORD *commanded to be done." Then Moses gave an order and they sent this word throughout the camp: "No man or woman is to make anything else as an offering for the sanctuary." And so the people were restrained from bringing more, because what they already had was more than enough to do all the work.*
> (Exodus 36:3–7)

When you skip a stone across the water, what happens when momentum no longer propels the rock? It sinks to the bottom, and you'll never find that stone again. Your heavenly Father's name reveals to you a God who overflows with tender mercies. Your Lord and Savior knows your weaknesses and advocates for you before the Father. When you admit your weaknesses, failings, and sin He is faithful and just to forgive your sin and separate you from the wrong you have done. Jesus tramples that sin under His feet. It's removed from us, like that rock that sinks into the deep. The Father gives you His name and takes away your disgrace.

Now forgiven, cleansed, healed, and restored you are made a pillar in God's house.[11] You are ready to do your part in rebuilding the house of the congregation; the house of prayer, praise, and worship. In His name you are strengthened and restored. You're safe in His sanctuary where you come to worship in a way that is spiritual and real.

> *You will again have compassion on us; you will tread our sins underfoot and hurl all our iniquities into the depths of the sea.*
> (Micah 7:19)

Think about the most pleasant hiking path you've ever enjoyed. You walk through the dense alpine trees enjoying the mixed scents the forest brings your way on gentle mountain breezes. You pick a few huckleberries for a quick morning snack. The crisp, clear air chills as you make your ascent to the summit where you can stand on the highest rock to see all around you for many miles. The elk bugles, the coyotes howl, and squirrels scurry about. You've discovered a delightful path to follow.

But there is a more pleasant way to walk that is eternally satisfying. It's the way of uprightness, and justice where the wind of the Spirit blows. This trek is the way of love, peace, comfort, joy, and strength. This narrow road is the way of life, liberty, freedom, and saving grace. And best of all, at the end of this life's pathway your portion awaits you—the wealth of heaven is stored up for you. They are beyond what you can even imagine,

> *I walk in the way of righteousness, along the paths of justice, bestowing a rich inheritance on those who love me and making their treasuries full.*
> (Proverbs 8:20–21)

By His stripes we are healed. By His suffering the Church is restored and made whole. We are the body of Christ and His house is revived in contrite hearts. The healing begins with repentance that prepares our hearts to partake of Christ as we come to the Lord's Table. We come to receive the bread.

---

11. Revelation 3:12.

Indeed, His body was broken so that we might be made whole; a unified body that works in harmony with Christ as its Head. We are made whole as we partake of Christ at His Table that He has prepared for us. We are forgiven so that we might be healed and restored to a healthy, fully functioning body. In His body, the Church, we are made complete as functioning parts of the whole.

The houses of Judah, Simeon, and Benjamin were joined together with Manasseh, Ephraim, Dan, Rueben, Gad, Zebulun, Naphtali, Asher, and Issachar. They were one—living stones on the High Priest's breastplate. Today we are the rocks that cry out with praise. Each generation of sons and daughters are made into refined building stones of the house for our Father's holy name. We are one house joined together like two sticks made into one.[12] The houses of the Smiths, Jones, Müllers, Rodriguez, Jungs, Diaminis, and Melnyks build one house for the name of the Almighty. Each generation builds upon the last until every nation has heard the Good News Gospel and this house of prayer and praise is restored and complete.[13]

> *All you Israelites, praise the LORD; house of Aaron, praise the LORD; house of Levi, praise the LORD; you who fear him, praise the LORD. Praise be to the LORD from Zion, to him who dwells in Jerusalem. Praise the LORD.* (Psalm 135:19–21)

All truth is established on the foundations of creation. As we take a walk through Bible history we see Noah the preacher, we observe Abraham in his faithfulness, and then watch as Israel is established as a holy nation with its ritual requirements and feasts. The histories of our faith all point the way forward to Christ. The sacrifices and feasts point the way to a Savior. Those who commemorate ancient Hebrew festivals must be constantly vigilant to be sure they don't go backwards into a lesser covenant. Instead, they must go forward to exalt Christ who is revealed in the celebrations. This warning is necessary because human nature leads us into depending on doing things just right because our own efforts are more self-satisfying. We like being in control.

Steadfast workers under the Old Covenant built a house for God's holy name. The faithful who came before us left behind a great legacy to build on. We don't go back to reconstruct a house built in Christ's shadow. Instead, we abide with Christ in a house that is part of a new and better covenant. We have come out of the shadow and live in the reality of Christ.

Will you build your part of the wall with unproven sandstone that crumbles into ruin and is left for future generations to rebuild? Or will you

---

12. Ezekiel 37:17.
13. Matthew 24:14.

embrace Christ, by whose stripes the Church is healed, and then build with precious, refined building stones?

> *When they see among them their children, the work of my hands, they will keep my name holy; they will acknowledge the holiness of the Holy One of Jacob, and will stand in awe of the God of Israel.*
> (Isaiah 29:23)

The faith of a little child, even in the midst of tragic circumstances, is strong enough to begin a good work of healing and restoration. Ezra and Nehemiah stood strong in a child-like faith while in exile in a foreign land. They gathered a remnant of God's people and set out to accomplish the impossible task of rebuilding Jerusalem and its temple.

The Israelites had suffered the consequences of their unrepentant and hardened hearts for seventy years. Then, with the consequences of their sin paid in full measure, they set out to rebuild what their rebellion had left in ruins. We too, like them, can rise up from the rubble of our sin and depravity. As forgiven and cleansed sons and daughters we find strength in Christ to tackle the task of building and rebuilding.

In Christ we can put the past behind us. The years of our wandering ways are forgotten because God is faithful to His promises. Our heavenly Father waits for us to come home. He constantly looks down the road for us to return from our rebellious ways. The Good Shepherd goes out to search for us and He celebrates our return with heaven's angels.

By Jesus' stripes we are healed. This means flesh and blood people are healed of sin's sickness and bodily infirmities. The people healed by Jesus' stripes are welcomed into the Church. We, the Church, are restored and made whole by His suffering, death, and resurrection. Now we are all made a part in the body of Christ. We are made whole in His Church. Christ Jesus makes us new creations to serve as healthy and strong, fully functioning parts of the body, His Church. Each generation of His sons and daughters are made parts in His healed and restored Church so that we may build with precious stones until the house is complete.

Will you come with a contrite heart to be forgiven and healed so that you may enter into this good work of building a house for God's holy name?

Chapter 24

Restoring the Temple

Q & A

1. How much faith do we need to begin the work of rebuilding the house for our Father's holy name?

   _____
   _____
   _____

2. Where does the work of restoration begin?

   _____
   _____
   _____

3. Describe our Father as He waits for us to return from our wandering ways.

   _____
   _____
   _____

4. How is the Church restored and made whole?

   _____
   _____
   _____

5. What are the building materials for the house we build for God's holy name?

   _____
   _____
   _____

My Journal Notes:

25

A Redemptive Name

Key Scriptures:

- "For your Maker is your husband—the LORD Almighty is his name—the Holy One of Israel is your Redeemer; he is called the God of all the earth." (Isaiah 54:5)

- "But these are written that you may believe that Jesus is the Messiah, the Son of God, and that by believing you may have life in his name." (John 20:31)

If you grew up in a family that moved away every time you started to put down roots and make new friends, it becomes a major challenge to get back that feeling of belonging; a sense of home. But for those who are in Christ, home is where your Father dwells. The table where you feast on Christ is your dwelling place.

Our heavenly Father's desire is for you to dwell in His house forever. In this study you'll come to know God's nurturing nature and His heart that reaches out to be a Father to the fatherless. Because of His love for family, He places the lonely in a house and home with a mom, dad, brothers, or sisters, and even more important, our heavenly Father brings us into His eternal family. In this family, your life is changed forever.

We'll learn that when a child is born into a family to carry on the family name, there is cause for celebration. Even more so, when a child is born into our Father's house, a child who will carry on His holy name, the angels in heaven rejoice. The teaching in this lesson is an inspiration for the learner to serve with the faith of an adopted child and carry the Redeemer's name to the far reaches of the Earth, starting in your own home.

As you meditate on the following Scriptures, you'll come to see that even the worst of us are offered redemption in Jesus Christ. He cleans us up, gives us new garments, and brings us to rest in our new home.

> ## Study Prayer
>
> *Heavenly Father, we come to you as living stones being built into a spiritual house. Redeem us to serve as a holy priesthood, offering spiritual sacrifices acceptable to you through Jesus Christ.*
>
> A prayer inspired by 1 Peter 2:5

Have your spiritual roots been yanked up and left to wither and dry out in the scorching sun? Do you have a sense of everyone turning their backs on you and leaving you behind? Do you feel like a scorned child, spurned by his own father and mother?[1] If feelings of rejection hold you in their grip, take hope! There is the One who will never leave you nor forsake you.[2] Your God is a Father to the fatherless and protector of widows.[3] He nurtures when a mother cannot. He settles the lonely in families.[4] He is Provider even when there is great want. We have a guarantee of these great promises and it is written in His name: "Redeemer."

God's provision and redemption are greater than your everyday needs. He is Provider and Savior to all who will call on His name from today and into all eternity.[5] He supplies your personal needs today and places an even higher priority on your eternal destiny. His greatest desire is for you to dwell in His house with Him forever. Yes, your eternal destiny is more important than any material thing here on earth. Your Bridegroom, Jesus Christ, is preparing a place for you to abide with Him forever. Keep in mind that having a forever place is more important than a McMansion on a cul-de-sac today. Remember that even Abraham, the forerunner of your redemptive faith, failed at times. But God is faithful even when you are not. Hold onto that sure promise and continue to abide in this house you build for His holy name: "Redeemer."

> *But you are our Father, though Abraham does not know us or Israel acknowledge us; you, LORD, are our Father, our Redeemer from of old is your name.* (Isaiah 63:16 ESV)

When a first child or grandchild is born to carry on the family name the celebrations are joyful and festive. This occasion is better than any New Year celebration. Our festivities begin with a child's first breath and get more elaborate with every birthday party from one to eighteen. By the time the child turns twenty-one we start to settle down and just add candles to the cake.

---

1. Isaiah 49:15.
2. Deuteronomy 31:8, Psalm 27:10.
3. Psalm 68:5.
4. Psalm 68:6
5. Romans 10:13.

Consider the angels as they celebrated the birth of Jesus our Savior. A host of angels encompassed the shepherd priests who watched over the temple's sacrificial lambs through the night. Heaven's chorus sang out: "Glory to God in the highest heaven, and on earth peace to those on whom his favor rests."[6] The shepherds surely sang with them because a Savior was born to take away the sins of the world. The Redeemer came down to earth to be the Light of the World. Indeed, He is Immanuel who is God with us. We can sing with the angels because our Redeemer is the firstborn of all creation. We rejoice in our Savior, singing with heaven's choir as we gather on the first day of every week—the day of new beginnings.

She will give birth to a son, and you are to give him the name Jesus, because he will save his people from their sins.
(Matthew 1:21)

All established nations send ambassadors to every other nation on earth to promote their agendas and advocate for their interests. The kingdom of heaven is the greatest of all realms and it sends out representatives to every tribe and nation to proclaim the Good News message of redemption.[7] This is our calling as Christians. Some of us are sent out as disciples to venture out as far as the local school bus garage where we serve as a witness to other mechanics. Others are called to go as kingdom representatives and live the Gospel before carpenters and masons at a building site. A few serve to exemplify the Gospel for their fellow teachers at school. The most daring ambassadors may be sent to minister God's words of saving grace to native tribes who are hidden in mountainous jungles.

When we are sent as ambassadors, we go in the authority of The Name. The words we proclaim are empowered by the Spirit of Christ. Our ambassador credentials give us authority to baptize all those who come to saving faith into the name of the Father, Son, and Holy Spirit. Jesus' command authorizes us to go out with boldness and do the work of the kingdom of heaven as God's royal envoys.

Therefore go and make disciples of all nations, baptizing them in the name of the Father and of the Son and of the Holy Spirit.
(Matthew 28:19)

It's unlikely that anyone would attempt to represent their country without proper credentials. With officially signed and stamped documents your words carry the full weight of the nation behind you as you speak on behalf of the country you represent.

---

6. Luke 2:14.
7. 2 Corinthians 5:20.

Ambassadors sent out from the kingdom of heaven can't go without proper authority or sufficient resources. We must not attempt the work by our own means, because our strength is inadequate for the job. Jesus' teaching shows us the way to step out boldly in the power of His name. By the anointing, gifting, and empowering work of the Holy Spirit, God is more than able to use even the weakest of us to accomplish the work of the Great Commission.

> *He told them, "This is what is written: The Messiah will suffer and rise from the dead on the third day, and repentance for the forgiveness of sins will be preached in his name to all nations, beginning at Jerusalem. You are witnesses of these things. I am going to send you what my Father has promised; but stay in the city until you have been clothed with power from on high."*
> (Luke 24:46–49)

When the crowds heard Peter's powerful anointed proclamation of Jesus who they crucified and who rose up in resurrection power, the throngs who gathered in Jerusalem felt "cut to the heart." As if with one voice the people cried out in despair, "What shall we do?"[8] This desperate question revealed their repentant hearts and their deep-felt need of Christ who offered forgiveness and cleansing from their sins. Even those who stood in the mob before Pontius Pilate screaming out, "Crucify, crucify," were offered forgiveness. The temple soldiers who arrested Jesus in the garden could be forgiven in Jesus' name. Mercy and forgiveness were offered to the guards at Jesus' tomb who accepted bribes to lie about Jesus' resurrection.

Then in the waters of baptism repentant sinners became one with Christ and His body the Church. Each one received the indwelling Holy Spirit. Now, stand back and review this awesome scene. The people came running when they heard an incredible rush of wind. They came in ignorance of their sinful condition. They heard Peter speak to them about their hardened hearts. They listened to the truth of the Gospel and cried out for someone to save them from their wretched condition. Over three thousand men and their families obeyed the Gospel's call, came to saving faith, and were baptized into Christ. Each one was given a new name, a family name that made them part of the eternal kingdom of heaven.

> *Peter replied, "Repent and be baptized, every one of you, in the name of Jesus Christ for the forgiveness of your sins. And you will receive the gift of the Holy Spirit."*
> (Acts 2:38)

Looking at our past lives from a spiritual perspective we see that we were brought to Christ all messed up and covered with the world's filth. Our lives

---
8. Acts 2:37.

were stained with sin's corruption, and (spiritually speaking) we looked like someone who had been rolling around in a coal bin. We smelled like we had been wallowing in a pig pen. But we came with a repentant heart because the Spirit planted the seed of faith in our hearts.

Now it's time to start serving as sons and daughters of the Most High God who keeps our hearts separate from the world. We submit to the Father's melting and molding to make us useful vessels.[9] In Bible terms this is called sanctification. Our heart, soul, and spirit are made useful in the kingdom of heaven. In Christ we get a complete makeover that has nothing to do with new clothes, a new hairstyle, or makeup. Indeed, we are made new creations in Christ and then shaped into usable vessels. We were once defiled and filthy, but by faith in Jesus Christ we are made new. By the power of the Word we are washed in the waters of baptism, forgiven and raised up in resurrection power. By the teaching of the Word we come into agreement with the holy Scriptures so that we may live in keeping with God's precepts. Now that we are one with our Lord Jesus Christ we come before the Father justified. We can enter through the gates to the Father's house with thanksgiving and come before Him in His courts with praise.[10]

> *And that is what some of you were. But you were washed, you were sanctified, you were justified in the name of the Lord Jesus Christ and by the Spirit of our God.*
> (1 Corinthians 6:11)

In the beginning Creator God set in place a strong foundation for all good things that were to come on planet Earth and in the heavens above. He established the laws of science and nature. The Almighty provided the Rock as a foundation for good governance of nations, societies, communities, and commerce. As the Word spoke creation into being He established righteousness, justice, and mercy as the touchstones of His sovereign rule.[11] He provided precepts to show us how to live and prosper in this bountiful creation. The Father welcomes us into His rest to honor His creation. With the Creator's rest established as a foundation; laborers, working animals, and the farmland are given time to be refreshed. He set all these good things in place for our benefit and for His glory and honor of His name.

The foundations our Father set in place make a lot of people angry today. In the third chapter of Genesis, Adam and Eve defied what God established. Too often, the Creator's foundation wasn't good enough for people to build on, so they built on sand instead. God provided a natural world that abounds

---

9. Isaiah 64:8.
10. Psalm 100:4.
11. Psalm 89:14.

with crops to feed the hungry, but instead of honoring the Creator we turn away to idolize nature. Then our idolatry turns against us and we come to fear that nature is going to destroy us.

And yet there is great hope for those who will exalt the God of creation and build on the foundations of His creation. The house we build for His holy name overflows with favor for all who are redeemed by the blood of the Lamb of God.

> *The nations were angry, and your wrath has come. The time has come for judging the dead, and for rewarding your servants the prophets and your people who revere your name, both great and small–and for destroying those who destroy the earth.*
> (Revelation 11:18)

If you feel like a 5th wheel on a 4-wheel drive ATV, there is great hope for you. Do feelings of rejection weigh you down? Are you feeling like your spiritual roots have been yanked up and they're wilting in the hot sun? Our Father's promises are greater than the rejection you suffer. His name is more than sufficient to cover you and carry you back home from every setback and wrong path.

You can rejoice because you have a Redeemer who came to pay the debt of your sin with His blood that He shed on a cruel Roman cross. His blood is sufficient, continuing to save all who will answer His call even today. Right now, you can answer as He calls out your name. Come and stand with Mary, mother of Jesus, who proclaimed in prophetic song, "My soul exalts the Lord, and my spirit has rejoiced in God my Savior."[12]

As redeemed souls who get molded into useful vessels, we are sent as ambassadors to represent our Redeemer. This work starts close to home.[13] Now, with the proper credentials and the anointing, gifting, and empowering of the Holy Spirit, we can minister in the spirit to accomplish the work of the Great Commission.

On the day of Pentecost, Peter spoke to the crowds in Jerusalem as a witness of Christ's forgiveness. Jesus forgave and restored him after denying Him three times. Peter proclaimed forgiveness to those who arrested Jesus, to those who pressed a crown of thorns on His head, and to those who drove the nails in His hands. Peter's words still ring true and there is forgiveness and redemption for your sins, so that even the shame and stain of your sins are cleansed away.

All redeemed sons and daughters are molded and shaped into useful vessels, worthy vessels for the work of the Great Commission. He is the Potter

---
12. Luke 1:46–47 NASB.
13. Acts 1:8.

and we are the clay that He makes into beautiful and precious building stones for building the house for our Father's holy name.

Chapter 25

A Redemptive Name

Q & A

1. Your needs are greater than your resources. Who, then, will be your source?

2. What does Mary's prophetic song teach us about our Redeemer?

3. What is the significance of being sent as ambassadors in Jesus' name?

4. Describe the wonders of Christ's redemption even for those who have done great harm.

My Journal Notes:

26

A House Built True to Plan

Key Scriptures:

- "By wisdom a house is built, and through understanding it is established; through knowledge its rooms are filled with rare and beautiful treasures. (Proverbs 24:3–4)

- For in Scripture it says: "See, I lay a stone in Zion, a chosen and precious cornerstone, and the one who trusts in him will never be put to shame." (1 Peter 2:6)

Doing the job right the first time gives a builder great satisfaction. That kind of success is only possible because the Master Builder and His crew are intimately familiar with every page of the plans. No detail of the design has been overlooked and the house is beautifully constructed as a result. This study rolls out the blueprint for a house that we will build according to plan. This safe and secure shelter is prepared for all who will come to dwell there.

Remember when you started planning your house, drawing on a napkin on your date night out; you kept in mind that the kitchen and bathrooms needed to be separated. The kid's play room wouldn't be compatible with dad and mom's office space and library. Your growing boys and girls needed separate bedrooms.

When you see the beauty and functionality of your new house, you're ashamed of the drafty old one-room shack you lived in. You won't have to take a bath in a tin tub by the kitchen stove any more. A house that brings the family together under one roof with the necessary separations is an awesome house for a family to enjoy.

We'll learn that the house we build for our Father's holy name is designed so that what is holy is kept separate from what is common. When we see the plan for this house, we see a dwelling place that keeps things in the right place. When our eyes are opened to understand the beauty and functions of this house, the old way of doing things, our own way of worshiping, brings us to shame.

> **Study Prayer**
>
> *Father in heaven, hear our penitent prayer. Open our eyes to see the desolation we have caused by building in our own strength and by our own abilities. Bring our hearts to repentance, forgive us, cleanse us, and then strengthen us so that we may build what is true and right. We present our petition before you because You, O Lord, are righteous, just, and merciful.*
>
> A prayer inspired by Daniel 9:18

There's great satisfaction in a job well done. When the building inspector comes to check, he rolls out the blueprint, and then looks around to be sure everything is according to code. You bask in the confidence of receiving a pass because there is an imprint of every notation, line, and angle on the plan fixed in your mind and you know every inch is built right. As the inspection proceeds, you're certain that the foundation is up to standard, the hurricane straps are secure, and the roof will carry the weight of the tile. Everything is according to spec.

The inspector's permit to occupy is an important step. With his approval, we can move in and enjoy the excitement of our new home. Our house has many rooms for each family member to enjoy their space. Every good home provides necessary separations while bringing the family all together under one roof.

The house we build in the kingdom realm is an eternal house and must be constructed according to God's perfect plan. We built stone upon precious stone on the Rock who is Christ Jesus. When the Master Builder comes to measure the work we've done, it must be according to His design and measure up to the standard of His measuring rod. This house is strong and secure. A house built to plan brings us together as God's children. It is carefully built so that all that is holy is kept separate from what is common.

Israel's Rechabite tribe offers us an example. They served as workers for constructing an eternally strong house. They promised to be loyal to their ancestor's vow to never build brick and stone houses, they planted no crops in fields, and never drank wine or beer. Instead, they lived in tents and built a strong spiritual house.

Jeremiah was instructed to test the descendants of Rechab by offering them wine in a room of the temple. But they would not yield to the temptation even from a prophet sent by the God of Abraham. Generation after generation they stayed true to their ancestor's vow. Their families lived in temporary dwellings. The Rechabites, by staying true to their vows, contributed in a mighty way to building a house for God's holy name. They remained truly separated to a holy God for the work of the temple.

By means of true instruction and knowledge of God we are strengthened to build a holy temple. This sanctuary provides a holy dwelling place for God's name. The temple we build is a spiritual house—a mighty fortress. We live in a tent that is our mortal body, while we build an eternal house where the shekinah glory of the Lord may dwell. In this house all those who are cleansed by the Blood of the Lamb, washed in the waters of baptism, cleansed by the fire of the Spirit dwell in peace. We lift up holy hands in prayer and every petition is heard in heaven and treasured as incense in golden bowls. The holy Scriptures reveal God's plan, teaching us to place stone upon stone to build a house for the honor and glory of His holy name.

> *For it is precept upon precept, precept upon precept, line upon line, line upon line, here a little, there a little.*
> (Isaiah 28:10 ESV)

David commissioned King Solomon to build a house for God's holy name. He used large quarried stones, skillfully chiseled rock for the pillars and capitals, and great timbers from Lebanon; all according to God's plan. With the approved materials he built a house for God's holy name. We, the church, are commissioned to build a house for our heavenly Father's holy name with refined precious, living stones. Today, as we put our hands to the work of building, it's important for us to understand the design and purpose of this dwelling place.

Solomon's inspired prayer of dedication for the temple offers us a complete picture of all that God intends for the spiritual house we build. This is a house of promise. Our Lord God promises that His name will always be there to cover His gathered sons and daughters. Our Lord and Savior is present with us in this dwelling. The house we build for His holy name is a place where His people gather to pray. Our community prayers, lifted up in unison and in harmony with the Spirit of Christ, are most surely heard and received with favor.

By God's righteous judgments administered in this sanctuary we come to know the fear of the Lord. This is a place of forgiveness where mercy is greater than justice. Here is our resting place where the congregation is clothed with salvation. People come burdened with guilt, but go home with the weight of their sin lifted away. In this abiding place, all who are called by God's holy name confess His holy name, because this is their very own family name.

In this house the Almighty's sons and daughters come together to be taught the right way to live and the Father sends showers of blessings on their inheritance. In this dwelling place our God deals with each one according to his or her actions. He calls our hearts to repentance and forgives us as we have forgiven others. It is here that we rejoice in God's goodness. It's a sanctuary that is built as a refuge for aliens and those who seek refuge. They come under the safe covering of God who is their Deliverer.

This is a house of abundance where our sacrifices and offerings are received. Our Lord and Master caps all of these good things with a promise: "My eyes and my heart will always be there." Indeed, in this house we come together in His holy presence—in the presence of our Jesus Christ, our High Priest who ministers before us.[1] As we gather in His presence, serving as His priests, we are called to separate ourselves and unburden our shoulders of what is common.

> *Now my eyes will be open and my ears attentive to the prayers offered in this place. I have chosen and consecrated this temple so that my Name may be there forever. My eyes and my heart will always be there.*
> (2 Chronicles 7:15–16)

Every generation of those who are called by the Almighty's holy name are taught and trained so they may serve as builders of the house for God's holy name. But when godly people turn away from what they have been taught and reject the right way to live, they may build, but they will not live there.[2] The walls they construct will not meet the standard of the Good Shepherd's rod. What they have established must be torn down so that it may be rebuilt with tried and tested precious stones.

Consider Israel's seventy years of exile. The weight of their sin required many years to complete Yahweh's imposed consequences. Then, once again, their hearts turned toward God's holy house, the temple in Jerusalem. They turned from their sin bent ways and in repentance their hearts were stirred into action and their feet carried them home. The groundwork of repentance prepared the way for the foundation of Jerusalem's temple to be set in place.

When the pilgrims arrived in Jerusalem the chaos overwhelmed them. Heaps of ruin looked like impossible mountains. But they took the fire scorched stones in hand and each one began to rebuild the walls of Jerusalem close to their own houses. Their work teaches us that rebuilding always begins close to home—right in our own family.

> *He has granted us new life to rebuild the house of our God and repair its ruins.*
> (Ezra 9:9)

---

1. In depth study Scriptures: 1 Kings 8:22–9:3, 2 Chronicles 6, 7.
2. Zephaniah 1:13.

The sanctuary our God inhabits in all His glory is a house built by those who are called by His holy name according to plan. When we hear the call to gather, we assemble in Jesus' name to worship in spirit and truth. We worship by means of an outpouring of the Holy Spirit. Our common, everyday gifts are not sufficient for true and real worship. Our exaltations must flow out from our spirit so we may worship the triune God in truth and according to all He has revealed Himself to be. Our worship exalts the Lord our God with singing of Psalms, hymns, and spiritual songs. The words of our songs go with us into our daily lives to light our pathway and keep our feet from slipping.

God's glory will not dwell in a divisive house. His holy presence is not manifested in a house that does not meet the standard of the Good Shepherd's measuring rod. With righteousness as the standard, the house is built true to plan. This truth is evident in Ezekiel's vision of a temple. The sanctuary, courts, and priest's quarters are meticulously measured to be sure that holy and common are kept separate. With everything in order, God's glory returns to the temple.

LORD, I love the house where you live, the place where your glory dwells.
(Psalm 26:8)

When you're in the middle of a construction project, when you close your eyes at night you see blueprints on the inside of your eyelids. In your dreams you remember where you forgot to nail down the framing for the kitchen wall. In the same way, building a spiritual house touches every moment of your life, day and night.

The house we build for our Father's holy name must be perfect in every detail, even as He is perfect.[3] We build in His strength and not in our own because on our own "perfect" is impossible. We must construct this house by the power of the Spirit of Christ and not by human might or mortal strength.[4]

We set ourselves apart as a holy people with a holy purpose, just as the Rechabite tribe did in ancient Israel. While dwelling in tents and living as roving shepherds, they built a solid house. They served their God Almighty by building an eternal house for His holy name.

King Solomon's prayer of dedication for the temple shows us the beauty, glory, and benefits of this eternal house we build for His name. His petition inspires us to come and dwell in our Father's holy presence—where His glory dwells in this holy abode. We learned that God's glory will not dwell in a divisive house. His holy presence inhabits a house built according to the design that meets the standard of the Good Shepherd's measuring rod. This is a house that separates what is holy from what is common.

---
3. Matthew 5:48.
4. Zechariah 4:6.

Teach my people the difference between the holy and the common and show them how to distinguish between the unclean and the clean.
(Ezekiel 44:23)

Chapter 26

A House Built True to Plan

Q & A

1. Describe the house that we are building true to plan.

___

2. Why are separations important in the house we build for our Father's holy name?

___

3. How does the building plan help us see that it's vital to separate the holy from what is common?

___

4. What does the Rechabite tribe teach us about how to build this awesome house?

___

My Journal Notes:

27

Blow the Trumpet in Zion

Key Scriptures:

- "Come, let us bow down in worship, let us kneel before the LORD our Maker." (Psalm 95:6)

- "Blow the trumpet in Zion, declare a holy fast, call a sacred assembly." (Joel 2:15)

During the Feast of Trumpets, the priests read Psalm 29 to the congregation. Hebrew tradition teaches that David wrote this Psalm while meditating on the Lord during a massive storm. The skies filled with dark clouds. Thunder, lightning, and torrents of rain inspired him to worship the Almighty. Again, in our day, the Father's voice sounds out like a great blast of a trumpet to gather His people.

In composing this Psalm David doesn't use the Hebrew words Elohim (God) nor does he use Adonai. He may have been thinking about the neighboring nation's idolatrous elohim (gods) and avoided using references that might mistakenly be attributed to someone other than the one true and eternally existent God. Instead, he wrote of Yehovah's voice sounding with trumpet-like thunder. The Lord inspired him to proclaim the God [לֵא 'êl] of glory whose voice thunders over the mighty waters.

This study resonates with Psalm 29's trumpet call that gathers the people for the feast. It's an exaltation, a song to honor the God of glory. The words of David's song call us to come with contrite hearts to worship the Lord God and be taught so we may know the splendor of His holiness. The prophet Haggai concludes this chapter's teaching so we may know the vital nature of God's call to worship. Let's walk step by step, verse by verse through David's powerful song.

> **Study Prayer**
>
> *O LORD, raise up a leader to serve as your signet, your chosen servant who will lead us as we rebuild this house for your holy name.*
>
> A prayer from Haggai 2:23.

All those who answer the trumpet's call gather as a people of praise. The most powerful praise comes from the mouths of our children and infants. Indeed, the cry of a newborn child can silence the Almighty's adversaries and the avenger.[5] The kingdom's citadels are reinforced with praise. The mighty army of the Lord is strengthened for battle with songs of rejoicing going before them. The battle is not ours, it is the Lord's, and it is already won. Now the choir of priests can march out on the front line singing out: "Give thanks to the LORD, for his love endures forever."[6]

May all those who are washed in the blood of Christ lift up voices with the angels of heaven and give witness to the name that is above all names. May this royal priesthood of faith exalt God who is glory and strength and who dwells in all who abide in Him. We do not come empty handed but with hands lifted up in praise and our voices shouting out His glory. We come in reverent awe to cast our crowns at His feet. We commit into His nail scarred hands all that He has ordained for us; scepters of leadership and the keys of the kingdom.[7]

We exalt Him because we are a people who are called by His holy name.

Ascribe to the LORD, you heavenly beings, ascribe to the LORD glory and strength. (Psalm 29:1)

At the sound of the ram's horn the people gather to worship Almighty God who made this vast universe. He created this green orb called Earth, the great oceans and seas, and the water that springs up to irrigate its fields and forest to provide for humankind. Assembling a redeemed people to worship our God of glory is the whole essence of the eternal Gospel.[8] Our Father reveals Himself to all who are called by His holy name. The wind of the Spirit fills us so we may breathe out with songs of praise and glory due His name. We lift up holy hands to extol Him. Shouts of joy and gladness ring out from our worship assemblies. Beautiful songs of exaltation resonate from the doors of this house of worship. Can our praise and worship give full honor to the glory due His name? Our worship gatherings today may sound like a first choir practice before everyone learns the musical score. Our songs are preparation for singing in heaven's choir where ten-thousands of voices will sing with the angels before the Throne of God.

---

5. Psalm 8:2. This verse, together with Psalm 127:5 and 1 Timothy 2:15, offers a perfect example of Scripture interpreting Scripture.
6. 2 Chronicles 20:21.
7. Scepters are symbolic of strength to lead and power to rule. Swords are images of the authority of the Scriptures. Keys are for those who minister under authority of Christ, administering His mercy and forgiveness.
8. Revelation 14:6–7.

What are the effects and blessings that come to the kingdom when we praise and worship the Father, Son, and Holy Spirit who is holy? The building stones of the walls in heaven's kingdom cry out and the beams of the house echo with our choruses and hymns sung to glorify His name.[9] With every note and word we sing as harmonious congregations and the walls of God's eternal kingdom are strengthened. The sounds of our wind instruments, horns, and strings harmonizing with our voices serve a great purpose. Every note is like vibrating the cement when constructing a house to increase the density and strength of the concrete.

Ascribe to the LORD the glory due his name; worship the LORD in the splendor of his holiness.
(Psalm 29:2)

Like a ram's horn that trumpets over the waves of the sea, God's people are gathered from the far corners of the Earth. In their towns and villages they come together to worship, serve, and minister before Christ Jesus our High Priest. The Great I AM is the object of our worship and we exalt Him in all the glory that is due His name. We come before Him to worship in the beauty of His holiness.

The New Moon serves as the Creator's faithful witness in the sky, announcing the festive gatherings along with the sounding of the shofar. We hear God's thunderous voice calling us together to celebrate the promise that's as sure as His name.

The voice of the LORD is over the waters; the God of glory thunders, the LORD thunders over the mighty waters.
(Psalm 29:3)

So many Christians believe that they must limit the way God speaks to the written canon of Scriptures. The Holy Spirit powerfully speaks through the written words of the Apostles and prophets in every one of the sixty-six books of the Bible. Every sermon and teaching can be proven true or false when tested by the inspired writers of every book from Genesis to Revelation. Every prophetic word must be inspired in the holy Scriptures and then tested by the same measure. Is there some new truth or revelation that is not written in the Bible? Certainly not! There is nothing new under the sun.[10]

Our challenge is that we forget or misinterpret what the Scriptures teach. We tend to force fit God's word to meet our own purpose. We need constant reminders of truths to live by in our daily lives. Because of this, the Almighty anoints men and women who will speak out to admonish, correct, and

---
9. Habakkuk 2:11.
10. Ecclesiastes 1:9.

encourage us in the moment according to the Scriptures. We need anointed prophets, teachers, pastors and evangelists who will boldly speak out with the majestic and awesome voice of the Lord—speaking only what they hear the Spirit speaking in our time of need.

> *The voice of the Lord is powerful; the voice of the Lord is majestic.*
> (Psalm 29:4)

We worship in His sanctuary, a safe fortress encompassed in the hollow of His hands. The world around us is crumbling into ruin, but we are safe in His house. Though storms, warfare, and pandemics rage around us we are comforted in the Rock, Christ Jesus, who is our refuge. The voice of the Almighty speaks and the mountains skip like rams, the hills like lambs.[11] Thousands may fall all around us, but our eternal soul and spirit will not be touched by the calamity.[12]

Why does the sea rage? Why are the waters held back? As the earth shakes around us and droughts threaten, our eyes are opened to see the pathway through to the other side. We put disasters behind us and see our way to enter into Christ victorious.

> *The voice of the Lord breaks the cedars; the Lord breaks in pieces the cedars of Lebanon.*
> (Psalm 29:5)

A blazing lightning flash blinds our eyes for a moment, but the voice of the Lord enlightens our eyes, opens our hearts, and reveals His might and power. His name is fearsome and awesome and His revelation power comes like a powerful flash of heaven's light in the dark clouds of a stormy night.

In our darkest hours, when pandemics press in and disasters assault us, there is light from above that comes like flashes across the sky from east to west to announce the coming of our Redeemer, our Savior, and Lord. At the thundering sound of His voice the mountain of the Lord leaps with joy.

> *He makes Lebanon leap like a calf, Sirion like a young wild ox. The voice of the Lord strikes with flashes of lightning.*
> (Psalm 29:6–7)

In the Desert of Kadesh the tribes of Israel refused to enter the Promised Land. They sent spies into Canaan to explore the land. But the spies from ten tribes came back with an evil report that discouraged the people. They became too frightened to face the giants of the land in the name of the Lord. They forgot about the Lord God who parted the Red Sea for them to cross

---

11. Psalm 114:4.
12. Psalm 91:7.

over. They pushed aside all memories of the Great I AM who gave them water from the rock. Their Provider gave them bread to eat in the wilderness, but they gathered, prepared, and ate the bread with ungrateful hearts.

Oh Lord, shake your people as we tremble with fear, stuck in this Desert called Kadesh. Awaken us with your resounding voice to break our ungrateful hearts. May your mighty presence speak to us, break us out of our rebellious resolve, and bring us to the Water from the Rock.

The voice of the LORD shakes the desert; the LORD shakes the Desert of Kadesh.
(Psalm 29:8)

In the Bible oak trees are a symbol of might, unswaying confidence, resilience in storms, and the strength of knowledge. They signify the enduring might of uprightness, and especially the righteousness of Jesus Christ.

When storms rage, thunder roils through the clouds, lightning bolts flash across the horizon, and tornadoes devastate the woodlands, all those who come into the safety of His temple shout out and rejoice in His name. The house built for His name is a fortress built to protect and shield all who are called by His holy name. Whose house will you dwell in, the house of wrath or the house of rejoicing?

The voice of the LORD twists the oaks and strips the forests bare. And in his temple all cry, "Glory!"
(Psalm 29:9)

The Almighty remains seated above Earth's waters, restraining the floods of judgment so they will never destroy the earth again as they did in Noah's day. The God of Justice is faithful to His promise and will never again overthrow the wicked of the earth with a flood.[13] When rain comes to water and refresh the earth God's rainbow appears in the sky to remind us of His promise to all humankind.

Our heavenly Father reigns supreme over sea and sky. The Almighty is sovereign over all the heavens and earth. He is our King, our Lord, and He holds us in the hollow of His loving hands to keep us safe through every one of earth's calamities.

The LORD sits enthroned over the flood; the LORD is enthroned as King forever.
(Psalm 29:10)

The house we build stands firm while the thundering, glorious voice of the Almighty roars. When He speaks, the house built upon the Rock stands firm while dwellings built on sand are washed away. The Almighty's powerful

---

13. Genesis 9:11, Isaiah 54:9.

voice breaks the majestic and stately cedars, even the great cedars of Lebanon. But the eternal house built on the Rock will not be shaken. When waters come like a pent-up flood, the Great I AM sits enthroned over them so that we will not be engulfed. We will not be swept away like those whose evil ways grieved the Creator in Noah's day.

Join the work crew. Let's put on our hard hats, strap on our tool belts, power up our tools and work together to build a house where we may dwell with our Lord Almighty. This is a house of blessing for all who abide there. It's a sanctuary where God's people overflow with praise.[14] This house has a bountiful garden that flourishes with a cornucopia of fragrant fruit of the Spirit. Stone upon stone we build a house for the glory and honor of the name of our Lord, God, and King.

> *The LORD gives strength to his people; the LORD blesses his people with peace.* (Psalm 29:11)

The Old Testament prophets spoke to the people, prophesying in the name of the Lord. God promised to send His only Son, Jesus, as Immanuel. When the Son of God came to walk among us, He only spoke what He heard the Father speaking, and proclaimed all truth and righteousness in His name.

It's good for us to honor our heavenly Father, rightly using His name. It's best to glorify our Lord Jesus by revering His name. To honor and revere His name it's important for us to exalt the name of our Lord God by submitting ourselves to serve as building stones for the house in which His name is lifted up. This is a strong house with each stone tried and tested in the fires of affliction. This is a temple where we live our lives in keeping with the name inscribed on our hearts. We rebuild with stones salvaged from the ruins of life. This home is where peace, comfort, joy, and strength are restored to us. God's blessings encompass all who continue to abide in this holy place.

With great signs and wonders the Lord Almighty made a name for Himself.[15] He glorified His name as He called Israel as a holy nation and delivered them from the bondage of slavery in Egypt. When they were unfaithful, He was longsuffering and showed them mercy for the honor of His name. He forgave them their many trespasses and saved them from powerful kings for the sake of His name.[16] His awesome name is exalted above all names and we are called to live, minister, serve, and in every way worship and glorify His awesome name.

Now is the time. This is the day for us to come together and build a dwell-

---

14. Psalm 84:4.
15. Jeremiah 23:20.
16. Psalm 106:8.

ing place where the most glorified name in all the Earth is exalted. We've suffered a full measure of despair and destruction. Now, let this house be built and let our covenant renewed. There is power in the name for all those who are called by Jesus' name and who walk by faith in agreement with the new name written on our hearts.

> *"Now give careful thought to this from this day on–consider how things were before one stone was laid on another in the Lord's temple. When anyone came to a heap of twenty measures, there were only ten. When anyone went to a wine vat to draw fifty measures, there were only twenty. I struck all the work of your hands with blight, mildew and hail, yet you did not return to me," declares the Lord. "From this day on, from this twenty-fourth day of the ninth month, give careful thought to the day when the foundation of the Lord's temple was laid. Give careful thought: Is there yet any seed left in the barn? Until now, the vine and the fig tree, the pomegranate and the olive tree have not borne fruit." "From this day on I will bless you."*
> (Haggai 2:15–19)

Zion's watchman blows his trumpet to call God's people to a repentant fast. We gather together in weakness, barely able to utter a note to sing God's praise. We're humbled to see that even the cry of a new-born child silences those who stand opposed to the Lord our God. We come into His glory with a child-like faith and we're strengthened to sing out, "Arise, O Lord, may your enemies be scattered."

We are a called and chosen nation, a holy people who serve as a royal priesthood to exalt God in all His glory and majesty. We submit ourselves to Christ who enlightens us to speak out the Gospel message and minister the keys of the kingdom. By the revelation of Jesus Christ and by means of the Holy Spirit, we lift up our spirits to worship in spirit and truth.

The Father reveals Himself to all whom the Holy Spirit indwells. We lift up our spirits in praise and lift our hands to worship the "splendor of His holiness." As servants of the Most High God we come together to exalt God in all the glory that is due His name. The sound of the trumpet calls us to gather in a holy assembly to receive the ministries of Christ Jesus our High Priest, and to worship, serve, and minister before Him.

As we minister and serve, we cannot limit how God chooses to speak to His people. Yes, God's word is absolutely adequate to teach, admonish, and correct His people. Yet, our Father is more than able to speak in so many ways through those whom He chooses to speak through, whether, pastor, preacher, teacher, evangelist, elder, deacon, deaconess, or anyone of any stature whom He chooses to use as His spokesperson.[17] Our heavenly Father is able to speak in the moment to an immediate need in the Church. He is more than able to proclaim His word in many ways to strengthen us in the moment of our need and in the moment when we are weak and wavering in our faith. By His Word, the house we build on the Rock, Christ Jesus, stands firm while the dwellings built on sand are left desolate.

Let us come together with contrite hearts to be forgiven, cleansed and revived in the power and strength of the Spirit so we may build a house where we dwell together in the awesome presence of the Spirit. Let's work together as one in Christ to build a house that separates what is holy from what is common where His glory may dwell.

Give careful thought to how things are now before the foundation of God's house were set in place—a foundation established upon the groundwork of repentance. Our hearts feel a deep and empty void that we try to fill with worship according to our own preferences, traditions, and rules. We filled the silence with our own words spoken out from our intuitions and personal impressions. But there is a great hope held out to us in Jesus' nail scarred hands. He is quick to forgive repentant hearts. He is faithful to restore His people to His house that overflows with all rich spiritual blessings.

---

17. Job 33:14.

Chapter 27

Blow the Trumpet in Zion

Q & A

1. How is it possible that the cry of a newborn child in a manger sounds out like a trumpet to silence all those who stand opposed to the Lord our God?

2. How will you answer the trumpet's call to come and serve in the royal priesthood of the kingdom?

3. What is the powerful effect of the revelation of Jesus Christ upon all those who are His bride?

4. How does God speak to His people in our day?

5. Describe the blessings of this house when the foundation is set in place and the builders stand ready to build.

My Journal Notes:

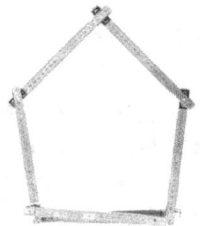

The Capstone

Key Scripture:

- "This is what the Lord says: 'Heaven is my throne, and the earth is my footstool. Where is the house you will build for me? Where will my resting place be?'" (Isaiah 66:1)

When meditating on the plan for the house we build for our Father's holy name, it becomes obvious that this is not a dwelling that can be built with common hands or by human initiative. Those who build a place by their own means must support it with promises of their own making and create a redeemer in their own image. Their house is built through their own strength, by their own means, and with their own materials, but they will never live in it. Jesus spoke against what the Pharisees built, saying, "Look, your house is left to you desolate."[1]

Instead of building with seven pillars of wisdom, the religious leaders of Jesus' day built on seven bags of sand.[2] The house they constructed never measured up because it was made with sticks, hay, and straw.[3] The Great I AM will never dwell in man-made sanctuaries that cannot pass the test of fire. The Almighty's throne, his footstool, and His resting place will only inhabit an eternal house built true to plan; a temple that separates what is holy from what is common.

Consider this example of separating what is holy from the common: A teacher who teaches math, English, reading, and writing skills to fourth-graders has a special, God-given gift for instructing children. She's good at what she does because she has a common gift for teaching—a secular calling. If this same teacher tried to teach children at church, this common talent would not measure up to the task of teaching for the purpose of changing lives for eternity. If she attempts to present the Gospel by means of her common talent rather than by the spiritual gift of teaching, her work has a limited effect. It is an affront to the Gospel and regarded as profane before a holy God. Indeed, we need the

---
1. Matthew 23:38.
2. Jesus spoke seven woes against the religious leaders in Matthew 23:13–32.
3. 1 Corinthians 3:12–13.

anointing, gifting, and empowering work of the Spirit poured out upon us to effectively accomplish the impossible work of the Great Commission.

> *But you will receive power when the Holy Spirit comes on you; and you will be my witnesses in Jerusalem, and in all Judea and Samaria, and to the ends of the earth.* (Acts 1:8)

The first stones of this dwelling place were set in place by Adam and Eve, Earth's first inhabitants. By faith, they laid the first stones upon the foundation who is the Word of creation. The first couple had a son named Seth and he grew up to revere the name of their Creator God. Adam and Eve passed on their faith, and in doing this they prepared the way for one more precious stone to be set in place for this eternal house for God's holy name. As time passed, men and women on the Earth became corrupt and violent. They refused to build using the Word of creation as their foundation. To preserve His creation from their destructive violence the Lord Almighty put an end to the wicked inhabitants of the Earth with a mighty flood. But He saved a remnant who would continue to build His kingdom. He sealed them from the storm of His wrath, keeping them safe in the ark with all the animals that came two by two.

Noah and his sons turned over a new leaf and began again.[4] By faith he built the ark that sealed him, his family, and the animals from God's just and righteous wrath. After the flood they would build again, but not a floating, temporary kind of construction. They lived by faith in a new world. They built this house for God's holy name by passing on their faith and trust in God their Redeemer to every new generation. Once again, they bore children who would fill the earth and subdue it.[5]

Stone upon precious stone the house for His name continued to be built through the generations. Then, many years after God separated Israel as a holy nation, David and Bathsheba begat Solomon. God's forgiveness and mercy are abundantly evident as God raised up a royal son who built the courtyards, and the temple walls. Solomon built a temple in the city of Jerusalem that prefigured the great city whose Builder and Maker is God. Building the temple showed them the way forward to Christ the Promised Messiah who came to offer up His body and blood for the redemption of humankind.

The high priest who served in Jerusalem's temple wore a breastplate with twelve precious stones set in golden filigrees. Each stone had the name of one of Israel's patriarchs inscribed on it, representing one clan that gathered to camp around their tribal banner. This breastplate with its precious stones served to foreshadow Christ who now serves as our High Priest. In

---

4. Genesis 8:11.
5. Genesis 1:28.

this Old Testament prefiguring of Messiah we see Jesus, our High Priest and soon coming King. Our Savior is girded with a breastplate of righteousness, worn like a golden sash upon His chest. Each one of our names—the names of all His sons and daughters, are engraved on costly stones and set in place on this priestly garment.[6] He wears our names close to His heart, and by the fire of His presence we are cleansed and made righteous in God's sight.[7] We are held so close that we hear His heartbeat and we know His voice. In this close proximity we are melted and molded into useful vessels to serve in the Church. Our vessels are made strong in Christ for the work of the Great Commission—building stone upon stone.

All those who are in Christ are the precious building stones for the house raised up for His holy name.[8] The Father's desire is that His dwelling place be renowned, in keeping with every attribute revealed in His name. We build this house guided by Wisdom as our Master Builder.[9] His house must be celebrated as a safe dwelling where all who will come may find mercy, forgiveness, and saving grace. The Great I AM desires that the house for His name be looked upon as a place of prayer, worship, and thanksgiving. This abode must be well-known as a house of safe refuge. God's people are called to represent this house to the nations as a holy dwelling place so that all who desire to encounter our Savior may come.

Christ Jesus is welcomed to minister His living and active presence as our High Priest in this house. He is welcomed to minister in the fullness of His majesty. Within this lodging our Redeemer is lifted up and exalted so that He may draw all people to the cross where He suffered and died. The Father's house must be known as the place where the thirsty may come to Springs of Living Water. It must never be known for water from self-dug wells that can only satisfy for a moment.[10] The first yearnings of all who suffer, whether physical pain or wounded souls, ought to recall the renown of our Father who dwells among us in the house we build for His name.

The power of The Name is not manifested by saying the Lord God's name correctly or by uttering His name just like Noah, David, or Solomon. In fact, the Father's name cannot be properly or precisely spoken in any of Earth's languages. But people of every language on Earth will confess that Jesus Christ is Lord in their own words and dialects.[11]

---

6. Revelation 1:13.
7. Daniel 10:5–6.
8. For an in-depth study on the indwelling Christ, see author's book, *The Mystery Which is Christ in You.*
9. Proverbs 9:1.
10. Jeremiah 2:13.
11. Philippians 2:11.

The power of the Name is not manifested by shouting it out with forceful vigor. When we speak out Jesus' name, we can only speak it with power because we abide in Him, and live lives that honor Him. Restoring the Father's name is best accomplished by living our lives as a reflection, manifestation, and a portrayal of His name.

We must constantly be reminded that we cannot build the walls of this house with unproven, unfinished, or unrefined stones because they crumble and give way. Inferior materials collapse under pressure and we are left with gaps in the walls. But take heart. Our Lord Jesus stands in the gap and oversees the rebuilding of the house for His name.[12] We can build a fortified house on the founding Rock who is Christ Jesus. As we build this house with precious stones, we restore the renown of our heavenly Father's holy name.

> *Your people will rebuild the ancient ruins and will raise up the age-old foundations, you will be called Repairer of Broken Walls, Restorer of Streets with Dwellings.* (Isaiah 58:12)

We are called to be diligent in the work of building the walls of this house as a mighty fortress. We can't build a house with our own customized Gospel message, man-made teachings, or promises of our own making. We all have to work out of the same tool box and use the same measuring tape. It doesn't work for one church to say, "This is the way of salvation," while another church says, "They don't do it right. I doubt they're even saved." We can't agree on salvation or what true worship is because our services are inspired by our own instincts and our personal preferences. The sermons we hear support us in our complacency, validate us in our self-indulgence, and justify us in our misdeeds. We demand music to our own liking but the words we sing blow away like the smoke of a candle, having no effect on our daily lives. Instead, we ought to fear our Father's holy justice. We must build according to the Spirit and in all truth and righteousness.

Most Christians realize that the Church in our day is broken. But we're experts at pointing fingers at others and overlooking our own failings. What if the church at Ephesus pointed their fingers at the people in Philadelphia, saying, "You're so weak. Your strength is not enough for this work"?[13] If we act like the church at Sardis we would cast blame on the church of Pergamum, saying; "That food you eat; you've got it all wrong." Looking at the faults of others so we can ignore our own failings is an age-old human weakness. We feed our self-righteous complacency by accusing our neighbor of their wrongs. We put on our rose-colored glasses, delighting in the beautiful dwelling we

---
12. Ezekiel 22:30.
13. Revelation 3:8

have built. Then we look through our bifocals, looking down on our neighbor's work, saying, "They're the problem." Meanwhile, the house we are called to build is rife with gaps in the walls; but we can't see them.

A house is not built by looking at the poor job our neighbor is doing. Certainly, the house we build for the Father's holy name is only weakened by ignoring our own failings. We are called to repent, turn away from our self-serving righteousness, and come to our Redeemer to receive His forgiveness and mercy. When we are forgiven, cleansed, and strengthened in the Spirit we are ready to build on the Rock who is Christ Jesus, our Lord and Savior.

Is it a time for you yourselves to be living in your paneled houses, while this house remains a ruin?
(Haggai 1:4)

By the leading of the Holy Spirit and in the light of Christ we grip our tools in hand and begin this good work of building. We build a house for our Father's holy name, stone upon precious stone. We only build with tested and proven stones, putting aside every man-made material that will never meet the test of time. We will not build for any other name, or any other god. We do this good work in the strength of the Spirit so we can build an eternal house, a temple, a sanctuary that withstands every storm. We construct a house whose gates will stand against every assault of the enemy. When our Good Shepherd comes with His measuring rod, we stand confident as He examines our work.

When we build a house for the name that is above every name, it must be true to plan. The Father's design keeps all that is holy separate from what is common. When we consider His plan, if we are ashamed of the building we have done by our own means, the whole design will be revealed to us.[14]

This house is a holy sanctuary and it must be built according to plan so that our Lord Almighty's splendor and the glory of His holy name will once again return to inhabit His temple of worship. This is a house that measures up according to the measurements of the Master Builder's rod; a dwelling place that gathers and separates. In this house we come together to worship in spirit and truth. We don't build by speaking the Father's name a certain way. This dwelling isn't for the name of any other savior, nor is it constructed according to our own design. Instead, we build with justice, love, compassion, and mercy. We do this good work, walking humbly with our God.[15]

The temple we work to complete serves as a refuge where every tongue spoken on planet Earth confesses that Jesus Christ is Lord in their own lan-

---
14. Ezekiel 43:10–11.
15. Micah 6:8, Zechariah 7:9.

guage and dialect. Out of every nation will come precious, tried and tested stones to build this mighty house; one sanctuary for one people, for the name of our Father, Son, and Holy Spirit.

And the glory of the LORD filled the temple.
(Ezekiel 43:5)

May the living stones of this house shout out our Redeemer's holy name in their nation's native tongue.

Jesus Christ is Lord

Jezu Krishti është Zot

Isus Hrist je Gospod

Ježíš Kristus je Pán

Jesus Kristus er Herre

Is é Íosa Críost Tiarna

Yesus Kristus adalah Tuhan

Jesucristo es el Señor

Jesosy Kristy no Tompo

Chrystus jest Panem

Iisus Hristos este Domnul

Jesus Kristus är Herre

Ісус Христос є Господом

Ujesu Kristu uyiNkosi

耶穌基督是主[16]

---

16. In the following order; English, Albanian, Bosnian, Czech, Danish, Indonesian, Irish, Spanish, Malagasy, Polish, Romanian, Swedish, Ukrainian, Zulu, and Chinese. (Google translate)

My Journal Notes:

Definitions

Holy and Common

Holy is defined by the Hebrew word קדוֹשׁ, qadosh: to be separate, set apart, and consecrated.

What is separated to the Father, Son, and Holy Spirit is holy. Water set apart for a holy purpose such as baptism is holy. The bread and wine (or juice from the grape) set apart to Christ at the Lord's table are holy. People who are set apart to God are a holy people. God's chosen people are set apart as holy so they may worship and minister in His name. We fulfill our sacred calling by means of the anointing, gifting, and empowering work of the Holy Spirit who sets us apart as a royal priesthood, and a holy nation.

Common in Hebrew is חֹל chôl.

Defined as created, natural things given for the good of humankind providing their daily needs. Rain that falls on the just and the unjust is good and common rain.[1] God-given common things and common callings are excellent in their place, but they profane what is holy when they are used in place of what is holy.

When Jesus taught His disciples about how hard it is for wealthy people to enter God's kingdom, they asked, "Who then can be saved?" Jesus answered, "With man this is impossible but with God all things are possible." We must understand that our God-given common abilities and talents do not make a way to bring a soul to repentance and saving grace. A soul saved by grace is only possible by means of the Spirit of Christ who anoints, gifts, and empowers His people to accomplish this impossible task of redeeming a lost soul.[2] Attempting to do the work of the kingdom in our own strength profanes what is holy and is an affront to a holy God. We cannot depend on common strength, talents, or abilities to accomplish the eternal work of the kingdom of heaven.[3] It's impossible.[4]

---

1. Matthew 5:45.
2. Matthew 19:25-26.
3. Ezekiel 22:26.
4. Additional Study Scriptures: Ezekiel 44:23, 1 Samuel 21:5–6, Ezekiel 22:26, 42:20, 44:23.

Because you have depended on your own strength and on your many warriors, the roar of battle will rise against your people, so that all your fortresses will be devastated.
(Hosea 10:13–14)

Historic Names of Our Heavenly Father

Yahweh, Yehovah, Jehovah, Yehovah, Yahvah, Yahowah, YHWH, YHVH:

Most Bible translations today use "Lord" rather than the ancient Hebrew name for our heavenly Father. The practice began with observant Jewish worshippers who replaced God's name with Adonai, which means "Lord" in English. Changes began before the "years of silence" that preceded Jesus' birth. Observant Jews began this practice out of reverence, because they feared mispronouncing the unpronounceable name of YHWH. Concern came from their interpretation of the commandment that says, "You shall not misuse the name of the Lord your God, for the Lord will not hold anyone guiltless who misuses his name."[5] Established Jewish practice carried this through to the early Christian Church and the inspired writers of the New Testament wrote the Father's name in Greek, the language of slaves and the poor. To this day there is no language on earth that can correctly pronounce God's name just as YHWH spoke His name to Moses.

Today, all English Bible versions of the Old Testament translate the Hebrew, "Yehovah," as Lord.[6] The Greek word κύριος, kýrios, is lord, ruler, or master. The early Christian church adopted this practice because they had no other Lord or Master than Jesus Christ. In writing his psalm, David used the one Hebrew name that is unique to the Creator, and this name is Yehovah, also spoken as Yahweh. This name is translated as Lord in English Bibles and refers to the self-existent and eternal God as revealed to Moses at the burning bush.

God said to Moses, "I AM who I AM. This is what you are to say to the Israelites: 'I AM has sent me to you.'" God also said to Moses, "Say to the Israelites, 'The Lord, the God of your fathers–the God of Abraham, the God of Isaac and the God of Jacob–has sent me to you.' This is my name forever, the name you shall call me from generation to generation."
(Exodus 3:14–15)

---

5. Exodus 20:7.
6. From Psalm 34:8. The original Hebrew "Yehovah" is translated in Greek as κύριος, kýrios, and in English as Lord in 1 Peter 2:3.

Historic Names of Jesus

Yeshua, Yahoshua, יְהוֹשֻׁעַ, Iēsous, and Y'shua

The name of Israel's promised Messiah, Yeshua HaMashiach. Yeshua is the Alpha and Omega, Immanuel, Prince of Peace, Mighty God, Everlasting Father, Head of the Church, Son of God, the Bread of Life, the Living Water, Deliverer, Savior, Redeemer, Healer, Teacher, Bridegroom, the Cornerstone, and the Capstone.

> *For to us a child is born, to us a son is given, and the government will be on his shoulders. And he will be called Wonderful Counselor, Mighty God, Everlasting Father, Prince of Peace.*
> (Isaiah 9:6)

> *You are to call him Jesus. He will be great and will be called the Son of the Most High.*
> (Luke 1:31–32)

Historic Names of the Holy Spirit

In Hebrew the Spirit is רוּחַ rûwach.

The Holy Spirit has many descriptive and awesome names and titles. He is the Spirit of Christ, Spirit of Jesus, Spirit of God, Spirit of the Lord, Spirit of Truth, Spirit of Holiness, Spirit of Revelation, Spirit of Grace, Breath of the Almighty, Comforter, Eternal Spirit, Spirit of Life, Spirit of Prophecy, Spirit of Adoption, Spirit of Counsel, Spirit of Might, Spirit of Knowledge, Spirit of the Fear of the Lord, Spirit of Judgment, Spirit of Glory, and the Seven Spirits of God.[7]

> *The Spirit of the Lord will rest on him–the Spirit of wisdom and of understanding, the Spirit of counsel and of might, the Spirit of the knowledge and fear of the Lord.*
> (Isaiah 11:2)

Restore the Sacred Name Movements.

An emphasis on the ancient Hebrew names for our heavenly Father and our Savior began with the Church of God in the 1930s. Restoration teaching states that any other name than Yahweh or Yahoshua for our Savior is blasphemy.

---

[7]. In order of reference: Romans 8:9, Acts 16:7, Genesis 1:2, Isaiah 11:2, John 14:16–17, Romans 1:4, Ephesians 1:17, Hebrews 10:29, Job 33:4, John 14:16, Hebrews 9:14, Romans 8:2, Revelation 19:10, Romans 8:15, Isaiah 11:2, Isaiah 4:4, 1 Peter 4:4, Revelation 1:4.

Several splinter churches have come out from the original Church of God movement, to include: Assemblies of Yahweh, the House of Yahweh, and Yahweh's Restoration Ministry. Some adherents to this doctrine also believe that Yeshua came to bring all the scattered nations into Israel, thus restoring all of God's children under Israel's covenant. There are some Restoration Christians who believe we should also reestablish Shabbat worship, kosher food laws, and observance of Jewish festivals. Strict observance of the historic festivals with their sacrifices and observances is impossible today. Learning about them serves to teach us how ancient Israel celebrated the festivals as a means of looking forward to Christ.

Concluding Study Prayer

Father in heaven, we ask one thing from you, Oh LORD; this alone do we desire: that we may serve as precious, living stones in the house of the LORD all the days of our lives, where we may gaze on the beauty of the LORD and seek You in Your temple.

A prayer inspired by Psalm 27:4.

www.ingramcontent.com/pod-product-compliance
Lightning Source LLC
Chambersburg PA
CBHW050313120526
44592CB00014B/1897